Oracle ERP Essentials

Accounts Receivable: From Basics to Advanced

Kiet Huynh

Table of Contents

CHAPTER I
Introduction to Oracle ERP and Accounts Receivable Module

1.1 Overview of Oracle ERP

1.1.1 Definition and Role of Oracle ERP

Oracle ERP (Enterprise Resource Planning) is a comprehensive suite of integrated applications designed to automate and manage the core business processes of an organization. Developed by Oracle Corporation, this ERP solution provides a unified system for finance, human resources, supply chain, manufacturing, and other essential functions. By integrating these diverse functions into a single system, Oracle ERP enables organizations to streamline operations, improve efficiency, and enhance decision-making capabilities.

Definition:

Oracle ERP is an integrated software platform that combines multiple business applications into a cohesive system. It is designed to manage and automate various business processes, ensuring that data flows seamlessly across different departments and functions. This integration helps eliminate data silos, reduce redundancies, and provide a single source of truth for the organization.

Role of Oracle ERP:

1. Centralized Data Management:

Oracle ERP consolidates data from various business functions into a single database. This centralization ensures consistency, accuracy, and accessibility of data across the organization. With a unified data repository, organizations can reduce errors, avoid duplicate data entries, and ensure that all departments are working with the same information.

2. Streamlined Business Processes:

By automating routine tasks and standardizing workflows, Oracle ERP helps streamline business processes. Automation reduces the time and effort required to complete tasks, allowing employees to focus on more strategic activities. Standardized workflows ensure that processes are consistent across the organization, leading to improved efficiency and productivity.

3. Enhanced Decision-Making:

Oracle ERP provides comprehensive reporting and analytics capabilities, enabling organizations to gain valuable insights into their operations. Real-time data and advanced analytics help decision-makers identify trends, spot opportunities, and make informed decisions. With accurate and timely information, organizations can respond quickly to changing market conditions and stay ahead of the competition.

4. Improved Financial Management:

One of the core functions of Oracle ERP is financial management. The system offers robust tools for managing accounts payable, accounts receivable, general ledger, budgeting, and financial reporting. By automating financial processes and providing real-time visibility into financial performance, Oracle ERP helps organizations maintain financial health and achieve their financial goals.

5. Effective Supply Chain Management:

Oracle ERP includes powerful supply chain management capabilities that help organizations optimize their supply chain operations. The system enables efficient procurement, inventory management, order fulfillment, and logistics planning. By improving supply chain visibility and collaboration, Oracle ERP helps organizations reduce costs, enhance customer satisfaction, and ensure timely delivery of products and services.

6. Human Capital Management:

Managing human resources is another critical function of Oracle ERP. The system provides tools for recruiting, onboarding, performance management, payroll, and employee self-service. By automating HR processes and providing insights into workforce performance, Oracle ERP helps organizations attract and retain talent, improve employee engagement, and align workforce strategies with business goals.

7. Compliance and Risk Management:

Oracle ERP helps organizations comply with regulatory requirements and manage risks effectively. The system includes features for audit trails, access controls, and compliance reporting. By ensuring data integrity and providing tools for monitoring and reporting, Oracle ERP helps organizations mitigate risks and avoid costly compliance violations.

8. Scalability and Flexibility:

Oracle ERP is designed to scale with the growth of an organization. Whether a small business or a large enterprise, the system can accommodate the increasing complexity and volume of business operations. Additionally, Oracle ERP offers flexibility in deployment options, including on-premises, cloud, and hybrid models, allowing organizations to choose the solution that best fits their needs.

9. Integration with Other Systems:

Oracle ERP seamlessly integrates with other Oracle products and third-party applications. This interoperability ensures that organizations can leverage their existing IT investments and build a cohesive technology ecosystem. Integration with other systems enhances data sharing and collaboration, further improving operational efficiency and decision-making.

Key Components of Oracle ERP:

1. Financial Management:

The financial management module of Oracle ERP includes features for managing general ledger, accounts payable, accounts receivable, fixed assets, cash management, and financial reporting. These tools help organizations maintain accurate financial records, manage cash flow, and generate insightful financial reports.

2. Supply Chain Management:

The supply chain management module encompasses procurement, inventory management, order management, and logistics. It enables organizations to optimize their supply chain operations, reduce costs, and ensure timely delivery of goods and services.

3. Human Capital Management:

The human capital management module includes tools for recruiting, onboarding, talent management, payroll, and employee self-service. It helps organizations manage the entire employee lifecycle, from hiring to retirement.

4. Manufacturing:

The manufacturing module provides tools for planning, scheduling, and managing production processes. It helps organizations optimize manufacturing operations, reduce production costs, and improve product quality.

5. Project Management:

The project management module includes features for planning, executing, and monitoring projects. It helps organizations manage project resources, timelines, and budgets, ensuring successful project delivery.

6. Customer Relationship Management:

The customer relationship management module includes tools for managing sales, marketing, and customer service activities. It helps organizations build strong customer relationships, improve customer satisfaction, and drive sales growth.

7. Enterprise Performance Management:

The enterprise performance management module provides tools for budgeting, forecasting, and performance reporting. It helps organizations align their strategies with business goals and monitor performance against key metrics.

8. Procurement:

The procurement module includes features for managing supplier relationships, sourcing, and purchasing activities. It helps organizations optimize procurement processes, reduce costs, and ensure compliance with procurement policies.

Benefits of Oracle ERP:

1. Improved Efficiency:

By automating and streamlining business processes, Oracle ERP helps organizations improve operational efficiency. Employees can complete tasks faster and with fewer errors, leading to increased productivity.

2. Better Collaboration:

Oracle ERP facilitates collaboration across departments by providing a unified platform for communication and data sharing. Teams can work together more effectively, share information seamlessly, and coordinate activities efficiently.

3. Enhanced Visibility:

With real-time data and advanced analytics, Oracle ERP provides enhanced visibility into business operations. Decision-makers can access accurate and up-to-date information, enabling them to make informed decisions and respond quickly to changes.

4. Cost Savings:

By optimizing processes and reducing redundancies, Oracle ERP helps organizations achieve cost savings. Automation reduces the need for manual intervention, while improved efficiency and productivity lead to lower operational costs.

5. Scalability:

Oracle ERP is designed to grow with the organization. As the business expands, the system can accommodate increasing complexity and volume of operations. This scalability ensures that organizations can continue to use Oracle ERP as they grow.

6. Compliance:

Oracle ERP helps organizations comply with regulatory requirements by providing tools for audit trails, access controls, and compliance reporting. The system ensures data integrity and helps organizations avoid costly compliance violations.

7. Strategic Advantage:

By providing insights into business operations and enabling informed decision-making, Oracle ERP gives organizations a strategic advantage. Decision-makers can identify opportunities, mitigate risks, and drive business growth.

In summary, Oracle ERP plays a critical role in modern organizations by providing a comprehensive and integrated solution for managing business processes. Its robust features, scalability, and flexibility make it a valuable tool for organizations of all sizes and industries. By implementing Oracle ERP, organizations can achieve improved efficiency, better collaboration, enhanced visibility, and significant cost savings, ultimately driving business success.

1.1.2 Key Modules in Oracle ERP

Oracle ERP is composed of several key modules, each designed to address specific business functions and processes. Understanding these modules is crucial for leveraging the full potential of the ERP system. Here are the main modules in Oracle ERP:

Financial Management

1. General Ledger (GL):

The General Ledger module is the core of Oracle's financial management system. It provides a centralized repository for all financial transactions and enables organizations to maintain accurate financial records. The GL module supports multiple currencies, complex financial structures, and comprehensive reporting capabilities. It allows for the creation of financial statements, balance sheets, and income statements, providing a clear view of the organization's financial health.

2. Accounts Payable (AP):

The Accounts Payable module manages the organization's obligations to vendors and suppliers. It handles the entire procure-to-pay process, from invoice receipt and validation to payment processing and vendor management. The AP module ensures timely and accurate payment of invoices, helps manage cash flow, and provides tools for monitoring outstanding liabilities.

3. Accounts Receivable (AR):

The Accounts Receivable module, which is the focus of this book, manages the organization's customer invoices and payments. It handles the entire order-to-cash process, from invoice generation and distribution to payment receipt and reconciliation. The AR module helps improve cash flow management, reduces days sales outstanding (DSO), and provides tools for managing customer credit and collections.

4. Cash Management:

The Cash Management module enables organizations to manage their cash inflows and outflows effectively. It provides tools for cash forecasting, bank reconciliation, and liquidity management. This module helps ensure that the organization has sufficient cash to meet its operational needs and financial obligations.

5. Fixed Assets:

The Fixed Assets module manages the lifecycle of an organization's fixed assets, from acquisition to disposal. It handles asset tracking, depreciation calculations, and asset retirement. This module ensures accurate asset valuation and provides tools for managing capital expenditures and asset-related financial reporting.

6. Tax Management:

The Tax Management module provides tools for managing and calculating taxes across various jurisdictions. It supports multiple tax regimes, including VAT, GST, and sales tax. This module helps ensure compliance with tax regulations and provides accurate tax reporting.

Supply Chain Management

1. Procurement:

The Procurement module manages the organization's purchasing processes, from requisition to purchase order generation and supplier management. It helps streamline procurement operations, ensures compliance with procurement policies, and provides tools for managing supplier relationships and contracts.

2. Inventory Management:

The Inventory Management module manages the organization's inventory levels, ensuring that the right products are available at the right time. It handles inventory tracking, stock replenishment, and warehouse management. This module helps optimize inventory levels, reduce carrying costs, and improve order fulfillment.

3. Order Management:

The Order Management module handles the entire order processing lifecycle, from order entry to order fulfillment and shipping. It provides tools for managing customer orders, tracking order status, and coordinating with other modules such as Inventory Management and Accounts Receivable. This module helps ensure timely and accurate order processing and improves customer satisfaction.

4. Manufacturing:

The Manufacturing module manages the organization's production processes, including planning, scheduling, and execution. It provides tools for managing bills of materials, work orders, and production costs. This module helps optimize manufacturing operations, improve production efficiency, and reduce manufacturing costs.

Human Capital Management

1. Core HR:

The Core HR module manages employee information, including personal details, employment history, and job assignments. It provides tools for managing employee records, organizational structures, and HR processes. This module helps ensure accurate and up-to-date employee information and supports HR decision-making.

2. Payroll:

The Payroll module manages the organization's payroll processes, including salary calculations, deductions, and payments. It handles payroll processing for multiple pay periods, tax calculations, and compliance with payroll regulations. This module helps ensure accurate and timely payroll processing and provides tools for managing payroll-related financial reporting.

3. Talent Management:

The Talent Management module provides tools for managing employee recruitment, performance, and development. It handles job postings, applicant tracking, performance reviews, and succession planning. This module helps attract and retain top talent, improve employee performance, and support career development.

Project Management

1. Project Financial Management:

The Project Financial Management module manages the financial aspects of the organization's projects. It provides tools for project budgeting, cost tracking, and financial reporting. This module helps ensure that projects are completed within budget and provides insights into project financial performance.

2. Project Execution:

The Project Execution module manages the planning and execution of the organization's projects. It handles project scheduling, resource allocation, and task management. This module helps ensure that projects are completed on time and within scope and provides tools for monitoring project progress.

Customer Relationship Management

1. Sales:

The Sales module manages the organization's sales processes, from lead generation to deal closure. It provides tools for managing sales opportunities, tracking customer interactions, and forecasting sales performance. This module helps improve sales efficiency, increase revenue, and enhance customer relationships.

2. Marketing:

The Marketing module manages the organization's marketing campaigns and activities. It provides tools for campaign planning, execution, and analysis. This module helps optimize marketing efforts, improve campaign effectiveness, and generate leads for the sales team.

3. Service:

The Service module manages the organization's customer service operations. It provides tools for managing service requests, tracking customer issues, and ensuring timely resolution. This module helps improve customer satisfaction, enhance service quality, and support customer retention.

Analytics and Reporting

1. Business Intelligence (BI):

The Business Intelligence module provides tools for data analysis, reporting, and visualization. It enables organizations to generate actionable insights from their data, create custom reports, and build interactive dashboards. This module helps improve decision-making, identify trends, and monitor business performance.

2. Financial Reporting:

The Financial Reporting module provides tools for generating financial statements, regulatory reports, and management reports. It supports multiple reporting standards and allows for the customization of report formats. This module helps ensure compliance with financial reporting requirements and provides insights into the organization's financial performance.

Governance, Risk, and Compliance

1. Risk Management:

The Risk Management module provides tools for identifying, assessing, and mitigating risks across the organization. It helps manage risk registers, perform risk assessments, and develop risk mitigation plans. This module helps ensure that risks are effectively managed and supports the organization's risk management framework.

2. Compliance Management:

The Compliance Management module provides tools for managing compliance with regulatory requirements and internal policies. It helps monitor compliance status, manage compliance activities, and generate compliance reports. This module helps ensure that the organization adheres to regulatory standards and minimizes compliance risks.

3. Internal Controls:

The Internal Controls module provides tools for managing and monitoring internal controls across the organization. It helps ensure that controls are in place to prevent fraud, errors, and non-compliance. This module supports the organization's internal control framework and helps maintain the integrity of financial and operational processes.

1.1.3 Benefits of Implementing Oracle ERP

Implementing Oracle ERP (Enterprise Resource Planning) offers numerous benefits to organizations of various sizes and industries. These benefits span operational efficiency, strategic advantages, financial management, and compliance. In this section, we will explore the key benefits of implementing Oracle ERP in detail.

Streamlined Business Processes

One of the primary benefits of implementing Oracle ERP is the streamlining of business processes. Oracle ERP integrates various functions such as finance, supply chain, human resources, and customer relationship management into a single cohesive system. This integration eliminates the need for disparate systems and manual processes, leading to more efficient operations. By automating routine tasks and workflows, organizations can reduce errors, save time, and focus on more strategic activities.

For example, in the Accounts Receivable module, the process of generating invoices, tracking payments, and managing collections can be automated, ensuring accuracy and timeliness. This not only improves cash flow management but also enhances customer satisfaction by providing timely and accurate billing information.

Enhanced Data Visibility and Reporting

Oracle ERP provides enhanced data visibility across the organization. With real-time access to critical business data, decision-makers can make informed choices quickly. The system offers comprehensive reporting and analytics capabilities, allowing users to generate detailed reports, analyze trends, and gain insights into various aspects of the business.

In the context of Accounts Receivable, users can generate reports on outstanding invoices, aging reports, and cash flow projections. These reports help in identifying overdue payments, assessing the financial health of the organization, and making data-driven decisions to improve collections and reduce bad debt.

Improved Financial Management

Oracle ERP significantly improves financial management by providing a unified view of financial data. It supports accurate and timely financial reporting, budgeting, and forecasting. The system ensures compliance with accounting standards and regulatory requirements, reducing the risk of errors and financial discrepancies.

In the Accounts Receivable module, Oracle ERP helps manage customer invoices, payments, and credit limits efficiently. By integrating with other financial modules, such as Accounts Payable and General Ledger, it provides a holistic view of the organization's financial position. This integration facilitates accurate financial reporting and aids in better cash flow management.

Scalability and Flexibility

Oracle ERP is designed to scale with the growth of the organization. Whether a company is expanding its operations, entering new markets, or undergoing mergers and acquisitions, Oracle ERP can adapt to changing business needs. The system's modular architecture allows organizations to add or modify modules as required, ensuring that the ERP system evolves with the business.

For instance, as a company grows and adds new customers, the Accounts Receivable module can handle an increased volume of transactions without compromising performance. This scalability ensures that the ERP system continues to support the organization's needs, regardless of its size or complexity.

Enhanced Collaboration and Communication

Oracle ERP fosters enhanced collaboration and communication within the organization. By providing a centralized platform for sharing information and coordinating activities, it breaks down silos and promotes cross-functional collaboration. Employees from different departments can access the same data, collaborate on projects, and communicate more effectively.

In the Accounts Receivable context, sales, finance, and customer service teams can work together seamlessly. Sales teams can access customer payment histories to negotiate terms, finance teams can track outstanding invoices and manage collections, and customer service teams can provide timely support based on accurate billing information. This collaboration leads to improved customer relationships and more efficient operations.

Better Compliance and Risk Management

Compliance with regulatory requirements and managing risks are critical concerns for organizations. Oracle ERP helps ensure compliance by providing tools for monitoring, reporting, and auditing financial transactions. The system supports adherence to accounting standards, tax regulations, and industry-specific compliance requirements.

In the Accounts Receivable module, Oracle ERP ensures that all financial transactions related to invoicing, payments, and collections are accurately recorded and reported. It provides audit trails and controls to prevent fraud and errors, reducing the risk of financial misstatements and legal issues.

Increased Productivity and Efficiency

Implementing Oracle ERP leads to increased productivity and efficiency across the organization. By automating routine tasks, reducing manual data entry, and streamlining processes, employees can focus on more value-added activities. The system's user-friendly interface and intuitive workflows further enhance productivity by reducing the learning curve and making it easier for users to perform their tasks.

For example, in the Accounts Receivable module, automating the invoice generation process eliminates the need for manual entry, reduces errors, and speeds up the billing cycle. This efficiency translates into faster payments, improved cash flow, and reduced administrative overhead.

Enhanced Customer Experience

Oracle ERP plays a crucial role in enhancing the customer experience. By providing accurate and timely information, improving communication, and streamlining processes, organizations can deliver better service to their customers. In the Accounts Receivable module, timely and accurate invoicing, efficient payment processing, and effective collections contribute to a positive customer experience.

For instance, customers appreciate receiving accurate invoices promptly and having multiple payment options available. Automated reminders for overdue payments and efficient handling of disputes and refunds further enhance customer satisfaction. By leveraging Oracle ERP, organizations can build stronger relationships with their customers and foster loyalty.

Cost Savings and Return on Investment (ROI)

Implementing Oracle ERP can lead to significant cost savings and a high return on investment (ROI). By streamlining processes, reducing manual work, and improving efficiency, organizations can lower operational costs. The system's ability to integrate various functions reduces the need for multiple standalone systems, resulting in cost savings related to maintenance, support, and training.

In the Accounts Receivable module, automating collections and reducing the time spent on manual tasks can lead to faster payments and reduced days sales outstanding (DSO). This improvement in cash flow management directly impacts the organization's bottom line. Additionally, the insights gained from enhanced reporting and analytics can help identify cost-saving opportunities and drive strategic decision-making.

Strategic Decision-Making

Oracle ERP provides the tools and insights necessary for strategic decision-making. With access to real-time data and advanced analytics, decision-makers can evaluate various scenarios, assess risks, and make informed choices that align with the organization's goals. The system supports strategic planning, performance management, and continuous improvement initiatives.

In the context of Accounts Receivable, organizations can analyze customer payment patterns, assess credit risks, and develop strategies to optimize collections. By leveraging data-driven insights, they can make informed decisions that improve cash flow, reduce bad debt, and enhance overall financial performance.

Integration with Emerging Technologies

Oracle ERP is designed to integrate with emerging technologies such as artificial intelligence (AI), machine learning (ML), and the Internet of Things (IoT). These technologies can further enhance the capabilities of the ERP system, providing advanced analytics, predictive insights, and automation.

For example, AI and ML can be used in the Accounts Receivable module to predict customer payment behavior, identify potential delinquencies, and recommend collection strategies. IoT integration can help track shipments and ensure timely delivery, improving the overall order-to-cash process. By embracing these technologies, organizations can stay ahead of the competition and drive innovation.

Globalization and Multinational Support

For organizations with a global presence, Oracle ERP offers robust support for multinational operations. The system can handle multiple currencies, languages, and regulatory requirements, ensuring compliance and efficiency across different regions. This capability is essential for organizations operating in diverse markets and dealing with international customers and suppliers.

In the Accounts Receivable module, Oracle ERP supports multi-currency invoicing, global tax compliance, and cross-border transactions. This flexibility enables organizations to manage their global accounts receivable processes seamlessly, reducing complexity and ensuring accuracy.

Continuous Improvement and Adaptability

Oracle ERP supports continuous improvement and adaptability, allowing organizations to refine their processes and adapt to changing business environments. The system's flexibility and scalability enable organizations to implement best practices, optimize workflows, and incorporate feedback from users.

For example, organizations can continuously monitor the performance of their Accounts Receivable processes, identify bottlenecks, and implement improvements. This iterative approach ensures that the ERP system evolves with the business, driving ongoing efficiency gains and better financial performance.

1.2 The Role of the Accounts Receivable Module

The Accounts Receivable (AR) module is an integral part of the Oracle ERP system, designed to manage and streamline the process of tracking customer payments and outstanding invoices. This module plays a crucial role in maintaining the financial health of an organization by ensuring accurate and timely billing and collection of receivables.

1.2.1 Primary Functions of Accounts Receivable

The primary functions of the Accounts Receivable module can be categorized into several key areas, each contributing to the efficient management of customer-related financial transactions. These functions include invoice management, receipt processing, credit management, collections, and reporting and analysis.

Invoice Management

Invoice management is the core function of the Accounts Receivable module. It involves creating, maintaining, and tracking customer invoices. The process starts when a sale is made, and an invoice is generated to request payment from the customer. The AR module automates this process, ensuring that invoices are accurate, timely, and compliant with organizational policies and regulations.

1. Invoice Creation: The module allows users to create invoices based on sales orders, contracts, or manual entries. It supports various invoice types, including standard invoices, credit memos, debit memos, and recurring invoices. This flexibility ensures that all types of customer transactions can be accurately billed.

2. Invoice Tracking: Once invoices are created, the AR module tracks their status, including issued, pending, paid, and overdue invoices. This tracking capability helps organizations monitor their receivables and take appropriate actions to ensure timely payments.

3. Invoice Customization: The module provides tools to customize invoice formats and templates, allowing businesses to include necessary details such as payment terms, due dates, and customer-specific information. This customization ensures clarity and professionalism in customer communications.

4. Automated Invoicing: The AR module can automate the invoicing process for recurring transactions or subscription-based services. This automation reduces manual effort, minimizes errors, and ensures that invoices are sent out on time.

Receipt Processing

Receipt processing is another critical function of the Accounts Receivable module. It involves recording and applying customer payments to outstanding invoices. Efficient receipt processing ensures that the organization's cash flow is accurately reflected and helps in maintaining a healthy financial position.

1. Payment Recording: The AR module supports various payment methods, including checks, electronic transfers, credit cards, and cash. It allows users to record payments received and match them to the corresponding invoices. This feature helps in keeping the receivables ledger up-to-date.

2. Payment Application: Once payments are recorded, the module automatically or manually applies them to the appropriate invoices. This process includes handling partial payments, overpayments, and prepayments. Accurate payment application reduces discrepancies and ensures that customer accounts are correctly balanced.

3. Bank Reconciliation: The AR module facilitates bank reconciliation by matching recorded payments with bank statements. This reconciliation process helps in identifying any discrepancies between the organization's records and the bank's records, ensuring accuracy in financial reporting.

4. Refund Processing: In cases where customers overpay or return goods, the AR module manages refund processing. It tracks refund requests, approves them based on organizational policies, and ensures that refunds are issued promptly.

Credit Management

Credit management is essential for controlling the risk associated with extending credit to customers. The Accounts Receivable module provides tools to manage credit policies, evaluate customer creditworthiness, and monitor credit limits.

1. Credit Policies: The module allows organizations to define and enforce credit policies. These policies may include criteria for credit approval, credit limits, payment terms, and

conditions for extending credit to customers. By adhering to these policies, businesses can minimize the risk of bad debts.

2. Credit Evaluation: Before extending credit, the AR module helps evaluate a customer's creditworthiness. It may involve assessing credit scores, payment history, and financial stability. This evaluation ensures that credit is granted to reliable customers, reducing the likelihood of defaults.

3. Credit Limits: The module enables setting credit limits for each customer based on their credit evaluation. It automatically monitors customer transactions and alerts users when a customer is approaching or exceeding their credit limit. This proactive approach helps in maintaining control over receivables.

4. Credit Hold: In cases where customers exceed their credit limits or have overdue invoices, the AR module can place their accounts on credit hold. This hold prevents further sales to the customer until the outstanding issues are resolved, mitigating the risk of accumulating bad debts.

Collections Management

Effective collections management ensures that overdue invoices are promptly addressed and payments are collected in a timely manner. The Accounts Receivable module provides tools and workflows to streamline the collections process.

1. Collections Strategies: The module allows organizations to define and implement collections strategies based on customer profiles, invoice aging, and payment history. These strategies may include automated reminders, escalation procedures, and personalized follow-ups.

2. Dunning Letters: The AR module can automatically generate and send dunning letters to customers with overdue invoices. These letters serve as formal reminders, urging customers to settle their outstanding balances. The module supports multiple dunning levels, escalating the tone and urgency of reminders as invoices age.

3. Collections Workflows: The module provides customizable collections workflows that guide users through the process of contacting customers, negotiating payment terms, and resolving disputes. These workflows ensure consistency and efficiency in collections efforts.

4. Payment Plans: For customers facing financial difficulties, the AR module supports setting up payment plans. These plans allow customers to pay their outstanding balances in installments, helping to recover receivables while maintaining positive customer relationships.

Reporting and Analysis

Accurate reporting and analysis of accounts receivable data are crucial for making informed financial decisions. The Accounts Receivable module offers comprehensive reporting and analytical tools to monitor performance, identify trends, and ensure compliance.

1. Standard Reports: The module provides a wide range of standard reports, including aged receivables, invoice summaries, payment histories, and credit limit utilization. These reports offer insights into the status and health of the organization's receivables.

2. Custom Reports: Users can create custom reports tailored to their specific needs. The module's reporting tools allow for the customization of report templates, data filters, and presentation formats. Custom reports provide flexibility in analyzing receivables data from different perspectives.

3. Key Performance Indicators (KPIs): The AR module includes dashboards and KPIs that highlight critical metrics such as days sales outstanding (DSO), collection effectiveness index (CEI), and bad debt ratio. These KPIs help in tracking performance and identifying areas for improvement.

4. Compliance Reporting: The module ensures compliance with regulatory requirements by generating necessary reports for audits and financial disclosures. It tracks and documents all transactions, providing a clear audit trail for regulatory scrutiny.

5. Trend Analysis: By analyzing historical data, the AR module helps identify trends in customer behavior, payment patterns, and credit risk. Trend analysis supports proactive decision-making and strategic planning.

1.2.2 Integration with Other Oracle ERP Modules

The integration of the Accounts Receivable (AR) module with other modules in Oracle ERP is essential for a seamless and efficient financial management process. Integration ensures that data flows smoothly between different departments and functions, minimizing errors and redundancies while maximizing efficiency and accuracy. This section explores the key areas of integration between the AR module and other Oracle ERP modules, highlighting the benefits and practical applications of these integrations.

1.2.2.1 Integration with General Ledger (GL)

The General Ledger (GL) module is the central repository for all financial data within an organization. Integration between AR and GL is crucial for accurate financial reporting and compliance. The AR module generates various financial transactions, such as invoices, receipts, and adjustments, which need to be recorded in the GL for proper financial tracking.

Benefits of Integration with GL:

1. Real-time Financial Data: Transactions in the AR module are automatically posted to the GL, providing real-time updates to financial statements.

2. Accurate Financial Reporting: Integration ensures that all revenue-related transactions are accurately reflected in the financial statements, supporting compliance with accounting standards.

3. Streamlined Month-End Closing: Automated posting reduces manual intervention, speeding up the month-end closing process.

Practical Applications:

- Invoice Posting: When an invoice is created in AR, the corresponding revenue and receivable accounts in GL are updated.

- Receipt Application: Applying customer receipts in AR updates the cash and receivables accounts in GL.

- Adjustments and Write-offs: Adjustments made in AR, such as discounts or write-offs, are automatically reflected in GL, ensuring financial accuracy.

1.2.2.2 Integration with Order Management (OM)

The Order Management (OM) module handles the creation, processing, and fulfillment of sales orders. Integration with AR is essential to ensure that sales orders are accurately invoiced and that revenue is recognized appropriately.

Benefits of Integration with OM:

1. Seamless Order-to-Cash Process: Integration ensures that sales orders are converted to invoices without manual intervention, streamlining the order-to-cash cycle.

2. Accurate Revenue Recognition: Sales orders are invoiced promptly, ensuring timely and accurate revenue recognition.

3. Enhanced Customer Experience: Customers receive accurate and timely invoices, improving customer satisfaction and reducing disputes.

Practical Applications:

- Sales Order Invoicing: When a sales order is fulfilled in OM, an invoice is automatically generated in AR, reflecting the order details.

- Order Adjustments: Changes to sales orders, such as returns or discounts, are automatically updated in AR, ensuring accurate invoicing and revenue recognition.

- Credit Holds: Integration allows AR to place credit holds on sales orders in OM if a customer exceeds their credit limit, mitigating financial risk.

1.2.2.3 Integration with Inventory Management (IM)

The Inventory Management (IM) module tracks the movement and value of inventory items. Integration with AR is critical for ensuring that sales of inventory items are accurately invoiced and that inventory values are updated accordingly.

Benefits of Integration with IM:

1. Accurate Inventory Valuation: Sales transactions in AR reduce the inventory quantities and update the inventory value in IM.

2. Consistent Data: Integration ensures that inventory data is consistent across both modules, reducing discrepancies.

3. Streamlined Sales Process: Sales transactions automatically update inventory records, simplifying inventory management.

Practical Applications:

- Inventory Deduction: When an invoice is generated for a sale, the corresponding inventory items are deducted from the inventory records in IM.

- Inventory Adjustments: Adjustments to inventory, such as returns or exchanges, are automatically reflected in both AR and IM, ensuring consistency.

- Cost of Goods Sold (COGS): Integration ensures that the cost of sold inventory items is accurately recorded in the financial statements.

1.2.2.4 Integration with Procurement and Payables (P2P)

The Procurement and Payables (P2P) module handles the purchasing and payment processes for goods and services. While the primary interaction between AR and P2P is less direct, integration is important for managing vendor and customer relationships, particularly in scenarios involving customer returns or rebates.

Benefits of Integration with P2P:

1. Efficient Returns Management: Integration allows for seamless processing of customer returns and vendor credits.

2. Accurate Financial Records: Transactions involving both customers and vendors are accurately recorded in both AR and P2P.

3. Enhanced Cash Flow Management: Integrated data provides a comprehensive view of both receivables and payables, aiding in cash flow management.

Practical Applications:

- Customer Returns: Returns processed in AR can generate vendor credits in P2P, ensuring accurate financial records.

- Rebates and Discounts: Rebates or discounts offered to customers may impact vendor agreements, necessitating updates in both AR and P2P.

- Intercompany Transactions: Integration facilitates accurate recording of transactions between different entities within the same organization.

1.2.2.5 Integration with Human Resources (HR)

The Human Resources (HR) module manages employee-related data and processes. Integration with AR is relevant in scenarios where employee sales or commissions need to be tracked and compensated accurately.

Benefits of Integration with HR:

1. Accurate Commission Tracking: Integration ensures that sales commissions are accurately calculated and paid to employees.

2. Consistent Employee Data: Employee information, such as department or role, is consistent across both modules.

3. Enhanced Reporting: Integrated data supports comprehensive reporting on sales performance and employee compensation.

Practical Applications:

- Commission Calculations: Sales transactions in AR are used to calculate employee commissions in HR, ensuring timely and accurate payments.

- Employee Sales Tracking: Sales data is linked to employee records, facilitating performance tracking and reporting.

- Expense Reimbursements: Integration allows for accurate recording and reimbursement of employee expenses related to customer sales or support.

1.2.2.6 Integration with Projects (PJ)

The Projects (PJ) module manages project-related financial and operational data. Integration with AR is important for invoicing project-related transactions and tracking project revenue.

Benefits of Integration with PJ:

1. Accurate Project Invoicing: Integration ensures that project-related transactions are accurately invoiced and recorded.

2. Comprehensive Project Financials: Project revenue and expenses are tracked accurately, supporting project profitability analysis.

3. Streamlined Billing Process: Project billing is automated, reducing manual intervention and errors.

Practical Applications:

- Project Invoicing: Transactions recorded in PJ, such as labor or materials, are invoiced through AR, ensuring accurate project billing.

- Revenue Recognition: Project-related revenue is recognized accurately in AR, supporting financial reporting.

- Project Financial Reports: Integration enables comprehensive financial reporting on project performance and profitability.

1.2.2.7 Integration with Customer Relationship Management (CRM)

The Customer Relationship Management (CRM) module manages customer interactions and data. Integration with AR is essential for providing a holistic view of customer relationships and financial transactions.

Benefits of Integration with CRM:

1. Enhanced Customer Insights: Integration provides a comprehensive view of customer interactions and financial transactions, supporting better decision-making.

2. Improved Customer Service: Customer service representatives have access to up-to-date financial data, enabling better support.

3. Targeted Marketing: Financial data from AR can be used to inform targeted marketing campaigns based on customer purchasing behavior.

Practical Applications:

- Customer Financial Data: Financial transactions in AR, such as invoices and payments, are accessible in CRM, providing a complete view of customer accounts.

- Sales Insights: Sales data from AR informs CRM activities, such as identifying high-value customers or targeting upsell opportunities.

- Customer Support: Integration ensures that customer service representatives can access financial data to resolve billing inquiries or disputes efficiently.

Conclusion

The integration of the Accounts Receivable module with other Oracle ERP modules is fundamental for achieving a streamlined and efficient financial management process. Each integration point brings specific benefits, from real-time financial data updates to enhanced customer insights, ensuring that organizations can manage their financial operations more effectively. By leveraging these integrations, businesses can improve accuracy, reduce manual effort, and support better decision-making across the organization.

1.2.3 Importance of Accounts Receivable in Financial Management

Accounts Receivable (AR) is a critical component of financial management within Oracle ERP, playing a pivotal role in ensuring the liquidity and financial health of an organization. This section explores the profound significance of Accounts Receivable, detailing its impact on various aspects of financial management.

Enhancing Cash Flow

One of the primary roles of Accounts Receivable is to facilitate cash flow management. By invoicing customers promptly and accurately, AR ensures that revenue is recognized and collected in a timely manner. This process directly impacts the organization's liquidity, allowing it to meet its financial obligations such as paying suppliers, employees, and other operating expenses.

Revenue Recognition and Reporting

Accounts Receivable plays a crucial role in revenue recognition, a cornerstone of financial reporting. Proper management of AR ensures that revenue is recorded accurately and in compliance with accounting standards. This not only supports transparent financial reporting but also enhances investor confidence and regulatory compliance.

Working Capital Management

Effective management of Accounts Receivable is essential for optimizing working capital. AR represents funds that are due to the organization but have not yet been received. By efficiently managing AR, organizations can minimize the time it takes to convert sales into cash, thereby reducing the need for external financing and improving overall financial stability.

Customer Relationships and Satisfaction

The Accounts Receivable function directly impacts customer relationships and satisfaction. Timely and accurate invoicing, along with responsive handling of billing inquiries and disputes, contributes to positive customer experiences. This, in turn, fosters long-term customer loyalty and enhances the organization's reputation in the marketplace.

Credit Management and Risk Mitigation

Accounts Receivable involves assessing and managing credit risks associated with customers. Effective credit management practices, such as establishing credit limits, monitoring creditworthiness, and implementing collections strategies, help mitigate the risk of bad debts and financial losses. This proactive approach safeguards the organization's financial health and profitability.

Compliance and Audit Readiness

Maintaining accurate Accounts Receivable records is crucial for regulatory compliance and audit readiness. Proper documentation of transactions, adherence to accounting principles, and timely reconciliation of AR balances ensure that the organization can demonstrate transparency and accountability during audits. This reduces the risk of penalties, fines, and legal liabilities.

Strategic Decision Making

Data derived from Accounts Receivable activities provides valuable insights for strategic decision-making. Analysis of AR aging, collection trends, and customer payment behaviors enables management to identify opportunities for process improvements, pricing adjustments, and resource allocation. These insights support informed decision-making that drives business growth and profitability.

Operational Efficiency and Automation

Modern Oracle ERP systems offer automation capabilities that streamline Accounts Receivable processes. Automated invoicing, payment reminders, and collections workflows improve operational efficiency, reduce manual errors, and accelerate cash conversion cycles. This allows AR teams to focus on strategic activities that add value to the organization.

Continuous Improvement and Adaptability

Accounts Receivable operations benefit from continuous improvement initiatives. Regular review of AR policies, procedures, and performance metrics allows organizations to adapt to changing market conditions, customer expectations, and regulatory requirements. Continuous improvement fosters agility and resilience, positioning the organization for sustained success in dynamic business environments.

Conclusion

In conclusion, Accounts Receivable is far more than a transactional function within Oracle ERP—it is a cornerstone of financial management that influences cash flow, revenue recognition, working capital, customer relationships, risk management, compliance, strategic decision-making, operational efficiency, and continuous improvement. By recognizing the critical importance of Accounts Receivable and implementing best practices supported by Oracle ERP functionalities, organizations can optimize financial performance, mitigate risks, and achieve sustainable growth.

1.3 Key Features of the Accounts Receivable Module

1.3.1 Overview of Key Features and Functionalities

The Accounts Receivable (AR) module in Oracle ERP is designed to manage and streamline the processes associated with customer invoicing, payment collections, and credit management. It is a critical component of the financial management system, offering a range of features that enhance efficiency, accuracy, and financial control. This section provides an in-depth overview of the key features and functionalities of the AR module, highlighting how they contribute to effective accounts receivable management.

1.3.1.1 Invoice Management

Invoice management is the core function of the AR module. This feature allows businesses to create, process, and manage customer invoices with ease. Key functionalities include:

- Invoice Creation: Users can generate invoices based on sales orders, contracts, or manual entries. The system supports different types of invoices such as standard, credit memos, and debit memos.

- Recurring Invoices: The AR module allows for the creation of recurring invoices for ongoing services or long-term contracts, automating the billing process and ensuring timely invoicing.

- Batch Invoicing: This feature enables the processing of multiple invoices in a batch, saving time and reducing manual effort. Batch invoicing is particularly useful for businesses with high transaction volumes.

- Invoice Templates: Customizable invoice templates ensure that all necessary information is included and presented in a professional format. Templates can be tailored to meet specific business requirements.

1.3.1.2 Payment Processing

Efficient payment processing is essential for maintaining healthy cash flow. The AR module provides several tools to manage and record customer payments:

- Receipt Management: The system supports various methods of payment, including cash, checks, credit cards, and electronic funds transfer (EFT). Users can record and apply payments to customer accounts quickly.

- Automatic Payment Matching: The AR module can automatically match payments to open invoices based on predefined criteria, reducing the need for manual reconciliation and minimizing errors.

- Partial Payments and Overpayments: The system handles partial payments and overpayments efficiently, ensuring that customer accounts are accurately updated and any discrepancies are managed.

- Payment Terms: Users can define and manage payment terms for different customers, including due dates, early payment discounts, and late payment penalties. This helps in maintaining clear payment expectations and improving collections.

1.3.1.3 Credit Management

Managing customer credit is crucial for minimizing financial risk and ensuring timely payments. The AR module offers robust credit management features:

- Credit Limits: Businesses can set credit limits for customers based on their creditworthiness and payment history. The system monitors outstanding balances and alerts users when a customer exceeds their credit limit.

- Credit Holds: If a customer's account exceeds their credit limit or has overdue invoices, the system can automatically place a credit hold on the account, preventing further sales orders until the issue is resolved.

- Credit Scoring: The AR module can integrate with credit scoring systems to assess and assign credit scores to customers, providing valuable insights into their financial stability and payment behavior.

- Customer Credit Reviews: Regular credit reviews can be scheduled and managed within the system, ensuring that credit policies are consistently applied and updated based on customer performance.

1.3.1.4 Collections Management

Effective collections management is essential for reducing delinquent accounts and improving cash flow. The AR module provides comprehensive tools for managing collections:

- Collection Strategies: Users can define and implement collection strategies tailored to different customer segments. These strategies may include automated reminders, personalized collection letters, and follow-up calls.

- Dunning Letters: The system can generate and send dunning letters to customers with overdue accounts, reminding them of their outstanding balances and encouraging prompt payment.

- Promise to Pay: Customers can make promises to pay within a specified timeframe. The AR module tracks these promises and alerts users if the payment is not received as agreed.

- Dispute Management: The system provides tools for managing and resolving invoice disputes. Users can log disputes, track their status, and communicate with customers to reach a resolution.

1.3.1.5 Reporting and Analysis

Accurate and timely reporting is essential for effective accounts receivable management. The AR module includes a range of reporting and analysis tools:

- Standard Reports: The system offers a variety of standard reports, including aging reports, payment histories, and customer statements. These reports provide valuable insights into the status of accounts receivable and help identify potential issues.

- Custom Reports: Users can create custom reports tailored to specific business needs. The reporting tools allow for the selection of specific data fields, filters, and formats, ensuring that the reports meet the organization's requirements.

- Dashboards and Analytics: The AR module includes dashboards that provide a visual representation of key performance indicators (KPIs) such as days sales outstanding (DSO), collection effectiveness index (CEI), and overdue balances. These dashboards help users monitor performance and make data-driven decisions.

- Audit Trails: The system maintains detailed audit trails of all transactions and changes, ensuring transparency and accountability. This is particularly important for compliance and audit purposes.

1.3.1.6 Integration with Other Modules

Seamless integration with other Oracle ERP modules enhances the functionality of the AR module and ensures data consistency across the organization:

- Sales Order Management: The AR module integrates with the Sales Order Management module to automate the invoicing process based on sales orders. This ensures accurate billing and reduces manual effort.

- General Ledger: Integration with the General Ledger (GL) ensures that all accounts receivable transactions are accurately recorded in the financial statements. This provides a comprehensive view of the organization's financial position.

- Cash Management: The AR module works with the Cash Management module to track and manage cash flows, providing real-time visibility into cash positions and liquidity.

- Inventory Management: Integration with Inventory Management allows for the accurate tracking of inventory levels and ensures that sales orders are fulfilled promptly.

1.3.1.7 User Interface and Navigation

A user-friendly interface and intuitive navigation are essential for efficient use of the AR module:

- Dashboard Interface: The AR module features a customizable dashboard that provides quick access to key information and frequently used functions. Users can personalize their dashboards to suit their roles and preferences.

- Menu Navigation: The system's menu navigation is designed to be intuitive and logical, making it easy for users to find and access the functions they need. This reduces the learning curve and improves productivity.

- Search and Filter Options: Powerful search and filter options allow users to quickly locate specific records or transactions. This is particularly useful for managing large volumes of data.

- Help and Documentation: The AR module includes comprehensive help and documentation resources, providing users with the information they need to perform their tasks effectively. This includes online help, user guides, and tutorials.

In conclusion, the Accounts Receivable module in Oracle ERP offers a comprehensive suite of features and functionalities designed to streamline invoicing, payment processing, credit management, and collections. By leveraging these tools, businesses can improve efficiency, enhance financial control, and maintain healthy cash flow. The module's integration with other ERP components ensures data consistency and provides a holistic view of the organization's financial health. With its user-friendly interface and powerful reporting capabilities, the AR module is an essential tool for effective accounts receivable management.

1.3.2 User Interface and Navigation

The user interface (UI) and navigation of the Oracle Accounts Receivable (AR) module are crucial for ensuring efficient and effective use of the system. A well-designed UI can significantly enhance user experience by making tasks more intuitive and less time-consuming. This section provides a detailed exploration of the key aspects of the AR module's user interface and navigation, covering the layout, key elements, and how to navigate through the module efficiently.

Layout and Design

The Oracle AR module's UI is designed to be user-friendly and consistent with the overall Oracle ERP suite. The layout typically includes the following components:

1. Navigation Pane: This is usually located on the left side of the screen and provides quick access to different areas of the AR module, such as customer records, invoices, receipts, and reports. The navigation pane helps users quickly switch between tasks without having to go through multiple screens.

2. Toolbar: Positioned at the top of the screen, the toolbar contains various buttons and menus that provide quick access to common functions and tools. These might include

options for creating new records, searching existing records, generating reports, and accessing help documentation.

3. Main Workspace: The central area of the screen is the main workspace where users perform their tasks. This area displays detailed information and forms for the current task, such as customer details, invoice forms, or payment processing screens.

4. Contextual Menus: Right-click menus and other contextual options provide additional functionality based on the specific area or task the user is working on. These menus help users perform actions relevant to the selected item without navigating away from the current screen.

Key Elements of the User Interface

1. Dashboards: Dashboards provide a visual overview of key metrics and performance indicators related to accounts receivable. They can be customized to display information such as outstanding invoices, overdue payments, and cash flow trends. Dashboards help users quickly assess the current state of AR processes and identify areas that need attention.

2. Forms and Fields: The AR module uses various forms to capture and display information. These forms are designed with fields that collect essential data, such as customer details, invoice amounts, and payment terms. The forms are organized logically to ensure that users can enter and retrieve information efficiently.

3. Search and Filter Options: To manage large volumes of data, the AR module provides robust search and filter options. Users can search for specific records using criteria such as customer name, invoice number, or date range. Filters can be applied to narrow down the search results and focus on relevant data.

4. Notifications and Alerts: The UI includes notifications and alerts to keep users informed about important events and tasks. For example, users may receive alerts for overdue invoices, pending approvals, or upcoming payment deadlines. These notifications help users stay on top of their responsibilities and take timely actions.

5. Reports and Analytics: The AR module includes built-in reporting and analytics tools that allow users to generate and view detailed reports. These reports provide insights into various aspects of accounts receivable, such as aging reports, payment histories, and customer balances. The reporting tools often include options for exporting data to other formats, such as Excel or PDF.

Navigation Techniques

Effective navigation is essential for maximizing productivity and minimizing errors. The Oracle AR module provides several navigation techniques to help users move through the system efficiently:

1. Menu Navigation: Users can navigate through the module using the main menu and sub-menus. The menus are organized hierarchically, making it easy to find specific functions and tasks. For example, under the "Transactions" menu, users might find options for creating invoices, recording receipts, and managing credit memos.

2. Quick Links: Quick links are shortcuts to frequently used functions and screens. These links are typically placed on the homepage or dashboard and provide one-click access to tasks such as creating a new invoice or viewing customer balances.

3. Search Functionality: The search bar allows users to quickly locate specific records or screens by entering keywords or phrases. Advanced search options enable users to refine their searches using multiple criteria, ensuring that they can find the information they need promptly.

4. Tabs and Sub-Tabs: Many screens in the AR module use tabs and sub-tabs to organize information into logical sections. For example, a customer record might have tabs for general information, contact details, payment terms, and transaction history. Tabs help users quickly navigate between different types of information without leaving the current screen.

5. Breadcrumbs: Breadcrumbs are a navigational aid that shows the user's current location within the module and the path taken to get there. They are typically displayed at the top of the screen and allow users to backtrack to previous screens or sections easily.

6. Keyboard Shortcuts: For users who prefer using the keyboard over the mouse, the AR module supports various keyboard shortcuts. These shortcuts enable users to perform common actions, such as saving a record or opening a new form, more quickly and efficiently.

Customizing the User Interface

The Oracle AR module allows for a high degree of customization to meet the specific needs of different organizations and users. Customizing the UI can enhance usability and ensure that the most relevant information is readily accessible. Key customization options include:

1. Personalized Dashboards: Users can customize their dashboards to display the most important metrics and reports for their role. For example, a collections manager might prioritize aging reports and overdue invoices, while an AR clerk might focus on daily receipt entries and customer communications.

2. Custom Fields and Forms: Organizations can add custom fields to forms to capture additional information specific to their processes. Custom forms can also be created to streamline data entry and ensure that all necessary information is collected.

3. Role-Based Access: The AR module supports role-based access controls, allowing administrators to define which users can access specific screens and functions. This ensures that users only see the information and tools relevant to their role, enhancing security and reducing complexity.

4. Saved Searches and Filters: Users can save their search criteria and filters for quick access in the future. This is particularly useful for recurring tasks, such as generating monthly reports or reviewing overdue invoices.

5. Themes and Layouts: The visual appearance of the UI can be customized to match the organization's branding or user preferences. Themes and layouts can be adjusted to improve readability and user comfort.

Training and Support

To ensure that users can effectively navigate and use the AR module, training and support are essential. Oracle provides various resources to help users become proficient with the system:

1. Training Programs: Oracle offers formal training programs, including instructor-led courses and online training modules. These programs cover the basics of using the AR module as well as advanced topics.

2. User Guides and Documentation: Comprehensive user guides and documentation are available to help users understand the features and functions of the AR module. These resources provide step-by-step instructions and best practices for performing various tasks.

3. Online Help and Tutorials: The AR module includes built-in help options, such as tooltips and tutorials, to assist users as they work. Online help resources are regularly updated to reflect new features and enhancements.

4. Community and Forums: Oracle's user community and forums provide a platform for users to share knowledge, ask questions, and find solutions to common issues. Engaging with the community can be a valuable way to learn from the experiences of other users.

5. Customer Support: For technical issues and more complex questions, Oracle's customer support team is available to provide assistance. Support options may include phone support, email support, and live chat.

In conclusion, the user interface and navigation of the Oracle Accounts Receivable module are designed to be intuitive and efficient, enabling users to perform their tasks with ease. By understanding the layout, key elements, and navigation techniques, users can maximize their productivity and ensure accurate and timely management of accounts receivable processes. Customization options further enhance the usability of the module, allowing organizations to tailor the UI to their specific needs. With proper training and support, users can become proficient in navigating the AR module and leveraging its full potential.

1.3.3 Benefits of Using Accounts Receivable Features

The Accounts Receivable (AR) module in Oracle ERP offers a wide array of features designed to streamline and optimize the management of customer receivables. By leveraging these features, businesses can enhance their financial operations, improve cash flow, and ensure better customer relationship management. Below are some of the key benefits of using Accounts Receivable features in Oracle ERP.

Enhanced Cash Flow Management

Effective management of accounts receivable is critical to maintaining a healthy cash flow. Oracle ERP's AR module provides tools for timely and accurate invoicing, efficient collections, and effective credit management, all of which contribute to improved cash flow.

- Timely Invoicing: Automated invoicing processes ensure that invoices are generated and sent to customers promptly. This reduces delays in payment cycles and accelerates cash inflow.

- Efficient Collections: With integrated collections strategies, businesses can follow up on overdue invoices systematically, reducing the days sales outstanding (DSO) and improving liquidity.

- Credit Management: By setting appropriate credit limits and monitoring customer creditworthiness, businesses can minimize bad debt and enhance cash flow predictability.

Improved Accuracy and Efficiency

Manual processing of accounts receivable can be prone to errors, which can lead to discrepancies and financial losses. The AR module in Oracle ERP automates many of these processes, ensuring greater accuracy and efficiency.

- Automated Data Entry: Automation reduces the need for manual data entry, minimizing errors and ensuring that all transactions are recorded accurately.

- Validation and Approval Workflows: Built-in validation checks and approval workflows ensure that invoices and payments are processed correctly, reducing the risk of errors and fraud.

- Reconciliation: The AR module facilitates the reconciliation of accounts receivable with the general ledger, ensuring that all transactions are accurately reflected in the financial statements.

Enhanced Customer Relationships

The AR module helps businesses manage customer interactions more effectively, leading to improved customer satisfaction and stronger relationships.

- Centralized Customer Information: All customer-related information, including contact details, transaction history, and credit terms, is stored in a centralized database, making it easier to access and manage.

- Efficient Dispute Management: The AR module provides tools for tracking and resolving disputes, ensuring that customer concerns are addressed promptly and satisfactorily.

- Flexible Payment Options: Offering a variety of payment options, such as electronic payments, credit card payments, and installment plans, can enhance customer satisfaction and encourage timely payments.

Better Financial Visibility and Reporting

Accurate and timely financial reporting is essential for making informed business decisions. The AR module in Oracle ERP provides robust reporting and analytical tools that offer valuable insights into the company's financial health.

- Comprehensive Reporting: Standard and customizable reports provide detailed insights into accounts receivable, including aging reports, collection performance, and customer payment behavior.

- Dashboards and KPIs: Real-time dashboards and key performance indicators (KPIs) enable managers to monitor the performance of the AR function and make data-driven decisions.

- Trend Analysis: Analytical tools allow businesses to identify trends in customer payments, assess the effectiveness of credit policies, and forecast future cash flows.

Compliance and Risk Management

Compliance with regulatory requirements and effective risk management are crucial for financial stability. The AR module helps businesses achieve these goals through robust compliance and risk management features.

- Tax Compliance: The AR module supports the configuration of various tax codes and jurisdictions, ensuring that invoices comply with tax regulations and that tax reporting is accurate.

- Audit Trails: Comprehensive audit trails provide a clear record of all transactions and changes, facilitating internal and external audits and ensuring accountability.

- Credit Risk Management: By monitoring customer creditworthiness and implementing appropriate credit controls, businesses can mitigate the risk of bad debt and financial losses.

Scalability and Flexibility

As businesses grow and evolve, their financial processes must adapt to changing needs. The AR module in Oracle ERP is designed to be scalable and flexible, supporting the growth and diversification of the business.

- Scalability: The AR module can handle increasing volumes of transactions and customers, ensuring that the system grows with the business.

- Customization: Businesses can customize the AR module to meet their specific requirements, including custom invoice templates, payment terms, and workflows.

- Integration: Seamless integration with other Oracle ERP modules and third-party systems ensures that the AR module can adapt to new business processes and technologies.

Operational Efficiency

The AR module's features enhance operational efficiency, allowing businesses to streamline their accounts receivable processes and reduce administrative overhead.

- Workflow Automation: Automation of routine tasks, such as invoice generation, payment matching, and dunning, frees up staff time for more strategic activities.

- Self-Service Portals: Customer self-service portals enable customers to view their invoices, make payments, and track their account status, reducing the need for manual intervention by AR staff.

- Document Management: Efficient document management features allow businesses to store, retrieve, and manage invoices, receipts, and other documents electronically, reducing paper usage and improving accessibility.

Enhanced Collaboration

Effective collaboration between departments is essential for the smooth functioning of the AR process. The AR module in Oracle ERP facilitates collaboration by providing a centralized platform for information sharing and communication.

- Shared Data: Centralized data storage ensures that all departments have access to the same accurate and up-to-date information, improving coordination and reducing errors.

- Integrated Communication Tools: Integrated communication tools, such as email notifications and workflow alerts, keep stakeholders informed and facilitate timely decision-making.

- Cross-Departmental Workflows: The AR module supports cross-departmental workflows, enabling seamless collaboration between finance, sales, customer service, and other departments involved in the AR process.

Conclusion

The benefits of using the Accounts Receivable features in Oracle ERP are manifold. From enhanced cash flow management and improved accuracy to better financial visibility and compliance, these features empower businesses to optimize their accounts receivable processes and achieve their financial goals. By leveraging the capabilities of the AR module, businesses can ensure efficient and effective management of customer receivables, leading to improved financial health and long-term success.

CHAPTER II
Setting Up the Accounts Receivable Module

2.1 Defining Company Parameters

2.1.1 Setting Up Basic Company Information

Setting up basic company information in the Oracle ERP Accounts Receivable (AR) module is a crucial step in ensuring the effective management of your organization's financial transactions. This foundational setup involves defining key details about your company, which will be used throughout the AR processes. This section will guide you through the steps to accurately configure this information, ensuring that your AR module operates smoothly and integrates seamlessly with other ERP modules.

1. Company Name and Legal Information

The first step in setting up basic company information is to input your company's name and legal details. This includes:

- Company Name: The official name of your organization as registered legally.

- Legal Entity: The specific legal structure of your company, such as corporation, partnership, or sole proprietorship.

- Registration Number: The official number provided upon registration of your company with the relevant authorities.

- Tax Identification Number (TIN): A unique identifier assigned to your company for tax purposes.

This information is critical for all transactions processed within the AR module, ensuring that all documentation and financial reports reflect the correct legal entity.

2. Address and Contact Information

Accurate address and contact details are essential for correspondence and compliance purposes. This information includes:

- Company Address: The official physical address of your organization. It is important to differentiate between the headquarters and any branch locations.

- Billing Address: The address where invoices and other financial documents should be sent.

- Contact Information: Key contact details such as phone numbers, email addresses, and fax numbers for various departments, including accounts receivable, finance, and customer service.

3. Financial Year and Reporting Periods

Defining the financial year and reporting periods is a critical aspect of setting up your company information. This involves:

- Financial Year Start and End Dates: The start and end dates of your financial year, which could vary depending on your organizational requirements or regulatory mandates.

- Reporting Periods: The intervals at which financial reports are generated. This could be monthly, quarterly, or annually. Consistent reporting periods are essential for accurate financial tracking and compliance.

4. Currency and Exchange Rates

Oracle ERP allows you to define the base currency in which your financial transactions will be recorded. This setup includes:

- Base Currency: The primary currency used by your organization for accounting purposes. All transactions will be recorded and reported in this currency.

- Exchange Rates: If your organization deals with multiple currencies, it is important to set up exchange rates. These rates can be updated regularly to reflect current market conditions.

5. Organizational Structure

Defining your organizational structure within Oracle ERP involves mapping out the different departments, divisions, and business units. This setup allows for better management and reporting of financial transactions. Key elements include:

- Departments and Divisions: Each department or division within your organization should be clearly defined. This helps in assigning responsibilities and tracking financial performance at a granular level.

- Business Units: If your organization operates multiple business units, it is important to set these up within the ERP system to ensure accurate financial reporting and accountability.

6. Tax Configuration

Setting up tax configurations is a crucial step to ensure compliance with local and international tax regulations. This setup includes:

- Tax Codes: Defining various tax codes applicable to your transactions.

- Tax Rates: Specifying the rates for each tax code.

- Jurisdictions: Identifying the different tax jurisdictions where your organization operates.

7. Chart of Accounts

The Chart of Accounts (COA) is the backbone of your financial reporting structure. Setting it up involves:

- Account Codes: Defining unique codes for each account in your financial system.

- Account Types: Categorizing accounts into assets, liabilities, equity, income, and expenses.

- Account Hierarchy: Organizing accounts into a hierarchical structure for easier reporting and analysis.

8. Defining Accounting Calendars

An accounting calendar is used to define the fiscal periods for your organization. This setup includes:

- Period Types: Monthly, quarterly, or annual periods.

- Period Names: Specific names for each period, such as Jan-2024, Feb-2024, etc.

- Period Status: The status of each period (open, closed, or future).

9. Setting Up Document Sequences

Document sequences ensure that all financial documents have unique identifiers. This setup includes:

- Document Categories: Defining categories such as invoices, receipts, and credit memos.

- Sequence Numbers: Assigning unique sequence numbers to each category for traceability.

10. Defining User Roles and Permissions

To ensure data security and proper access control, it is essential to define user roles and permissions. This setup includes:

- User Roles: Defining roles such as AR Clerk, AR Manager, and Financial Controller.

- Permissions: Assigning specific permissions to each role, such as view, create, edit, or delete transactions.

Detailed Steps for Setting Up Basic Company Information in Oracle ERP

1. Access the Setup Menu

Log in to your Oracle ERP system and navigate to the setup menu. This is typically located under the 'Administration' or 'Setup' section.

2. Enter Company Details

Go to the 'Company Information' section and enter the required details such as company name, legal entity, registration number, and TIN. Ensure that all information is accurate and up to date.

3. Add Address and Contact Information

Enter the physical address, billing address, and contact information. Double-check for accuracy to avoid any correspondence issues.

4. Define Financial Year and Reporting Periods

In the 'Financial Settings' section, specify the start and end dates of your financial year. Set up the reporting periods according to your organizational requirements.

5. Set Up Currency and Exchange Rates

Define the base currency for your organization. If dealing with multiple currencies, set up exchange rates in the 'Currency Settings' section.

6. Map Organizational Structure

In the 'Organizational Structure' section, define the departments, divisions, and business units. Assign responsibilities and reporting structures accordingly.

7. Configure Tax Settings

Set up tax codes, rates, and jurisdictions in the 'Tax Configuration' section. Ensure compliance with all relevant tax regulations.

8. Create Chart of Accounts

Define your Chart of Accounts in the 'Financial Settings' section. Assign account codes, types, and hierarchy for better financial management.

9. Define Accounting Calendars

Set up accounting calendars in the 'Calendar Settings' section. Define period types, names, and statuses for each fiscal period.

10. Set Up Document Sequences

In the 'Document Settings' section, define document categories and assign unique sequence numbers to each category.

11. Assign User Roles and Permissions

Go to the 'User Management' section and define user roles and permissions. Assign appropriate permissions to ensure data security and access control.

Best Practices for Setting Up Basic Company Information

- Data Accuracy: Ensure that all information entered is accurate and up to date. Incorrect data can lead to issues in financial reporting and compliance.

- Regular Updates: Periodically review and update company information to reflect any changes in organizational structure, address, or legal details.

- User Training: Provide training to users responsible for setting up and maintaining company information. This ensures that they understand the importance of accurate data entry and the impact on financial processes.

- Compliance Checks: Regularly review tax configurations and ensure compliance with local and international tax regulations. This helps in avoiding penalties and legal issues.

- Backup and Security: Implement robust backup and security measures to protect sensitive company information. Regularly back up data and restrict access to authorized personnel only.

By following these detailed steps and best practices, you can ensure that your basic company information is set up accurately in the Oracle ERP Accounts Receivable module. This foundational setup is crucial for the effective management of financial transactions and the seamless integration of the AR module with other ERP components.

2.1.2 Configuring Financial and Reporting Parameters

Configuring financial and reporting parameters in the Accounts Receivable (AR) module of Oracle ERP is a critical step that ensures accurate financial data recording, reporting, and compliance. This section delves into the specific parameters that need to be set up and the importance of each in the overall AR process.

Understanding Financial and Reporting Parameters

Financial parameters in the AR module determine how transactions are recorded and reported within the organization's financial system. These parameters include settings for currency, fiscal periods, accounting rules, revenue recognition methods, and reporting standards. Accurate configuration of these parameters is essential for maintaining the integrity of financial data and ensuring that the organization meets its reporting and compliance obligations.

Reporting parameters, on the other hand, govern how financial data is presented in various reports. This includes settings for report formats, data filters, and aggregation levels. Properly configured reporting parameters enable the generation of insightful and accurate reports that support decision-making processes within the organization.

Key Financial Parameters

1. Currency and Exchange Rates

  - Functional Currency: The functional currency is the primary currency used for recording transactions within the AR module. It is typically the currency of the country in which the company operates. Setting the functional currency correctly ensures that all transactions are recorded in a consistent currency, facilitating accurate financial reporting.

  - Exchange Rates: If the company deals with multiple currencies, it is essential to configure exchange rates. Exchange rates can be set up manually or imported from external sources. These rates are used to convert foreign currency transactions into the functional currency, ensuring accurate financial records.

2. Fiscal Periods and Calendars

  - Fiscal Year Setup: Defining the fiscal year is crucial for accurate financial reporting. The fiscal year can be aligned with the calendar year or set according to the company's specific requirements. Configuring the fiscal year correctly ensures that financial transactions are recorded in the appropriate periods.

  - Accounting Periods: Within the fiscal year, accounting periods (monthly, quarterly, or annually) need to be defined. Each accounting period represents a specific time frame for recording and reporting financial transactions. Accurate setup of accounting periods facilitates proper revenue recognition and financial analysis.

3. Chart of Accounts

- Account Segments: The chart of accounts is a structured list of all accounts used in the general ledger. Each account can have multiple segments (e.g., department, location, product line) that provide additional granularity. Configuring account segments accurately ensures detailed and meaningful financial reporting.

- Account Types: Defining account types (e.g., assets, liabilities, revenues, expenses) helps categorize financial transactions. Proper categorization is essential for generating accurate financial statements, such as the balance sheet and income statement.

4. Revenue Recognition Methods

- Revenue Recognition Rules: These rules determine when and how revenue is recognized in the financial statements. Different methods, such as accrual basis and cash basis, can be configured based on the company's revenue recognition policies. Accurate setup of revenue recognition rules ensures compliance with accounting standards and principles.

- Deferred Revenue: For transactions where revenue is received in advance but recognized over time (e.g., subscription services), configuring deferred revenue accounts is necessary. This ensures that revenue is recognized correctly over the applicable periods.

5. Tax Configuration

- Tax Codes: Defining tax codes is crucial for calculating and reporting taxes on transactions. Tax codes represent different types of taxes (e.g., sales tax, VAT) applicable to the company's operations. Accurate setup of tax codes ensures compliance with tax regulations and accurate tax reporting.

- Tax Jurisdictions: If the company operates in multiple regions with different tax laws, configuring tax jurisdictions is essential. Tax jurisdictions represent the geographical areas with specific tax rules. Accurate configuration ensures that the correct tax rates and rules are applied to transactions based on their location.

Key Reporting Parameters

1. Report Formats and Templates

- Standard Report Templates: Oracle ERP provides standard report templates for various financial reports (e.g., AR aging reports, revenue reports). Configuring these templates involves selecting the data fields, formatting options, and layout. Using standard templates ensures consistency and accuracy in reporting.

- Custom Report Templates: Companies may have unique reporting requirements that standard templates do not fulfill. In such cases, custom report templates can be created. Configuring custom templates involves defining the report structure, data sources, and filters. Accurate setup of custom templates ensures that specific reporting needs are met.

2. Data Filters and Parameters

- Date Filters: Configuring date filters allows users to generate reports for specific time periods (e.g., monthly, quarterly, annually). Accurate date filters ensure that the reports reflect the correct time frame, facilitating trend analysis and performance evaluation.

- Account Filters: Filtering reports by specific accounts or account segments (e.g., departments, regions) provides detailed insights into different aspects of the business. Configuring account filters accurately ensures that reports are relevant and useful for decision-making.

3. Aggregation Levels

- Summary Reports: Summary reports provide an overview of financial data at a high level. Configuring summary reports involves setting aggregation levels (e.g., total revenue, total expenses) that offer a quick snapshot of the company's financial performance. Accurate setup ensures that summary reports are concise and informative.

- Detailed Reports: Detailed reports break down financial data into specific transactions or account segments. Configuring detailed reports involves selecting the appropriate data fields and aggregation levels (e.g., transaction details, departmental expenses). Accurate setup ensures that detailed reports provide comprehensive insights.

Configuring Financial and Reporting Parameters in Oracle ERP

The configuration process in Oracle ERP involves several steps, each requiring careful attention to detail. Below is a step-by-step guide to configuring financial and reporting parameters in the AR module:

1. Accessing the Configuration Interface

- Navigate to the Accounts Receivable module in Oracle ERP.

- Access the setup or configuration menu, where financial and reporting parameters can be defined.

2. Setting Up Functional Currency and Exchange Rates

  - Define the functional currency for the company.

  - Configure exchange rates for any foreign currencies used in transactions.

  - Set up automatic updates for exchange rates if using external sources.

3. Defining Fiscal Periods and Calendars

  - Set up the fiscal year according to the company's requirements.

  - Define accounting periods within the fiscal year.

  - Ensure that the fiscal calendar is correctly aligned with the reporting periods.

4. Configuring the Chart of Accounts

  - Define account segments and their respective values.

  - Categorize accounts into different types (e.g., assets, liabilities, revenues, expenses).

  - Ensure that the chart of accounts reflects the company's financial structure.

5. Establishing Revenue Recognition Rules

  - Define revenue recognition methods based on company policies.

  - Configure rules for deferred revenue if applicable.

  - Ensure that revenue recognition rules comply with accounting standards.

6. Setting Up Tax Codes and Jurisdictions

  - Define tax codes for different types of taxes.

  - Configure tax jurisdictions based on the company's operating regions.

  - Ensure that tax setup complies with regulatory requirements.

7. Configuring Report Formats and Templates

- Select and customize standard report templates.

- Create custom report templates for specific reporting needs.

- Ensure that report formats are consistent and meet user requirements.

8. Defining Data Filters and Aggregation Levels

  - Configure date filters for generating reports for specific periods.

  - Set up account filters for detailed analysis.

  - Define aggregation levels for summary and detailed reports.

9. Testing and Validation

  - Generate sample reports to validate the accuracy of the configured parameters.

  - Verify that financial data is recorded and reported correctly.

  - Make any necessary adjustments to the configuration settings.

Best Practices for Configuring Financial and Reporting Parameters

1. Involve Key Stakeholders

  - Engage finance and accounting teams in the configuration process.

  - Ensure that the configured parameters align with business requirements and compliance needs.

2. Document Configuration Settings

  - Maintain detailed documentation of all configured parameters.

  - Document the rationale behind key configuration decisions for future reference.

3. Regularly Review and Update Parameters

  - Periodically review financial and reporting parameters to ensure they remain accurate and relevant.

  - Update parameters as needed to reflect changes in business operations or regulatory requirements.

4. Utilize Oracle Support Resources

  - Leverage Oracle's support resources, including documentation, forums, and customer support, for guidance on configuration settings.

  - Stay informed about updates and best practices for configuring financial and reporting parameters in Oracle ERP.

By following these guidelines and best practices, organizations can ensure that their financial and reporting parameters in the Accounts Receivable module are configured accurately and effectively. This not only enhances the accuracy of financial reporting but also supports informed decision-making and compliance with regulatory requirements.

2.1.3 Importance of Accurate Company Parameter Setup

Setting up accurate company parameters is critical for the smooth functioning of the Accounts Receivable (AR) module within Oracle ERP. These parameters form the foundation for how financial transactions are recorded, processed, and reported. Incorrect or incomplete setup can lead to a cascade of issues that affect the entire accounting process, leading to potential financial discrepancies, compliance issues, and operational inefficiencies. In this section, we will delve into the various reasons why accurate company parameter setup is vital and provide insights into best practices for ensuring precision in this critical task.

1. Financial Accuracy and Integrity:

Accurate company parameters are essential for maintaining financial accuracy and integrity. They determine how transactions are categorized, recorded, and reported. For example, the setup of fiscal calendars, accounting periods, and chart of accounts directly impacts how financial data is captured and presented. An incorrect setup could result in misclassified transactions, leading to inaccurate financial statements that do not reflect the true financial health of the organization. Accurate setup ensures that financial data is reliable, facilitating better decision-making and financial planning.

2. Compliance and Regulatory Adherence:

Companies operate under various regulatory frameworks that mandate specific financial reporting standards and practices. Accurate company parameter setup ensures compliance with these regulations. This includes setting up tax codes, legal entity configurations, and intercompany transaction rules. Compliance with regulatory requirements is non-negotiable, as non-compliance can result in legal penalties, fines, and damage to the company's reputation. Proper setup of parameters helps in adhering to these regulations, thereby mitigating the risk of non-compliance.

3. Streamlined Operations and Efficiency:

Efficient operations are driven by the seamless integration and functioning of various ERP modules. Accurate company parameters facilitate this by ensuring that data flows correctly between modules. For instance, accurate setup of customer credit limits, payment terms, and collection strategies in the AR module impacts how sales orders are processed and payments are collected. This integration is crucial for maintaining operational efficiency, as any discrepancies can lead to delays, increased workload for corrective actions, and overall inefficiency.

4. Improved Cash Flow Management:

Cash flow is the lifeblood of any business, and effective cash flow management is dependent on accurate company parameters. Parameters such as payment terms, discount policies, and dunning rules influence how quickly receivables are collected. By setting these parameters accurately, companies can optimize their cash flow, ensuring that they have sufficient liquidity to meet their obligations and invest in growth opportunities. Incorrect setup can lead to cash flow issues, affecting the company's ability to operate smoothly.

5. Enhanced Reporting and Analytics:

In today's data-driven business environment, accurate and timely reporting is crucial for strategic decision-making. Accurate company parameter setup ensures that financial data is correctly captured and reported, providing reliable insights for analysis. Parameters such as accounting periods, financial calendars, and reporting hierarchies impact how financial data is aggregated and presented. Accurate setup enables detailed and meaningful reporting, allowing management to identify trends, analyze performance, and make informed decisions.

6. Facilitating Audit and Internal Controls:

Audits are a necessary aspect of financial management, ensuring that financial statements are accurate and compliant with regulations. Accurate company parameter setup facilitates the audit process by providing a clear and reliable trail of financial transactions. Parameters such as audit trails, approval workflows, and segregation of duties are critical for maintaining internal controls and ensuring that financial data is accurate and tamper-proof. Proper setup helps in reducing the risk of fraud and errors, making audits more straightforward and less time-consuming.

7. Supporting Growth and Scalability:

As businesses grow and expand, their financial processes become more complex. Accurate company parameter setup is crucial for supporting this growth. Parameters such as multi-currency handling, intercompany transactions, and global tax compliance need to be accurately set up to support international operations and business expansion. Incorrect setup can hinder growth, leading to operational bottlenecks and financial mismanagement. Accurate parameters ensure that the AR module can scale with the business, supporting its growth and expansion strategies.

8. Best Practices for Accurate Company Parameter Setup:

To ensure accurate company parameter setup, it is important to follow best practices and adopt a systematic approach. Here are some best practices to consider:

- Thorough Planning and Documentation:

  Before setting up company parameters, it is important to thoroughly plan and document the required configurations. This includes understanding the business requirements, regulatory obligations, and operational workflows. Detailed documentation helps in ensuring that all necessary parameters are accurately set up and can be referenced for future updates and audits.

- Involving Key Stakeholders:

Involving key stakeholders, such as finance, compliance, and IT teams, in the setup process ensures that all perspectives are considered. Collaborative setup helps in identifying potential issues and ensuring that the parameters meet the needs of all departments. It also facilitates better communication and alignment across the organization.

- Regular Reviews and Updates:

Company parameters should be regularly reviewed and updated to reflect changes in business operations, regulatory requirements, and market conditions. Regular reviews help in identifying discrepancies and making necessary adjustments to ensure continued accuracy and compliance. This proactive approach helps in maintaining the integrity of financial data.

- Training and Knowledge Transfer:

Training staff on the importance of accurate company parameter setup and providing them with the necessary knowledge and tools is crucial. This includes training on how to configure parameters, understanding their impact on financial processes, and best practices for maintaining accuracy. Knowledge transfer ensures that the setup process is consistent and reliable.

- Utilizing Oracle Support and Resources:

Leveraging Oracle's support resources, such as documentation, training programs, and community forums, can help in ensuring accurate parameter setup. Oracle provides detailed guidelines and best practices for setting up various parameters, which can be invaluable in ensuring accuracy and compliance.

Conclusion:

Accurate company parameter setup is a foundational aspect of effective accounts receivable management within Oracle ERP. It ensures financial accuracy, regulatory compliance, operational efficiency, and supports business growth. By following best practices and adopting a systematic approach, companies can ensure that their company parameters are accurately set up, providing a strong foundation for their financial processes. This not only enhances the reliability and integrity of financial data but also facilitates better decision-making and strategic planning.

2.2 Establishing Customer Relationships

2.2.1 Creating and Maintaining Customer Records

Creating and maintaining accurate customer records is a critical function within the Accounts Receivable (AR) module of Oracle ERP. This process ensures that all necessary customer information is captured and maintained correctly, facilitating smooth financial transactions and effective customer relationship management. In this section, we will explore the detailed steps involved in creating and maintaining customer records, the importance of accurate information, and best practices for managing these records efficiently.

1. Introduction to Customer Records

Customer records form the backbone of the Accounts Receivable module, encompassing all the essential details about your clients or customers. These records include basic information such as customer names, addresses, and contact details, as well as more complex data like payment terms, credit limits, and tax information. Accurate and up-to-date customer records are essential for processing invoices, tracking payments, and managing customer interactions effectively.

2. Creating Customer Records

Creating a new customer record in Oracle ERP involves several steps, each requiring attention to detail to ensure the accuracy and completeness of the information. Here's a step-by-step guide to creating customer records:

  a. Accessing the Customer Creation Interface

   To create a customer record, navigate to the Accounts Receivable module and select the option to create a new customer. This will open the customer creation interface, where you can enter the necessary details.

  b. Entering Basic Customer Information

Start by entering the basic customer information. This includes:

- Customer Name: The full name of the customer or company.

- Customer Type: Specify whether the customer is an individual or a business entity.

- Contact Information: Include the primary contact person's name, phone number, and email address.

- Address Details: Provide the billing and shipping addresses. Ensure the addresses are accurate and formatted correctly for postal services.

c. Configuring Financial Information

Next, enter the financial details associated with the customer. This includes:

- Payment Terms: Define the payment terms agreed upon with the customer, such as Net 30, Net 45, or any custom terms.

- Credit Limit: Set a credit limit for the customer based on their creditworthiness and your company's credit policies.

- Tax Information: Enter the customer's tax identification number and specify any applicable tax codes.

d. Additional Information

In addition to the basic and financial information, you may need to enter additional details such as:

- Customer Classification: Categorize the customer based on criteria like industry, size, or geographical location.

- Salesperson Assignment: Assign a salesperson or account manager responsible for managing the customer relationship.

- Notes and Comments: Add any relevant notes or comments that may be useful for future reference.

3. Maintaining Customer Records

Maintaining customer records involves regular updates and reviews to ensure the information remains current and accurate. Here are some best practices for maintaining customer records:

a. Regular Updates

Schedule regular reviews of customer records to update any changes in contact information, addresses, or financial details. This can include changes in the customer's business structure, payment terms, or credit limits.

b. Monitoring Credit Limits

Continuously monitor customer credit limits to ensure they align with the customer's current financial status and payment history. Adjust credit limits as necessary based on the customer's payment performance and any changes in your company's credit policies.

c. Handling Customer Inquiries

Ensure that customer inquiries regarding their records are addressed promptly and accurately. This includes updating contact information, resolving discrepancies, and providing any requested documentation.

d. Archiving Inactive Customers

For customers who are no longer active, consider archiving their records rather than deleting them. This maintains a historical record for reference purposes while keeping the active customer list current and manageable.

4. Importance of Accurate Customer Information

Accurate customer information is crucial for several reasons:

a. Efficient Invoice Processing

Accurate customer records ensure that invoices are generated correctly and sent to the right addresses. This minimizes the risk of invoice disputes and delays in payment.

b. Effective Communication

Maintaining up-to-date contact information facilitates effective communication with customers. This is essential for resolving issues, providing updates, and maintaining strong customer relationships.

c. Compliance and Reporting

Accurate customer records are necessary for compliance with tax regulations and financial reporting requirements. This includes ensuring that tax identification numbers and tax codes are correctly entered and maintained.

d. Enhanced Customer Service

Up-to-date customer records enable your team to provide better customer service. With accurate information at their fingertips, your team can address customer inquiries more efficiently and effectively.

5. Best Practices for Managing Customer Records

Implementing best practices for managing customer records can significantly enhance the accuracy and efficiency of your Accounts Receivable processes. Here are some key best practices:

a. Implementing Data Validation Checks

Use data validation checks to ensure that all required fields are completed and that the information entered meets the expected format. This helps prevent errors and inconsistencies in customer records.

b. Regular Training for Staff

Provide regular training for staff responsible for creating and maintaining customer records. This ensures that they are familiar with the latest procedures and best practices, and can accurately enter and update customer information.

c. Utilizing Automation Tools

Consider utilizing automation tools to streamline the process of creating and updating customer records. Automation can help reduce manual data entry errors and improve the efficiency of record maintenance.

d. Establishing Clear Policies and Procedures

Establish clear policies and procedures for managing customer records. This includes guidelines for entering new customer information, updating existing records, and handling customer inquiries. Ensure that these policies are documented and communicated to all relevant staff.

6. Case Study: Implementing Effective Customer Record Management

To illustrate the importance and impact of effective customer record management, consider the following case study:

Company A's Challenge

Company A, a mid-sized manufacturing firm, was facing challenges with their Accounts Receivable processes due to inaccurate and incomplete customer records. Invoices were frequently sent to incorrect addresses, leading to payment delays and disputes. Additionally, customer inquiries were often mishandled due to outdated contact information.

Solution and Implementation

Company A decided to revamp their customer record management process by implementing the following steps:

- Conducted a thorough audit of existing customer records to identify and correct inaccuracies.

- Implemented data validation checks to ensure new records were accurate and complete.

- Provided training for staff on best practices for entering and maintaining customer information.

- Utilized automation tools to streamline the updating process and reduce manual errors.

- Established clear policies and procedures for managing customer records, including regular reviews and updates.

Results and Benefits

After implementing these changes, Company A saw significant improvements in their Accounts Receivable processes. Invoices were delivered accurately and on time, reducing payment delays and disputes. Customer inquiries were handled more efficiently, leading to improved customer satisfaction. Overall, the company experienced enhanced cash flow management and stronger customer relationships.

Conclusion

Creating and maintaining accurate customer records is a foundational aspect of the Accounts Receivable module in Oracle ERP. By following the detailed steps outlined in this section and implementing best practices, you can ensure that your customer records are accurate, up-to-date, and effectively managed. This will lead to more efficient invoice processing, better customer communication, compliance with regulations, and enhanced overall financial management.

2.2.2 Required Information for Customer Records

Creating and maintaining accurate customer records is essential for the effective management of the Accounts Receivable (AR) module in Oracle ERP. Properly maintained customer records ensure smooth invoicing, efficient payment processing, and effective communication with customers. This section will detail the required information for customer records, ensuring you capture all necessary data to maintain comprehensive and accurate records.

1. Basic Customer Information

The foundation of a customer record is the basic information about the customer. This includes:

- Customer Name: The legal name of the customer, which should be consistent with the name used in contracts and official documents.

- Customer Number: A unique identifier for the customer within the Oracle ERP system. This number helps in distinguishing customers and is crucial for reporting and transaction processing.

- Address Details: The customer's billing and shipping addresses. These addresses are important for sending invoices, shipping goods, and maintaining accurate records for tax purposes.

- Contact Information: This includes phone numbers, email addresses, and contact names. Having up-to-date contact information ensures that communication channels are open and effective.

2. Financial Information

Financial information is critical for managing credit limits, payment terms, and overall customer financial health. Key financial details include:

- Credit Limit: The maximum amount of credit extended to the customer. This helps in managing credit risk and ensuring that customers do not exceed their credit limits.

- Payment Terms: The agreed-upon terms for payment, such as Net 30, Net 60, or other negotiated terms. Payment terms affect cash flow and need to be clearly defined and consistently applied.

- Tax Information: Tax identification numbers, exemption certificates, and other relevant tax details. Proper tax information ensures compliance with tax regulations and accurate tax reporting.

- Currency Preferences: The preferred currency for transactions with the customer. This is particularly important for international customers and helps in avoiding currency conversion issues.

3. Customer Classification and Grouping

Classifying and grouping customers can help in segmenting the customer base and applying different strategies for different customer segments. Key classification information includes:

- Customer Type: Classifying customers as individuals, businesses, government entities, etc. This helps in tailoring communication and service strategies.

- Industry Classification: Identifying the industry in which the customer operates. Industry classification can help in understanding customer needs and potential risks.

- Customer Groups: Grouping customers based on similarities, such as size, purchasing behavior, or geographic location. Customer groups can simplify the management of large customer bases and enable targeted marketing and service efforts.

4. Account Management Information

Account management information helps in maintaining relationships with customers and managing accounts effectively. This includes:

- Account Manager: The internal representative responsible for managing the customer relationship. Having a designated account manager ensures consistent communication and relationship management.

- Preferred Communication Method: The customer's preferred method of communication, whether it is email, phone, or mail. Respecting communication preferences enhances customer satisfaction.

- Service Level Agreements (SLAs): Any agreed-upon service levels that dictate the quality and speed of service provided to the customer. SLAs are important for managing customer expectations and ensuring service quality.

5. Historical and Transactional Information

Maintaining historical and transactional information helps in understanding customer behavior and managing future interactions. This includes:

- Order History: Detailed records of past orders, including products purchased, quantities, and order dates. Order history provides insights into customer buying patterns.

- Payment History: Records of past payments, including dates, amounts, and payment methods. Payment history helps in assessing the customer's payment behavior and creditworthiness.

- Communication Logs: Records of past communications with the customer, including emails, phone calls, and meetings. Communication logs ensure that all interactions are documented and can be referenced when needed.

6. Compliance and Regulatory Information

Compliance and regulatory information are essential for ensuring that all interactions with the customer comply with relevant laws and regulations. This includes:

- Compliance Requirements: Any specific compliance requirements applicable to the customer, such as industry-specific regulations or international trade restrictions.

- Regulatory Documents: Copies of relevant regulatory documents, such as licenses, permits, and certifications. Keeping these documents on file ensures that all necessary compliance requirements are met.

- Data Privacy Preferences: The customer's preferences regarding data privacy and how their data should be handled. Respecting data privacy preferences is crucial for building trust and complying with data protection laws.

7. Additional Information

Additional information may be needed depending on the specific needs of your business and the nature of the customer relationship. This can include:

- Notes and Comments: Any additional notes or comments about the customer that may be relevant for account management. This can include preferences, special requests, or important considerations.

- Attachments: Any relevant documents or files that should be associated with the customer record. This can include contracts, agreements, or correspondence.

Importance of Comprehensive Customer Records

Maintaining comprehensive customer records is vital for several reasons:

1. Improved Customer Service: Having all relevant information at hand enables customer service representatives to provide quick and accurate responses to customer inquiries. It also helps in personalizing interactions and building stronger relationships with customers.

2. Enhanced Financial Management: Accurate financial information ensures that credit limits, payment terms, and tax details are properly managed. This helps in minimizing financial risks and optimizing cash flow.

3. Efficient Operations: Well-maintained customer records streamline various operations, such as order processing, invoicing, and collections. This reduces the chances of errors and improves overall efficiency.

4. Better Decision Making: Detailed customer information provides valuable insights that can be used for decision-making. For example, analyzing order history and payment behavior can help in identifying trends and making informed business decisions.

5. Compliance and Reporting: Accurate and complete records ensure compliance with legal and regulatory requirements. They also facilitate accurate and timely reporting, which is essential for audits and financial reporting.

Best Practices for Maintaining Customer Records

To ensure that customer records are comprehensive and accurate, consider the following best practices:

1. Regularly Update Records: Customer information should be regularly reviewed and updated to ensure accuracy. This includes verifying contact details, financial information, and other critical data.

2. Standardize Data Entry: Use standardized formats and fields for data entry to ensure consistency. This reduces the chances of errors and makes it easier to search and report on customer information.

3. Use Validation Rules: Implement validation rules to ensure that all required fields are completed and that the data entered is valid. This helps in maintaining data quality and accuracy.

4. Train Staff: Ensure that all staff members responsible for entering and maintaining customer records are properly trained. They should understand the importance of accurate data and be familiar with data entry procedures and validation rules.

5. Implement Data Governance Policies: Establish data governance policies that outline how customer data should be managed and protected. This includes defining roles and responsibilities, setting data quality standards, and implementing data security measures.

By capturing and maintaining comprehensive and accurate customer records, businesses can improve customer service, enhance financial management, and ensure compliance with regulatory requirements. This not only helps in managing current customer relationships effectively but also provides a strong foundation for future growth and success.

2.2.3 Importance of Accurate Customer Information

Accurate customer information is the cornerstone of effective Accounts Receivable (AR) management. In the Oracle ERP environment, the accuracy and completeness of customer data directly influence various business processes, from billing and collections to financial reporting and customer relationship management. This section delves into the importance of maintaining accurate customer information and the benefits it brings to an organization.

1. Enhancing Invoice Accuracy and Timeliness

One of the primary reasons for maintaining accurate customer information is to ensure the accuracy and timeliness of invoices. When customer details such as name, address, contact information, and payment terms are correct, it reduces the likelihood of errors during the invoicing process. Accurate invoices ensure that customers receive bills on time, leading to prompt payments and improved cash flow.

- Accurate Address Information: Ensures that invoices are sent to the correct location, minimizing delays in delivery and payment.

- Correct Contact Details: Facilitates effective communication with customers for resolving any invoice-related queries or disputes promptly.

- Precise Payment Terms: Helps in setting clear expectations regarding payment due dates and any applicable discounts for early payment.

2. Improving Customer Relationships

Accurate customer information plays a crucial role in building and maintaining strong customer relationships. When businesses have up-to-date and accurate customer data, they can personalize their interactions, offer better customer service, and foster trust and loyalty.

- Personalized Communication: Enables businesses to address customers by their correct names and tailor communication based on their preferences and history.

- Efficient Issue Resolution: Accurate records help in quickly identifying and addressing customer concerns, leading to higher satisfaction levels.

- Customer Loyalty Programs: Accurate data allows businesses to effectively implement and manage loyalty programs, rewarding customers for their continued business.

3. Facilitating Effective Collections Management

Effective collections management relies heavily on accurate customer information. Knowing the correct contact details and payment histories of customers enables AR teams to follow up on overdue accounts more efficiently.

- Targeted Follow-ups: Accurate information helps in reaching the right contact person, ensuring that collection efforts are directed appropriately.

- Payment History Analysis: Access to accurate payment histories aids in identifying patterns and determining the best approach for collections.

- Reduced Disputes: Correct data minimizes billing errors that could lead to disputes, streamlining the collections process.

4. Enhancing Financial Reporting and Analysis

Accurate customer data is essential for reliable financial reporting and analysis. The accuracy of accounts receivable balances and related financial metrics depend on the integrity of customer information.

- Reliable AR Aging Reports: Accurate customer data ensures that AR aging reports reflect the true status of outstanding receivables, aiding in effective credit management.

- Accurate Financial Statements: Reliable customer information contributes to the accuracy of financial statements, enhancing the overall credibility of financial reports.

- Informed Decision-Making: Accurate data supports better analysis and decision-making, allowing management to devise effective strategies for credit and collections.

5. Ensuring Compliance and Reducing Risk

Maintaining accurate customer information is critical for compliance with regulatory requirements and reducing operational risks. Inaccurate data can lead to non-compliance with tax regulations and other legal requirements, resulting in penalties and reputational damage.

- Regulatory Compliance: Accurate customer data ensures compliance with regulations such as the General Data Protection Regulation (GDPR) and industry-specific requirements.

- Audit Preparedness: Correct and complete customer records facilitate smoother audits and reduce the risk of discrepancies.

- Risk Management: Reliable customer information helps in assessing credit risk accurately, enabling businesses to make informed decisions on extending credit.

6. Supporting Marketing and Sales Efforts

Accurate customer information is invaluable for marketing and sales teams. It enables targeted marketing campaigns, efficient lead management, and better customer segmentation.

- Targeted Campaigns: Accurate data allows marketing teams to segment customers effectively and target them with relevant promotions and offers.

- Lead Management: Correct customer information aids in tracking and nurturing leads, increasing the chances of conversion.

- Sales Insights: Accurate data provides sales teams with insights into customer behavior and preferences, enabling more effective selling strategies.

7. Implementing Best Practices for Maintaining Accurate Customer Information

To ensure the accuracy of customer information, organizations should implement best practices and establish robust data management processes. Here are some recommended practices:

- Regular Data Audits: Conduct periodic audits to identify and rectify inaccuracies in customer records.

- Data Validation: Implement validation checks during data entry to prevent errors.

- Standardized Data Entry: Establish standardized procedures and formats for entering customer information.

- Ongoing Training: Provide training to employees on the importance of accurate data entry and management.

- Customer Self-Service Portals: Enable customers to update their information through self-service portals, ensuring data remains current.

Conclusion

In conclusion, accurate customer information is vital for the efficient operation of the Accounts Receivable module in Oracle ERP. It enhances invoice accuracy, improves customer relationships, facilitates effective collections management, enhances financial reporting, ensures compliance, supports marketing and sales efforts, and reduces operational risks. By implementing best practices for maintaining accurate customer data, organizations can optimize their AR processes and achieve better financial outcomes.

2.3 Configuring Payment Terms and Options

2.3.1 Setting Up Payment Terms for Customers

Setting up payment terms for customers in Oracle ERP's Accounts Receivable module is a crucial task that ensures both the organization and its customers have clear expectations regarding payment timelines. Payment terms define the conditions under which a sale is completed, including when payment is due and any discounts that may be available for early payment. This section will guide you through the process of configuring payment terms, explaining their significance, and demonstrating how to use Oracle ERP to manage them effectively.

Understanding Payment Terms

Payment terms are a set of conditions established by the seller that detail when payments for goods or services are expected. These terms are agreed upon at the time of the sale and are crucial for managing cash flow and ensuring timely payments. Common types of payment terms include:

- Net 30: Payment is due 30 days after the invoice date.

- Net 60: Payment is due 60 days after the invoice date.

- 2/10 Net 30: A 2% discount is available if payment is made within 10 days, with the full amount due in 30 days.

Importance of Payment Terms

Properly configured payment terms can significantly impact an organization's cash flow management. They help in:

- Improving Cash Flow: By setting terms that encourage early payments, businesses can improve their cash flow.

- Reducing Risk: Clear payment terms reduce the risk of late payments and bad debts.

- Enhancing Customer Relationships: Well-communicated payment terms foster trust and transparency between the business and its customers.

Configuring Payment Terms in Oracle ERP

To configure payment terms in Oracle ERP, follow these detailed steps:

Step 1: Access the Payment Terms Setup

1. Navigate to the Accounts Receivable Module: From the Oracle ERP main menu, navigate to the Accounts Receivable module.

2. Select Payment Terms: Within the Accounts Receivable module, locate and select the option for Payment Terms. This is usually found under the setup or configuration menu.

Step 2: Create a New Payment Term

1. Click on 'Create Payment Term': Select the option to create a new payment term. This will open a new form where you can define the details of the payment term.

2. Enter Payment Term Name: Provide a unique and descriptive name for the payment term. This name will be used to identify the term in transactions.

3. Define the Payment Duration: Specify the duration for the payment term. For example, if the term is Net 30, enter 30 days.

4. Add Early Payment Discounts (if applicable): If the payment term includes a discount for early payment, specify the discount percentage and the number of days within which the payment must be made to avail of the discount. For example, for 2/10 Net 30, enter a 2% discount and 10 days.

5. Set Due Date Calculation: Define how the due date will be calculated. Options may include the invoice date, the end of the month, or the receipt date.

Step 3: Define Installment Terms (if applicable)

If the payment term involves installment payments, follow these additional steps:

1. Enable Installments: Select the option to enable installment payments.

2. Specify Installment Details: Define the number of installments, the percentage of the total amount due in each installment, and the due dates for each installment.

Step 4: Review and Save the Payment Term

1. Review the Details: Before saving, review all the details to ensure accuracy.

2. Save the Payment Term: Once you are satisfied with the configuration, save the payment term. It will now be available for use in customer transactions.

Step 5: Assign Payment Terms to Customers

1. Navigate to Customer Records: Go to the customer management section within the Accounts Receivable module.

2. Select a Customer: Choose the customer to whom you want to assign the payment term.

3. Assign Payment Term: In the customer record, find the section for payment terms and select the appropriate term from the list.

4. Save the Customer Record: Save the changes to the customer record.

Best Practices for Configuring Payment Terms

While configuring payment terms, consider the following best practices to ensure optimal effectiveness:

1. Align with Business Strategy: Ensure that the payment terms align with your overall business strategy and financial goals. For example, if you aim to improve cash flow, consider shorter payment terms or early payment discounts.

2. Customize for Different Customer Segments: Different customers may require different payment terms based on their payment history, industry standards, and the nature of their business. Customize payment terms to cater to the needs of various customer segments.

3. Regularly Review and Update Terms: Periodically review and update payment terms to reflect changes in business conditions, market trends, and customer payment behaviors.

4. Communicate Clearly: Clearly communicate payment terms to customers at the time of sale and ensure they are documented in all relevant contracts and invoices.

5. Monitor Compliance: Use Oracle ERP's reporting and analytics tools to monitor customer compliance with payment terms and take proactive measures to address any issues.

Example of Configuring Payment Terms

To illustrate the process, let's walk through an example of setting up a payment term for a company that offers a 5% discount for payments made within 15 days, with the full payment due in 45 days.

1. Create a New Payment Term: Navigate to the Payment Terms setup in Oracle ERP and select the option to create a new payment term.

2. Enter Payment Term Name: Name the payment term "5/15 Net 45".

3. Define the Payment Duration: Enter 45 days as the payment duration.

4. Add Early Payment Discount: Enter a 5% discount and specify that it applies if payment is made within 15 days.

5. Set Due Date Calculation: Choose to calculate the due date from the invoice date.

6. Review and Save: Review the details and save the payment term.

7. Assign to Customers: Go to the customer management section, select the relevant customers, and assign the "5/15 Net 45" payment term.

By following these steps, you ensure that the payment term is correctly configured in Oracle ERP, allowing the company to benefit from improved cash flow and incentivizing customers to pay early.

Summary

Configuring payment terms in Oracle ERP's Accounts Receivable module is a vital task that influences cash flow, customer relationships, and overall financial health. By setting up clear and effective payment terms, businesses can ensure timely payments, reduce financial risk, and maintain healthy cash flow. The process involves understanding the significance of payment terms, navigating Oracle ERP to set them up, and adhering to best practices to maximize their benefits.

2.3.2 Different Payment Options Available

Configuring payment terms and options is a critical component in managing the Accounts Receivable (AR) module within Oracle ERP. The payment options available can significantly impact cash flow management, customer relationships, and overall financial health. This section explores the various payment options available in Oracle ERP's AR module, providing a comprehensive understanding of how to effectively set them up and leverage their benefits.

Understanding Payment Options in Accounts Receivable

Payment options in AR refer to the various methods and terms under which customers can settle their invoices. These options include different types of payment methods (e.g., cash, credit, electronic funds transfer) and terms (e.g., net 30, early payment discounts). Properly configuring these options ensures that the organization can efficiently manage its cash flow and offer flexibility to its customers.

Types of Payment Options

1. Cash Payments:

   - Immediate Payment: Customers pay the full invoice amount immediately upon receipt. This is common in retail settings or small transactions.

   - Benefits: Provides instant cash flow and minimizes credit risk.

   - Challenges: Not practical for large transactions or long-term customer relationships.

2. Credit Payments:

   - Credit Terms: Extending credit to customers, allowing them to pay within a specified period (e.g., net 30 days).

- Benefits: Enhances customer relationships and can drive sales volume.

- Challenges: Involves credit risk and requires effective credit management.

3. Electronic Funds Transfer (EFT):

   - Direct Bank Transfers: Customers can transfer funds directly from their bank accounts to the company's bank account.

   - Benefits: Secure, quick, and reduces the risk of payment delays.

   - Challenges: Requires integration with banking systems and may involve transaction fees.

4. Credit Card Payments:

   - Card Transactions: Customers pay using credit or debit cards.

   - Benefits: Widely accepted and convenient for customers.

   - Challenges: Involves processing fees and requires secure handling of card information.

5. Online Payments:

   - Payment Gateways: Utilizing online payment platforms like PayPal, Stripe, or other payment gateways.

   - Benefits: Convenient for online transactions and offers a wide range of payment options.

   - Challenges: Involves fees and requires integration with e-commerce platforms.

6. Mobile Payments:

   - Mobile Wallets: Customers use mobile payment solutions like Apple Pay, Google Wallet, or other mobile wallets.

   - Benefits: Convenient for mobile users and promotes quick payments.

   - Challenges: Requires secure integration with mobile payment providers.

7. Checks:

   - Traditional Checks: Customers issue paper checks as a form of payment.

   - Benefits: Traditional and familiar method for many businesses.

   - Challenges: Involves longer processing times and the risk of bounced checks.

Configuring Payment Options in Oracle ERP

Configuring these payment options within Oracle ERP involves several steps, including setting up payment methods, defining payment terms, and integrating with external payment systems. The following outlines the process for configuring each type of payment option:

1. Setting Up Payment Methods:

  - Navigation: Navigate to the AR setup module in Oracle ERP.

  - Configuration: Define each payment method, including cash, credit, EFT, credit cards, online payments, mobile payments, and checks.

  - Integration: Ensure integration with relevant financial institutions and payment gateways for seamless processing.

2. Defining Payment Terms:

  - Payment Terms: Configure the payment terms associated with each payment method. This includes setting due dates, early payment discounts, and late payment penalties.

  - Cash Terms: For immediate cash payments, no additional terms are necessary.

  - Credit Terms: Define terms like net 30, net 60, or custom terms based on customer agreements.

  - Discounts: Set up early payment discounts, such as 2/10 net 30, where a 2% discount is offered if payment is made within 10 days.

3. Integration with Banking Systems and Payment Gateways:

  - Bank Integrations: For EFT and direct bank transfers, integrate Oracle ERP with the company's bank. This ensures seamless transactions and automatic reconciliation.

  - Payment Gateways: For online and mobile payments, integrate with chosen payment gateways. Ensure secure handling of transactions and compliance with relevant regulations (e.g., PCI DSS for credit card payments).

4. Security and Compliance:

  - Data Security: Implement robust security measures to protect sensitive payment information. This includes encryption, secure access controls, and regular security audits.

- Compliance: Ensure compliance with financial regulations and standards, such as PCI DSS for credit card payments and AML (Anti-Money Laundering) regulations for large transactions.

Benefits of Proper Payment Option Configuration

1. Improved Cash Flow Management:

 - Efficiency: Efficiently configured payment options enable quicker receipt of funds, improving the organization's cash flow.

 - Flexibility: Offering multiple payment options provides flexibility to customers, enhancing satisfaction and fostering long-term relationships.

2. Enhanced Customer Relationships:

 - Convenience: Providing a variety of payment options makes it easier for customers to settle their invoices, leading to higher customer satisfaction and loyalty.

 - Negotiation: Flexible payment terms can be used as a negotiation tool to secure better deals or encourage early payments.

3. Reduced Credit Risk:

 - Credit Management: By setting clear credit terms and monitoring compliance, organizations can reduce the risk of bad debts and improve overall financial stability.

4. Streamlined Operations:

 - Automation: Automating the payment processing through integration with banking systems and payment gateways reduces manual effort and minimizes errors.

 - Reconciliation: Automated reconciliation processes ensure that payments are accurately matched with invoices, reducing discrepancies and improving financial reporting.

5. Data Insights and Reporting:

 - Analytics: Configured payment options provide valuable data for financial analysis and reporting. Organizations can track payment patterns, identify trends, and make informed decisions.

- Performance Metrics: Monitor key performance indicators (KPIs) related to payments, such as Days Sales Outstanding (DSO) and payment cycle times, to optimize financial performance.

Best Practices for Configuring Payment Options

1. Customer-Centric Approach:

   - Understand Customer Needs: Tailor payment options based on customer preferences and industry standards. Conduct surveys or gather feedback to understand customer needs better.

   - Offer Multiple Options: Provide a range of payment options to cater to different customer segments, ensuring convenience and flexibility.

2. Regular Review and Updates:

   - Periodic Review: Regularly review and update payment terms and methods to align with changing business needs and market conditions.

   - Feedback Loop: Establish a feedback loop with the finance team and customers to continuously improve payment processes.

3. Training and Support:

   - Staff Training: Ensure that finance and sales teams are well-trained on the configured payment options and processes. Conduct regular training sessions and provide up-to-date documentation.

   - Customer Support: Offer support to customers for any payment-related queries or issues. Provide clear instructions and assistance for using different payment methods.

4. Technology Integration:

   - Leverage Technology: Use advanced ERP features and integrate with modern payment solutions to streamline processes and enhance security.

   - Automation Tools: Implement automation tools for payment processing, reconciliation, and reporting to reduce manual effort and increase efficiency.

5. Compliance and Security:

- Adhere to Standards: Ensure that all payment processes comply with relevant financial regulations and standards. Regularly audit systems for compliance and security.

- Data Protection: Implement robust data protection measures to safeguard sensitive payment information and prevent fraud.

By understanding and effectively configuring the various payment options available in Oracle ERP's Accounts Receivable module, organizations can enhance their financial management, improve customer relationships, and achieve greater operational efficiency. Proper setup and ongoing management of payment options are essential for optimizing cash flow and ensuring the smooth functioning of the AR module.

2.3.3 Impact of Payment Terms on Cash Flow Management

In the realm of financial management, cash flow is paramount to the health and sustainability of any business. Managing cash flow effectively involves understanding and optimizing the inflow and outflow of funds. One of the critical components that can significantly influence cash flow is the payment terms set for customers. In Oracle ERP's Accounts Receivable module, configuring payment terms appropriately can have a profound impact on cash flow management, helping to maintain liquidity, reduce the cost of capital, and enhance overall financial performance.

Understanding Payment Terms

Payment terms define the conditions under which a customer must pay an invoice. They typically specify the amount of time a customer has to pay the invoice and any discounts available for early payment. Common examples of payment terms include "Net 30," which means payment is due 30 days after the invoice date, or "2/10 Net 30," which offers a 2% discount if paid within 10 days but requires full payment in 30 days if the discount is not taken.

The primary elements of payment terms include:

- Due Date: The date by which the invoice must be paid.

- Discount Rate: A percentage reduction offered for early payment.

- Discount Period: The time frame within which the discount is available.

- Late Fees: Penalties for overdue payments, which can be either a fixed amount or a percentage of the outstanding balance.

Influence on Cash Flow

Effective management of payment terms can lead to improved cash flow. Here are several ways in which payment terms impact cash flow management:

1. Accelerating Cash Inflows: By offering discounts for early payments, businesses can encourage customers to pay their invoices sooner, thereby accelerating cash inflows. For example, a 2% discount for payment within 10 days can incentivize customers to pay earlier, reducing the average collection period.

2. Reducing Bad Debt: Clear and consistent payment terms can reduce the risk of bad debt. When customers understand the expectations for payment and the consequences of late payments, they are more likely to comply, thus minimizing the likelihood of non-payment.

3. Improving Predictability: Standardized payment terms help businesses predict cash inflows more accurately. This predictability is crucial for planning and managing working capital needs, ensuring that there is enough cash on hand to meet operational expenses and invest in growth opportunities.

4. Enhancing Customer Relationships: Flexible payment terms can strengthen relationships with customers by accommodating their cash flow cycles. By offering terms that align with customers' financial situations, businesses can foster goodwill and encourage repeat business.

Strategies for Optimizing Payment Terms

To optimize payment terms for improved cash flow management, businesses should consider the following strategies:

1. Analyzing Customer Payment Behavior: Use historical data to understand customer payment patterns. Identify which customers are likely to take advantage of early payment discounts and which tend to pay late. This analysis can inform decisions on which customers to offer discounts to and which may require stricter terms.

2. Segmenting Customers: Different customers may warrant different payment terms based on their creditworthiness and payment history. High-risk customers might be given shorter payment terms or required to make advance payments, while low-risk, loyal customers might benefit from extended terms.

3. Incentivizing Early Payments: Offering attractive discounts for early payment can significantly improve cash flow. The discount should be sufficient to motivate early payment without eroding profit margins excessively. Regularly reviewing and adjusting discount rates based on their effectiveness can help maintain a balance between encouraging early payments and preserving profitability.

4. Implementing Late Fees: To discourage late payments, businesses can impose late fees. These fees should be clearly communicated to customers as part of the payment terms. Consistent enforcement of late fees can encourage timely payments and compensate for the cost of delayed cash inflows.

5. Leveraging Technology: Utilize the capabilities of Oracle ERP to automate the management of payment terms. The system can automatically apply discounts, calculate due dates, and generate reminders for overdue invoices. Automation reduces the administrative burden and ensures consistency in applying payment terms.

Case Study: Effective Payment Terms Management

Consider a company, ABC Electronics, that implemented a revised payment terms strategy using Oracle ERP. Previously, ABC Electronics had a standard Net 30 payment term for all customers. However, the company faced issues with delayed payments, resulting in cash flow challenges.

By analyzing customer payment behavior, ABC Electronics identified that 30% of their customers consistently paid late, while 20% were capable of early payments but lacked incentive. The company introduced a tiered payment terms approach:

- Tier 1: Net 15 with a 1% discount for payment within 10 days for customers with a history of early payments.

- Tier 2: Net 30 with no discount for customers with consistent payment behavior.

- Tier 3: Net 15 with a late fee of 2% per month for high-risk customers with a history of late payments.

After implementing these changes, ABC Electronics saw a 15% increase in early payments, a 10% reduction in overdue invoices, and a significant improvement in cash flow stability. The use of Oracle ERP's automated reminders and discount applications streamlined the process, ensuring accurate and timely execution of the new payment terms.

Monitoring and Reviewing Payment Terms

It is essential to regularly monitor and review the effectiveness of payment terms. Businesses should track key performance indicators (KPIs) such as Days Sales Outstanding (DSO), the percentage of invoices paid on time, and the uptake rate of early payment discounts. Regular reviews help identify areas for improvement and adjust strategies as needed to maintain optimal cash flow.

Conclusion

Configuring payment terms and options in Oracle ERP's Accounts Receivable module is a critical aspect of cash flow management. By understanding the impact of payment terms, implementing strategic measures, and leveraging technology, businesses can enhance their cash flow, reduce financial risk, and build stronger customer relationships. The case of ABC Electronics illustrates the tangible benefits of a well-thought-out payment terms strategy, demonstrating that with the right approach, businesses can achieve financial stability and growth.

2.4 Setting Up Tax Codes and Jurisdictions

Proper setup of tax codes and jurisdictions in Oracle ERP's Accounts Receivable (AR) module is crucial for ensuring compliance with local, national, and international tax regulations. This section delves into the specifics of defining tax codes within the Accounts Receivable module.

2.4.1 Defining Tax Codes in Accounts Receivable

Understanding Tax Codes

Tax codes are a critical component of financial systems, allowing businesses to apply the correct tax rates to transactions based on various factors such as location, product type, and customer classification. In the Oracle ERP AR module, tax codes ensure that sales and receivables are taxed appropriately according to governing laws.

Types of Tax Codes

Tax codes can vary significantly depending on the geographic location and the nature of the business transactions. Common types include:

- Sales Tax: Applied to the sale of goods and services, typically a percentage of the sale price.

- Value-Added Tax (VAT): A consumption tax applied to the value added at each stage of production or distribution.

- Goods and Services Tax (GST): Similar to VAT but often with different administrative processes.

- Excise Tax: Levied on specific goods, often those considered harmful (e.g., tobacco, alcohol).

- Service Tax: Applied specifically to service-based transactions.

Each of these tax types may have unique rates and reporting requirements.

Steps to Define Tax Codes

1. Access the Tax Setup Interface

   To begin defining tax codes in the AR module, navigate to the Tax Setup interface within Oracle ERP. This is typically found under the Financials or Tax Administration menus.

2. Create a New Tax Code

   - Navigate to the 'Create Tax Code' Option: Select the option to create a new tax code. This will open a form where you can enter the details of the tax code.

   - Enter Basic Information: Provide a name and description for the tax code. The name should be descriptive enough to distinguish it from other tax codes. For example, "US Sales Tax 7%" or "EU VAT 20%".

3. Define Tax Rate

   - Rate Percentage: Specify the tax rate percentage. For instance, if the sales tax rate is 7%, you would enter "7".

   - Effective Dates: Define the start and end dates for the tax rate. This is useful for managing changes in tax rates over time. For example, if a new tax rate comes into effect on January 1st, 2025, you would set that as the start date.

4. Specify Tax Jurisdiction

   - Geographic Scope: Indicate the geographic scope of the tax code. This could be a specific country, state, province, or city.

   - Jurisdiction Code: Enter the jurisdiction code that corresponds to the geographic area. This ensures that the correct tax rate is applied based on the location of the transaction.

5. Assign Tax Categories

   - Product and Service Categories: Assign the tax code to specific product or service categories. For example, the same tax rate may apply to all physical goods but a different rate to digital services.

   - Customer Categories: Similarly, assign the tax code to customer categories if different rates apply to different types of customers (e.g., business vs. individual).

6. Set Up Tax Rules and Conditions

- Taxability Rules: Define rules that determine when the tax code should be applied. For instance, certain goods might be exempt from tax if sold to non-profit organizations.

- Thresholds and Limits: Establish any thresholds or limits for the tax code. For example, certain taxes might only apply to transactions exceeding a specific amount.

Example Setup Scenario

Let's consider an example where a company needs to set up a VAT tax code for sales in the European Union with a standard rate of 20%.

1. Navigate to the Tax Setup Interface in Oracle ERP.

2. Create a New Tax Code named "EU VAT 20%".

3. Define the Tax Rate:

  - Rate Percentage: 20%

  - Effective Dates: Start Date: January 1, 2024 (no end date specified, as it is the current rate).

4. Specify the Tax Jurisdiction:

  - Geographic Scope: European Union

  - Jurisdiction Code: EU

5. Assign Tax Categories:

  - Product Categories: All physical and digital goods and services.

  - Customer Categories: All customers (no exemptions).

6. Set Up Tax Rules and Conditions:

  - No specific taxability rules or thresholds needed for this standard rate.

Ensuring Compliance and Accuracy

Accurate setup of tax codes is essential for compliance with tax regulations and for avoiding costly errors. Here are some best practices to ensure compliance and accuracy:

- Regular Updates: Tax rates and regulations can change frequently. Regularly update your tax codes to reflect the latest rates and rules.

- Validation Checks: Implement validation checks within Oracle ERP to ensure that tax codes are correctly applied to transactions.

- Audit Trails: Maintain comprehensive audit trails of all tax code setups and changes. This helps in tracking and verifying changes for compliance purposes.

- Training and Documentation: Provide thorough training for staff responsible for tax setup and maintain detailed documentation of tax codes and their application rules.

Advanced Tax Code Features

Oracle ERP offers advanced features for managing complex tax scenarios:

- Tax Exemptions and Exceptions: Set up specific exemptions or exceptions for certain products, services, or customer types.

- Multi-Jurisdiction Support: Manage tax codes across multiple jurisdictions, ensuring that transactions are taxed according to local regulations.

- Automated Tax Calculation: Utilize Oracle ERP's automated tax calculation features to minimize manual intervention and reduce errors.

- Integration with Third-Party Tax Engines: Integrate with third-party tax engines for real-time tax rate updates and compliance checks.

Testing and Verification

Before fully implementing new tax codes, it's crucial to test and verify their setup. Here's a suggested approach:

1. Test Environment: Use a test environment to create and apply the new tax codes.

2. Sample Transactions: Run sample transactions to ensure the tax codes are applied correctly.

3. Review Reports: Generate tax reports and review them for accuracy.

4. User Feedback: Collect feedback from users to identify any issues or areas for improvement.

Conclusion

Defining tax codes in Oracle ERP's Accounts Receivable module is a detailed process that requires careful attention to regulatory requirements and business needs. By following the steps outlined in this section, businesses can ensure accurate tax calculations, compliance with tax laws, and efficient financial operations. Regular updates, thorough testing, and continuous monitoring are essential to maintain the integrity of the tax setup in the AR module.

2.4.2 Types of Tax Codes and Jurisdictions

Setting up tax codes and jurisdictions correctly in Oracle ERP's Accounts Receivable module is crucial for ensuring compliance with various tax regulations and for accurate financial reporting. This section will delve into the different types of tax codes and jurisdictions that you may encounter, explaining their roles and how they should be configured within the system.

Overview of Tax Codes

Tax codes in Oracle ERP are used to define the tax rate that applies to transactions such as sales, purchases, and inter-company transfers. These codes are essential for calculating the correct amount of tax to be applied to each transaction, ensuring compliance with local, state, national, and international tax laws. There are several types of tax codes, each serving a specific purpose.

1. Sales Tax Codes

Sales tax codes are used to determine the tax rate applicable to the sale of goods and services. These codes are typically defined by the location where the sale occurs and can vary significantly depending on local laws. For instance, a sales tax code in California might be different from a sales tax code in New York, even for the same product or service.

- State Sales Tax Codes: These codes are applied based on state-level regulations. Each state may have its own tax rate and rules.

- Local Sales Tax Codes: In addition to state taxes, local jurisdictions such as cities and counties may impose additional sales taxes. Local sales tax codes reflect these additional rates.

- Special Sales Tax Codes: Some jurisdictions may have special tax rates for specific types of goods or services, such as food, clothing, or digital products.

2. Value Added Tax (VAT) Codes

VAT codes are used in countries where Value Added Tax is applicable. VAT is a consumption tax levied on the value added to goods and services at each stage of production or distribution. VAT codes help in calculating the correct VAT amount to be charged or reclaimed.

- Standard VAT Codes: These apply to most goods and services.

- Reduced VAT Codes: Some items may qualify for a reduced VAT rate, such as essential goods (food, medicine).

- Zero-Rated VAT Codes: Certain goods and services may be exempt from VAT, meaning a 0% rate is applied. However, these transactions are still reportable.

- Exempt VAT Codes: Items that are completely exempt from VAT and do not need to be reported.

3. Use Tax Codes

Use tax codes apply to the use, consumption, or storage of goods that were purchased without paying sales tax. This typically applies when goods are bought from out-of-state vendors where sales tax was not collected at the time of purchase.

- State Use Tax Codes: Similar to state sales tax codes, these are based on state regulations.

- Local Use Tax Codes: These may apply additional use taxes at the local jurisdiction level.

4. Excise Tax Codes

Excise tax codes are used for specific goods, such as alcohol, tobacco, and fuel, which are subject to additional taxes based on quantity rather than value. These taxes are often included in the price of the goods.

- Product-Specific Excise Tax Codes: Different codes for different excise-taxed products.

- Environmental Excise Tax Codes: Taxes on products with environmental impacts, such as carbon emissions.

Defining Tax Jurisdictions

Tax jurisdictions refer to the specific geographical areas where certain tax rules apply. These can include countries, states, provinces, cities, and special tax districts. Properly defining tax jurisdictions ensures that the correct tax codes are applied based on the location of the transaction.

1. Country-Level Jurisdictions

Country-level jurisdictions encompass national tax laws and rates. Each country has its own tax authority and regulations.

- National Tax Codes: Define the tax rates and rules that apply across the entire country.

- International Tax Codes: Special codes for international trade, ensuring compliance with cross-border tax regulations.

2. State and Provincial Jurisdictions

State and provincial jurisdictions define the tax rules within a specific state or province. In federated countries like the United States, each state may have its own tax authority and rules.

- State Tax Codes: Specific to state-level taxation.

- Provincial Tax Codes: Applicable in countries with provinces instead of states.

3. Local Jurisdictions

Local jurisdictions include cities, counties, and special tax districts. These smaller areas can impose additional taxes beyond those applied at the national or state level.

- City Tax Codes: Specific to city-level taxes.

- County Tax Codes: Specific to county-level taxes.

- Special District Tax Codes: Apply to specific areas with unique tax requirements, such as business improvement districts.

 4. Special Tax Zones

Special tax zones are areas that have unique tax rules to encourage or manage economic activity, such as free trade zones or economic development zones.

- Free Trade Zone Tax Codes: Areas with reduced or no taxes to promote trade.

- Economic Development Zone Tax Codes: Zones with special tax incentives for businesses.

Configuring Tax Codes in Oracle ERP

Configuring tax codes in Oracle ERP involves several steps to ensure that all relevant tax rates and rules are correctly applied to transactions. This process typically includes:

1. Defining Tax Codes: Create the specific tax codes required for different types of taxes. This involves setting the tax rate, the type of tax (sales, VAT, etc.), and any special conditions or exemptions.

2. Assigning Tax Codes to Products and Services: Link the defined tax codes to the relevant products and services. This ensures that the correct tax rate is applied based on what is being sold.

3. Mapping Tax Codes to Jurisdictions: Assign the tax codes to the appropriate jurisdictions. This step ensures that the tax rate applied depends on the location of the sale or transaction.

4. Testing and Validation: Before going live, it is crucial to test the tax configuration to ensure accuracy. This can involve running test transactions and verifying that the correct tax amounts are calculated.

5. Ongoing Maintenance: Tax laws and rates can change, so it is essential to regularly review and update the tax codes and jurisdictions in Oracle ERP to remain compliant.

Best Practices for Setting Up Tax Codes and Jurisdictions

Implementing tax codes and jurisdictions effectively requires adhering to best practices to ensure accuracy and compliance. Here are some recommended practices:

- Stay Updated with Tax Regulations: Regularly monitor changes in tax laws and regulations to ensure that the tax codes in Oracle ERP are always current.

- Standardize Tax Code Naming Conventions: Use a consistent naming convention for tax codes to make them easily identifiable and to avoid confusion.

- Automate Tax Calculations: Utilize Oracle ERP's automation features to ensure that tax calculations are consistent and accurate, reducing the risk of human error.

- Conduct Regular Audits: Periodically audit the tax setup in Oracle ERP to identify and correct any discrepancies.

- Provide Training for Staff: Ensure that the finance and accounting teams are well-trained in the use of Oracle ERP's tax features to maximize their effectiveness and compliance.

- Leverage Oracle Support and Updates: Take advantage of Oracle's support services and regular software updates to keep the system optimized and compliant with the latest tax requirements.

Conclusion

Properly defining and setting up tax codes and jurisdictions in Oracle ERP's Accounts Receivable module is fundamental for compliance with tax regulations and for accurate financial reporting. By understanding the different types of tax codes, their applications, and how to configure them within the system, businesses can ensure that they meet their tax obligations efficiently and accurately. Additionally, following best practices for tax setup and maintenance can help avoid common pitfalls and ensure ongoing compliance and accuracy in tax management.

2.4.3 Importance of Accurate Tax Setup for Compliance

Setting up accurate tax codes and jurisdictions in the Accounts Receivable (AR) module of Oracle ERP is crucial for ensuring compliance with various tax regulations and requirements. This section explores the importance of precise tax setup, the potential consequences of inaccuracies, and best practices for maintaining compliance.

Compliance with Legal Requirements

One of the primary reasons for accurate tax setup is to comply with legal requirements. Tax laws and regulations can vary significantly across different countries, states, and local jurisdictions. Ensuring that tax codes and jurisdictions are set up correctly helps businesses adhere to these legal requirements, thereby avoiding potential fines, penalties, and legal issues.

Global and Local Tax Regulations:

Businesses operating in multiple regions must comply with global and local tax regulations. Accurate tax setup ensures that the correct tax rates are applied to transactions based on the location of the sale or service. This includes Value-Added Tax (VAT), Goods and Services Tax (GST), sales tax, and other region-specific taxes.

Automated Tax Calculations:

Oracle ERP's AR module can automate tax calculations based on the defined tax codes and jurisdictions. This automation reduces the risk of human error and ensures that taxes are calculated accurately and consistently for each transaction. Automated tax calculations are especially important for businesses with a high volume of transactions, as manual calculations can be time-consuming and prone to errors.

Avoiding Financial Penalties

Inaccurate tax setup can lead to financial penalties from tax authorities. These penalties can be substantial and can negatively impact a company's financial health and reputation.

Underpayment and Overpayment of Taxes:

Incorrect tax setup can result in the underpayment or overpayment of taxes. Underpayment of taxes can lead to audits, fines, and penalties from tax authorities. On the other hand, overpayment of taxes can strain a company's cash flow and require additional administrative efforts to reclaim the overpaid amounts.

Audit Readiness:

Accurate tax setup ensures that businesses are prepared for tax audits. Tax authorities may conduct audits to verify that businesses are compliant with tax regulations. Having accurate and well-documented tax codes and jurisdictions simplifies the audit process and demonstrates the company's commitment to compliance.

Enhancing Financial Reporting Accuracy

Accurate tax setup is essential for generating precise financial reports. Financial reports provide critical insights into a company's financial performance and are used by internal and external stakeholders, including management, investors, and regulatory bodies.

Accurate Tax Reporting:

Correctly defined tax codes and jurisdictions enable accurate reporting of tax liabilities and tax payments. This includes generating tax reports for filing purposes, such as VAT/GST returns, sales tax reports, and other tax-related filings. Accurate tax reporting ensures that businesses meet their tax obligations and avoid discrepancies in their financial statements.

Improved Decision-Making:

Reliable financial reports, supported by accurate tax data, facilitate informed decision-making. Management can use these reports to assess the company's financial health, identify trends, and make strategic decisions. Investors and stakeholders also rely on accurate financial reports to evaluate the company's performance and make investment decisions.

Ensuring Customer Trust

Maintaining accurate tax setup is vital for building and retaining customer trust. Customers expect businesses to handle tax matters correctly and transparently. Inaccurate tax charges can lead to customer dissatisfaction and damage the company's reputation.

Transparent Invoicing:

Accurate tax setup ensures that invoices issued to customers reflect the correct tax amounts. Transparent and accurate invoicing builds customer trust and minimizes disputes related to tax charges. Clear and accurate tax information on invoices also helps customers with their own tax reporting and compliance.

Customer Satisfaction:

Customers are more likely to be satisfied with their purchases when they receive accurate invoices with correct tax calculations. This satisfaction contributes to customer loyalty and positive word-of-mouth referrals, ultimately benefiting the business.

Best Practices for Accurate Tax Setup

To ensure accurate tax setup and compliance, businesses should follow best practices in defining and maintaining tax codes and jurisdictions in the AR module of Oracle ERP.

Regularly Review Tax Codes:

Tax laws and regulations can change over time. Regularly reviewing and updating tax codes ensures that the system reflects the latest tax rates and rules. Staying informed about changes in tax regulations helps businesses maintain compliance and avoid unexpected issues.

Implement Robust Validation Processes:

Implementing robust validation processes for tax data entry reduces the risk of errors. This includes validating tax rates, checking the accuracy of tax jurisdictions, and ensuring that all necessary tax codes are correctly defined. Automated validation tools within Oracle ERP can assist in this process.

Conduct Periodic Audits:

Periodic internal audits of tax setup and transactions help identify and rectify any discrepancies. Internal audits provide an opportunity to review tax processes, verify the accuracy of tax calculations, and ensure that the system aligns with current tax regulations.

Provide Training and Resources:

Providing training and resources for staff responsible for tax setup and management is essential. Ensuring that employees understand the importance of accurate tax setup and are familiar with the system's functionalities helps maintain compliance and reduces the risk of errors.

Utilize Expert Advice:

Consulting with tax professionals or advisors can provide valuable insights and guidance on complex tax matters. Tax experts can assist in setting up tax codes and jurisdictions accurately and offer advice on best practices for compliance.

Leverage Oracle ERP Features:

Oracle ERP offers various features and tools to support accurate tax setup and compliance. Leveraging these features, such as automated tax calculations, tax reporting tools, and validation processes, enhances the accuracy and efficiency of tax management.

Conclusion

Accurate tax setup in the Accounts Receivable module of Oracle ERP is critical for ensuring compliance with tax regulations, avoiding financial penalties, enhancing financial reporting accuracy, and maintaining customer trust. By following best practices and leveraging the features of Oracle ERP, businesses can achieve accurate and compliant tax management, ultimately contributing to their overall financial health and success.

CHAPTER III
Managing Sales Orders in Accounts Receivable

3.1 Overview of Sales Orders

3.1.1 Definition and Importance of Sales Orders

Definition of Sales Orders

A sales order is a document generated by a seller to authorize a sale transaction. It is a critical component in the sales process, acting as a binding contract between the customer and the seller. The sales order specifies the details of the products or services being purchased, including quantities, prices, and delivery terms. It typically includes the following information:

1. Order Number: A unique identifier for the sales order.

2. Customer Information: Details about the customer, including name, address, and contact information.

3. Order Date: The date when the sales order was created.

4. Delivery Date: The expected date for the delivery of goods or services.

5. Product/Service Details: Description, quantity, unit price, and total price for each item.

6. Terms and Conditions: Payment terms, delivery terms, and any other conditions governing the sale.

7. Approval Status: Indicates whether the sales order has been approved and by whom.

Sales orders serve as a bridge between the sales and delivery processes, ensuring that both parties are clear on the terms of the sale and what is expected.

Importance of Sales Orders

1. Clarity and Accuracy in Transactions: Sales orders provide clear, written documentation of the agreed-upon terms of a sale. This helps to eliminate misunderstandings and discrepancies that can arise from verbal agreements. By detailing the products or services, quantities, prices, and delivery terms, sales orders ensure that both the seller and the customer have a mutual understanding of the transaction.

2. Inventory Management: Sales orders play a vital role in inventory management. They help businesses keep track of what products have been sold and what needs to be delivered. This information is crucial for maintaining accurate inventory levels, planning for restocking, and preventing stockouts or overstock situations.

3. Financial Management and Reporting: Sales orders are integral to financial management and reporting. They provide essential data for revenue recognition, accounts receivable management, and financial forecasting. By tracking sales orders, businesses can better understand their sales performance, identify trends, and make informed financial decisions.

4. Customer Relationship Management: Sales orders are a key touchpoint in the customer relationship management process. They offer insights into customer buying patterns and preferences, enabling businesses to tailor their sales and marketing strategies to better meet customer needs. Additionally, well-managed sales orders can enhance customer satisfaction by ensuring timely and accurate delivery of products and services.

5. Legal and Compliance Considerations: Sales orders can serve as legal documents in the event of disputes between the seller and the customer. They provide a clear record of what was agreed upon, which can be crucial in resolving conflicts. Furthermore, sales orders help businesses comply with regulatory requirements by providing an audit trail for sales transactions.

6. Workflow Automation and Efficiency: In modern business environments, sales orders often integrate with automated systems, streamlining the order processing workflow. Automated sales order systems can reduce manual data entry, minimize errors, and accelerate the order fulfillment process. This leads to increased operational efficiency and allows businesses to handle a higher volume of sales with greater accuracy.

7. Performance Measurement and Analysis: Sales orders provide valuable data for performance measurement and analysis. Businesses can analyze sales order data to assess the effectiveness of their sales strategies, identify high-performing products or services, and uncover areas for improvement. By leveraging sales order data, companies can drive continuous improvement and enhance their competitive advantage.

Detailed Breakdown of the Sales Order Lifecycle

1. Order Creation: The lifecycle begins with the creation of the sales order. This can be initiated by the sales team, a customer service representative, or directly by the customer through an online portal. The sales order captures all necessary information about the transaction.

2. Order Approval: Once the sales order is created, it typically goes through an approval process. This may involve review by sales managers, finance departments, or other stakeholders to ensure accuracy and compliance with company policies.

3. Order Fulfillment: After approval, the sales order is sent to the fulfillment team. This team is responsible for picking, packing, and shipping the products or delivering the services as specified in the order. The fulfillment process may also involve coordination with inventory management systems to ensure the availability of stock.

4. Invoice Generation: Upon fulfillment, an invoice is generated based on the sales order. The invoice is sent to the customer for payment. In some cases, the sales order and invoice may be linked in the system to facilitate tracking and reconciliation.

5. Payment and Collection: The customer makes payment according to the terms specified in the sales order. The accounts receivable team tracks the payment, applies it to the relevant invoice, and updates the financial records.

6. Post-Sale Support and Service: The lifecycle doesn't end with payment. Post-sale support and service are critical for maintaining customer satisfaction. This may involve handling returns, addressing customer inquiries, and providing ongoing support.

Sales Orders and ERP Integration

In the context of Oracle ERP, sales orders are deeply integrated with other modules such as Inventory, Shipping, Accounts Receivable, and General Ledger. This integration ensures seamless data flow across different business functions, enhancing overall efficiency and accuracy. For example:

- Inventory Integration: When a sales order is created, the inventory module is updated to reflect the committed stock. This helps in maintaining accurate inventory levels and planning for future stock requirements.

- Shipping Integration: The shipping module uses the sales order information to plan and execute the delivery process. This includes generating shipping documents, tracking shipments, and confirming delivery.

- Accounts Receivable Integration: The accounts receivable module uses sales order data to generate invoices, track payments, and manage customer accounts. This integration ensures accurate revenue recognition and financial reporting.

- General Ledger Integration: The general ledger module captures the financial impact of sales transactions, ensuring that all sales-related activities are accurately recorded in the company's financial statements.

Conclusion

Sales orders are a fundamental component of the sales process, serving as a critical link between the customer and the seller. They provide clarity, accuracy, and transparency in transactions, support effective inventory and financial management, and play a key role in customer relationship management. In the context of Oracle ERP, sales orders integrate seamlessly with other modules, enhancing overall operational efficiency and accuracy. Understanding the definition and importance of sales orders is essential for any business seeking to optimize its sales processes and achieve long-term success.

3.1.2 Sales Order Lifecycle

The sales order lifecycle is a critical component of managing sales orders within the Accounts Receivable module of Oracle ERP. This lifecycle outlines the various stages a sales order goes through from its inception to fulfillment, and it is essential for ensuring efficient order processing, accurate revenue recognition, and timely customer satisfaction. In this section, we will explore the stages of the sales order lifecycle in detail, highlighting best practices and key considerations for each stage.

1. Order Entry

The first stage in the sales order lifecycle is order entry. This involves capturing the customer's order details and entering them into the Oracle ERP system. Key steps in this stage include:

- Customer Information: Collecting and verifying the customer's information, such as name, address, and contact details.

- Product Selection: Identifying the products or services the customer wishes to purchase, including quantities, specifications, and any special instructions.

- Pricing and Discounts: Applying the appropriate pricing, discounts, and promotional offers to the order. This may involve validating pricing rules and ensuring compliance with company policies.

- Order Confirmation: Confirming the order details with the customer to ensure accuracy and completeness before proceeding to the next stage.

2. Order Validation

Once the sales order is entered into the system, it undergoes a validation process to ensure all necessary information is accurate and complete. This stage includes:

- Data Validation: Checking for completeness and accuracy of order data, such as product codes, quantities, pricing, and customer details.

- Credit Check: Verifying the customer's credit status to ensure they have the financial capacity to fulfill the order. This may involve checking credit limits and outstanding balances.

- Inventory Check: Ensuring that the requested products are available in inventory or can be procured in a timely manner. This step is crucial to avoid backorders and stockouts.

- Approval Workflow: If applicable, routing the order through an approval workflow to obtain necessary authorizations from relevant stakeholders, such as sales managers or finance departments.

3. Order Fulfillment

After the sales order is validated and approved, it moves into the fulfillment stage. This stage involves several key activities:

- Picking: Generating a pick list for warehouse staff to retrieve the ordered products from inventory. This process ensures that the correct items are selected for the order.

- Packing: Packaging the products securely to prevent damage during transit. This step may also involve labeling and preparing shipping documents.

- Shipping: Arranging for the shipment of the order to the customer. This includes selecting a carrier, scheduling pickup, and tracking the shipment until it reaches the customer.

- Delivery Confirmation: Confirming that the order has been delivered to the customer. This step may involve obtaining proof of delivery and updating the order status in the system.

4. Invoicing

Once the order is fulfilled, the next stage is invoicing. This involves generating an invoice for the customer based on the order details and shipping information. Key steps in this stage include:

- Invoice Generation: Creating an invoice document that includes details such as product descriptions, quantities, prices, discounts, taxes, and total amount due.

- Invoice Approval: Routing the invoice through an approval workflow, if necessary, to ensure accuracy and compliance with company policies.

- Invoice Distribution: Sending the invoice to the customer via their preferred method, such as email, postal mail, or electronic data interchange (EDI).

- Invoice Posting: Recording the invoice in the Accounts Receivable module to reflect the amount due from the customer.

5. Payment Processing

After the customer receives the invoice, the payment processing stage begins. This stage involves the following activities:

- Payment Receipt: Recording payments received from the customer. This may include various payment methods, such as checks, electronic funds transfers, credit cards, and cash.

- Payment Application: Applying the received payments to the corresponding invoices. This step ensures that outstanding balances are accurately updated.

- Reconciliation: Reconciling the payments with bank statements to verify that all payments have been correctly recorded and accounted for.

- Handling Discrepancies: Resolving any discrepancies or issues related to payments, such as partial payments, overpayments, or disputed charges.

6. Order Closure

The final stage in the sales order lifecycle is order closure. This stage involves completing all necessary activities to officially close the sales order. Key steps include:

- Order Status Update: Updating the order status in the system to reflect that it has been fully processed and closed.

- Documentation: Ensuring all relevant documentation, such as invoices, shipping receipts, and payment records, is properly filed and stored for future reference.

- Customer Follow-Up: Conducting any necessary follow-up with the customer to address any outstanding issues or to gather feedback on their experience.

- Reporting: Generating reports to analyze order performance, fulfillment efficiency, and customer satisfaction. These reports can provide valuable insights for continuous improvement.

Best Practices for Managing the Sales Order Lifecycle

Managing the sales order lifecycle effectively requires careful planning, attention to detail, and a focus on customer satisfaction. Here are some best practices to consider:

- Automate Processes: Utilize automation tools within Oracle ERP to streamline order processing, reduce manual errors, and improve efficiency. Automation can also help ensure compliance with company policies and regulatory requirements.

- Maintain Accurate Data: Ensure that customer and product data is accurate and up-to-date. Regularly review and clean up data to prevent issues during order processing.

- Monitor Inventory Levels: Keep a close eye on inventory levels to avoid stockouts and backorders. Implement inventory management practices such as just-in-time (JIT) replenishment and safety stock levels.

- Establish Clear Policies: Develop clear policies and procedures for order processing, including credit checks, pricing rules, and approval workflows. Communicate these policies to all relevant stakeholders.

- Provide Training: Offer regular training for staff involved in order processing, fulfillment, and customer service. Training can help ensure that employees are familiar with system features and best practices.

- Focus on Customer Service: Prioritize customer satisfaction by providing timely and accurate information, addressing issues promptly, and maintaining open communication channels with customers.

- Utilize Reporting Tools: Leverage the reporting capabilities of Oracle ERP to monitor order performance, identify trends, and make data-driven decisions. Regularly review reports to identify areas for improvement.

In conclusion, understanding and effectively managing the sales order lifecycle is crucial for the success of the Accounts Receivable module in Oracle ERP. By following best practices and leveraging the capabilities of Oracle ERP, organizations can ensure efficient order processing, accurate revenue recognition, and high levels of customer satisfaction.

3.1.3 Integration with Accounts Receivable

Integration between the Sales Orders module and the Accounts Receivable (AR) module in Oracle ERP is a critical aspect that enhances the efficiency and accuracy of financial processes within an organization. This integration ensures that all sales-related transactions are seamlessly reflected in the financial statements, providing a comprehensive view of the company's financial health. Below is an in-depth analysis of how Sales Orders integrate with Accounts Receivable and the benefits of this integration.

The Importance of Integration

The integration of Sales Orders with Accounts Receivable facilitates a smooth flow of information from the point a sales order is created to the point it is fulfilled and subsequently invoiced. This seamless flow of data eliminates the need for manual data entry, reducing errors and saving time. Moreover, it ensures that financial records are updated in real-time, providing accurate and up-to-date information for decision-making.

Key Integration Points

Sales Order Creation and Validation

When a sales order is created in the Sales Orders module, it undergoes a series of validations to ensure that all necessary information is captured. This includes customer details, product information, pricing, discounts, and payment terms. Once validated, the sales order is ready to be processed and eventually converted into an invoice in the Accounts Receivable module. The integration ensures that any updates or changes made to the sales order are automatically reflected in the AR module, maintaining consistency across the system.

Sales Order Fulfillment

As sales orders are fulfilled, the inventory levels are adjusted, and the fulfillment status is updated in the system. This information is crucial for the Accounts Receivable module, as it determines when an invoice should be generated. The integration ensures that once the order is fulfilled, the AR module is notified, and the process of invoicing can begin. This helps in maintaining accurate records of inventory and ensures that revenue is recognized in a timely manner.

Invoicing and Revenue Recognition

Once a sales order is fulfilled, the next step is to generate an invoice. The integration with Accounts Receivable allows for the automatic creation of invoices based on the sales order details. This includes the customer information, products or services delivered, pricing, taxes, and any discounts applied. The invoice is then sent to the customer for payment. This seamless transition from sales order to invoice helps in accurate and timely revenue recognition, which is crucial for financial reporting and analysis.

Payment Processing

After an invoice is generated and sent to the customer, the Accounts Receivable module tracks the payment status. When a payment is received, it is matched against the corresponding invoice. The integration ensures that the payment information is updated in both the Sales Orders and Accounts Receivable modules, providing a complete view of the transaction lifecycle. This helps in accurate cash flow management and ensures that the financial records reflect the actual state of receivables.

Benefits of Integration

Improved Accuracy and Efficiency

The integration between Sales Orders and Accounts Receivable eliminates the need for manual data entry, reducing the chances of errors. It also streamlines the process of order fulfillment and invoicing, saving time and resources. This improved efficiency allows the finance team to focus on more strategic tasks, such as financial analysis and planning.

Real-Time Financial Insights

With integrated systems, financial data is updated in real-time. This provides management with accurate and up-to-date information on sales, receivables, and cash flow. These real-time insights are crucial for making informed business decisions and for responding quickly to market changes.

Enhanced Customer Experience

Integration ensures that customer orders are processed and invoiced promptly, leading to faster delivery and accurate billing. This enhances the overall customer experience, leading to higher customer satisfaction and loyalty. Customers appreciate timely and accurate invoicing, as it simplifies their payment process.

Better Cash Flow Management

By integrating Sales Orders with Accounts Receivable, companies can better manage their cash flow. The real-time update of payment statuses and the seamless transition from sales order to invoicing help in accurate cash flow forecasting. This allows businesses to plan their financial activities more effectively and ensure they have the necessary liquidity to meet their obligations.

Streamlined Reporting and Compliance

Integrated systems facilitate streamlined reporting and ensure compliance with accounting standards and regulations. All sales and receivable data is consistently updated, making it easier to generate accurate financial reports. This is crucial for compliance with regulatory requirements and for maintaining transparency in financial reporting.

Implementation Considerations

Data Consistency and Accuracy

Ensuring data consistency and accuracy is crucial when integrating Sales Orders with Accounts Receivable. All data points, such as customer information, product details, and pricing, must be standardized across both modules. Implementing data validation rules and regular audits can help maintain data integrity.

System Configuration and Customization

Proper configuration and customization of the ERP system are necessary to ensure smooth integration. This includes setting up workflows, defining integration points, and configuring automated processes. Working with experienced ERP consultants can help in achieving the desired level of integration.

Training and Change Management

Training staff on the integrated system is essential for successful implementation. Users need to understand how the integration works and how to leverage it for their daily tasks. Additionally, effective change management practices should be in place to address any resistance to the new system and to ensure a smooth transition.

Conclusion

Integrating Sales Orders with Accounts Receivable in Oracle ERP brings numerous benefits, including improved accuracy and efficiency, real-time financial insights, enhanced customer experience, better cash flow management, and streamlined reporting and compliance. By leveraging this integration, companies can optimize their financial processes, reduce manual effort, and achieve greater operational efficiency. Implementing and maintaining this integration requires careful planning, proper system configuration, and ongoing training and support. However, the long-term benefits make it a worthwhile investment for any organization looking to enhance its financial management capabilities.

3.2 Creating and Processing Sales Orders

3.2.1 Steps to Create a Sales Order

Creating a sales order in Oracle ERP's Accounts Receivable module is a systematic process that involves several steps, each crucial to ensuring the order is accurate and meets customer requirements. This section will guide you through the detailed steps needed to create a sales order effectively.

Step 1: Access the Sales Order Module

To begin the process, log in to Oracle ERP and navigate to the Sales Order module. This module can be accessed from the main menu or dashboard, depending on your system's configuration. Ensure you have the necessary permissions to create and manage sales orders.

Step 2: Initiate a New Sales Order

Once in the Sales Order module, select the option to create a new sales order. This is typically found under the "Order Management" section. Click on the "Create Order" button to open the sales order creation form.

Step 3: Enter Customer Information

The first critical piece of information needed is the customer details. Select the customer from the existing customer database. If the customer is new, you will need to create a new customer record by entering relevant information such as the customer's name, address, contact details, and payment terms. Accurate customer information is vital for processing the sales order efficiently.

Step 4: Define the Sales Order Type

Next, select the type of sales order you are creating. Oracle ERP supports various types of sales orders, such as standard orders, drop shipments, and return orders. The order type dictates the subsequent steps and fields required, so it is essential to choose the correct type based on the transaction.

Step 5: Enter Order Details

In this step, you will input the specifics of the order. This includes:

- Order Date: The date on which the order is being placed.

- Delivery Date: The expected date for the delivery of the goods or services.

- Order Currency: The currency in which the transaction will be conducted.

- Payment Terms: The agreed terms for payment, which might include net 30 days, cash on delivery, etc.

Step 6: Add Line Items

The core of any sales order is the line items, which specify what the customer is ordering. For each line item, enter the following details:

- Item Code: The unique identifier for the product or service.

- Description: A brief description of the item.

- Quantity: The number of units ordered.

- Unit Price: The price per unit of the item.

- Discounts: Any applicable discounts or promotional pricing.

Step 7: Configure Shipping Information

Shipping details are critical to ensure the timely and accurate delivery of the order. Enter the shipping method (e.g., ground, air, express), shipping address, and any special shipping instructions. You may also need to specify the shipping terms, such as FOB (Free on Board) or CIF (Cost, Insurance, and Freight).

Step 8: Apply Taxes

Depending on the jurisdiction, different tax rates and rules may apply. Oracle ERP allows you to configure and apply the appropriate taxes to each line item and the total order. Ensure that the correct tax codes are used to maintain compliance with local regulations.

Step 9: Review and Confirm the Order

Before finalizing the order, review all the entered information carefully. Check for accuracy in customer details, order type, line items, shipping information, and taxes. This step is crucial to prevent errors that could lead to delays or issues in order fulfillment.

Step 10: Save and Submit the Order

Once you have verified all details, save the order. This action may trigger a workflow process for order approval, depending on your organization's policies. If the order requires approval, it will be routed to the appropriate personnel. Otherwise, the order can be submitted directly to initiate the fulfillment process.

Step 11: Order Confirmation

After the order is saved and submitted, an order confirmation is typically generated. This confirmation can be sent to the customer via email or printed for record-keeping. The confirmation includes all relevant details of the order, such as order number, customer information, items ordered, and expected delivery date.

Step 12: Monitor Order Status

Post-creation, it's essential to monitor the status of the sales order. Oracle ERP provides tools to track the progress of the order through various stages, such as processing, shipping, and delivery. Monitoring the status helps in ensuring that any issues are addressed promptly and that the customer is kept informed about the order's progress.

Step 13: Handle Order Modifications

Sometimes, changes may be required after the order has been created. Oracle ERP allows for modifications to the sales order, such as updating quantities, changing shipping addresses, or altering delivery dates. Ensure that any changes are communicated to the customer and that the order is re-approved if necessary.

Step 14: Finalize Order Fulfillment

As the order moves through the fulfillment process, ensure that all items are picked, packed, and shipped as per the specifications. The fulfillment team must update the order status in the system to reflect these actions. Any partial shipments or backorders should be documented and communicated to the customer.

Step 15: Close the Order

Once the order has been fully delivered and any necessary follow-ups are complete, the final step is to close the order in the system. This action moves the order from an active state to a closed state, indicating that the transaction is complete. Closing the order ensures that all related financial transactions, such as invoicing and revenue recognition, are accurately recorded.

By following these detailed steps, you can create and process sales orders in Oracle ERP's Accounts Receivable module efficiently and accurately. Proper handling of sales orders is crucial for maintaining customer satisfaction and ensuring smooth operations within the sales and finance teams.

3.2.2 Mandatory Fields and Information

Creating and processing sales orders in the Oracle ERP Accounts Receivable module involves several mandatory fields and information that ensure accuracy, efficiency, and compliance. These fields capture essential details about the customer, the products or services being sold, pricing, delivery instructions, and other critical data. In this section, we will explore each of these mandatory fields in detail, providing a comprehensive understanding of their importance and how to populate them correctly.

Customer Information:

- Customer Name: This is the legal name of the customer placing the order. It is crucial for identification, billing, and legal purposes. Ensuring the correct customer name avoids confusion and ensures proper documentation.

- Customer Address: The customer's billing and shipping addresses are required. These addresses are used for invoicing and shipping goods. Accurate address information ensures timely delivery and correct billing.

- Customer Contact Information: This includes the contact person's name, phone number, and email address. Having accurate contact details facilitates communication regarding order status, delivery schedules, and any issues that may arise.

- Customer Account Number: Each customer is assigned a unique account number within the Oracle ERP system. This number helps in tracking customer history, credit limits, and payment terms.

Sales Order Details:

- Sales Order Number: A unique identifier for each sales order. This number is auto-generated by the system and is crucial for tracking and referencing the order throughout its lifecycle.

- Order Date: The date when the sales order is created. This is essential for processing timelines, scheduling deliveries, and financial reporting.

- Requested Delivery Date: The date by which the customer expects to receive the goods or services. This helps in planning inventory, logistics, and meeting customer expectations.

- Order Type: Specifies the nature of the order, such as standard order, backorder, or rush order. This classification helps in prioritizing and processing orders according to their type.

Product/Service Information:

- Item Code/SKU: A unique identifier for each product or service being ordered. This ensures accurate selection and tracking of inventory.

- Description: A brief description of the product or service. While the item code provides identification, the description offers clarity on what is being ordered.

- Quantity: The number of units of each item being ordered. Accurate quantity information is crucial for inventory management, billing, and fulfillment.

- Unit of Measure: Defines the measurement unit for the quantity specified, such as pieces, kilograms, or liters. Consistency in units of measure ensures accurate billing and inventory tracking.

- Price per Unit: The selling price for each unit of the product or service. This information is used to calculate the total order value.

- Total Price: The total value of each line item, calculated as quantity multiplied by price per unit. This helps in determining the overall value of the sales order.

Pricing and Discounts:

- List Price: The standard price of the product or service before any discounts. This serves as a reference point for calculating discounts.

- Discounts: Any applicable discounts on the list price. Discounts can be in the form of percentage reductions or fixed amounts.

- Net Price: The final price after applying discounts. This is the amount that will be billed to the customer.

Shipping Information:

- Shipping Method: The mode of transportation for delivering the goods, such as air freight, ground shipping, or express delivery. This affects delivery times and costs.

- Shipping Address: The location where the goods are to be delivered. This may be different from the billing address.

- Freight Terms: Defines who is responsible for the shipping costs, such as FOB (Free On Board) or CIF (Cost, Insurance, and Freight). This affects the financial responsibilities and risk during transportation.

Payment Information:

- Payment Terms: The conditions under which payment is to be made, such as net 30 days or cash on delivery. These terms affect cash flow and credit management.

- Payment Method: The means by which payment will be made, such as bank transfer, credit card, or check. This information is necessary for processing payments and ensuring timely collection.

Tax Information:

- Tax Code: The applicable tax code for the items being sold. This ensures compliance with tax regulations and accurate tax calculation.

- Tax Rate: The percentage rate of the applicable tax. This is used to calculate the tax amount for the order.

- Tax Amount: The total tax amount for the order, calculated as the net price multiplied by the tax rate. This ensures accurate billing and compliance with tax laws.

Approval Information:

- Approver's Name: The name of the person authorized to approve the sales order. This is crucial for maintaining control and accountability within the organization.

- Approval Date: The date when the sales order was approved. This helps in tracking the timeline of order processing.

Special Instructions:

- Delivery Instructions: Any specific instructions related to the delivery of the order, such as special handling requirements or preferred delivery times. These instructions ensure that customer expectations are met.

- Comments: Any additional notes or comments related to the order. This field provides flexibility to include information that doesn't fit into the standard fields.

Attachments:

- Supporting Documents: Any documents that are relevant to the sales order, such as contracts, quotations, or specifications. Attaching these documents ensures that all relevant information is accessible and referenced as needed.

Importance of Accurate Data Entry

Accurate data entry for mandatory fields in sales orders is critical for several reasons:

- Order Accuracy: Ensuring that all mandatory fields are correctly populated reduces the risk of errors and discrepancies, leading to accurate order processing and fulfillment.

- Customer Satisfaction: Accurate and complete information helps in meeting customer expectations regarding delivery times, product specifications, and billing accuracy.

- Inventory Management: Correct quantity and product information facilitate efficient inventory management, preventing stockouts or overstock situations.

- Financial Accuracy: Accurate pricing, discount, and tax information ensure correct invoicing and financial reporting, which is essential for maintaining the company's financial health.

- Regulatory Compliance: Properly capturing tax codes and rates ensures compliance with tax regulations, avoiding legal issues and penalties.

- Operational Efficiency: Well-documented and accurate sales orders streamline the workflow, reducing the need for manual corrections and rework.

Populating Mandatory Fields in Oracle ERP

In the Oracle ERP system, populating mandatory fields for sales orders typically involves the following steps:

1. Accessing the Sales Order Module:

   - Navigate to the Sales Order module in Oracle ERP.

   - Select the option to create a new sales order.

2. Entering Customer Information:

   - Input the customer name, address, contact details, and account number.

   - Ensure that all information matches the customer records in the system.

3. Filling Sales Order Details:

   - Enter the sales order number, order date, requested delivery date, and order type.

   - Verify that the details align with customer requests and internal policies.

4. Specifying Product/Service Information:

   - Select the item code or SKU from the product catalog.

   - Enter the description, quantity, unit of measure, price per unit, and total price.

   - Double-check that the information matches the customer's order.

5. Applying Pricing and Discounts:

   - Enter the list price and any applicable discounts.

   - Calculate and input the net price for each item.

6. Providing Shipping Information:

   - Select the shipping method and enter the shipping address.

   - Define the freight terms based on the agreement with the customer.

7. Entering Payment Information:

   - Specify the payment terms and payment method.

   - Ensure that the payment conditions are clear and agreed upon with the customer.

8. Defining Tax Information:

   - Select the appropriate tax code and enter the tax rate.

- Calculate and input the total tax amount for the order.

9. Approval and Special Instructions:

   - Enter the approver's name and approval date.

   - Add any delivery instructions or comments relevant to the order.

10. Attaching Supporting Documents:

   - Upload any relevant documents to the sales order.

   - Ensure that all necessary documents are included for reference and verification.

Conclusion

Accurate and complete entry of mandatory fields in sales orders is crucial for effective order management in Oracle ERP. By understanding and properly populating these fields, organizations can ensure accurate order processing, improve customer satisfaction, and maintain efficient operational workflows. This attention to detail not only enhances the overall efficiency of the Accounts Receivable module but also supports the broader goals of financial accuracy and regulatory compliance.

3.2.3 Customizing Sales Order Templates

Customizing sales order templates in Oracle ERP is crucial for businesses to ensure that their sales documentation meets their specific operational, branding, and legal requirements. Tailoring these templates helps streamline the sales process, improve customer experience, and maintain consistency across all sales-related documents. This section will delve into the various aspects of customizing sales order templates, including understanding the template structure, utilizing Oracle ERP tools, and best practices for customization.

Understanding the Template Structure

Before diving into customization, it is essential to understand the basic structure of a sales order template. A typical sales order template in Oracle ERP comprises several key sections:

1. Header Section: This includes essential information such as the sales order number, date, customer details, and billing/shipping addresses.

2. Line Items Section: This section lists the products or services being sold, including details like item descriptions, quantities, unit prices, and total amounts.

3. Summary Section: This summarizes the sales order with totals, taxes, discounts, and the final payable amount.

4. Footer Section: This may include additional notes, terms and conditions, and signature lines for authorization.

Understanding these sections helps in identifying which parts of the template need customization based on business requirements.

Utilizing Oracle ERP Tools for Customization

Oracle ERP provides several tools and features that facilitate the customization of sales order templates. These tools enable users to modify the layout, add or remove fields, and apply branding elements. Key tools and features include:

1. Oracle BI Publisher: BI Publisher is a powerful reporting tool within Oracle ERP that allows users to create and customize templates using a variety of formats (e.g., RTF, PDF, Excel). It provides a user-friendly interface to design templates and generate dynamic reports.

2. Template Manager: The Template Manager in Oracle ERP enables users to manage and configure various templates. Users can upload new templates, modify existing ones, and set default templates for different transactions.

3. XML Publisher: XML Publisher allows for advanced customization using XML data. Users can create templates that pull data dynamically from Oracle ERP databases, enabling highly personalized sales order documents.

4. Oracle Forms and Reports: For more technical users, Oracle Forms and Reports offer a way to develop customized templates using PL/SQL and other programming languages. This tool is suitable for complex customizations that require specific business logic.

Steps to Customize Sales Order Templates

The process of customizing sales order templates involves several steps, from designing the template to deploying it in Oracle ERP. Below is a detailed guide to help you through the customization process:

1. Identify Requirements: Begin by gathering requirements from stakeholders, including sales, finance, and customer service teams. Determine what information needs to be included in the sales order, how it should be presented, and any specific branding elements that need to be incorporated.

2. Design the Template: Using a tool like Oracle BI Publisher, start designing the template. Create the layout based on the identified requirements. Ensure that all necessary sections (header, line items, summary, footer) are included and formatted correctly.

3. Incorporate Data Fields: Use XML data or direct database queries to incorporate dynamic fields into the template. These fields will pull real-time data from Oracle ERP, ensuring that the sales orders are accurate and up-to-date.

4. Apply Branding Elements: Add branding elements such as company logos, colors, and fonts to the template. This helps maintain a consistent brand image across all sales documents.

5. Test the Template: Before deploying the template, conduct thorough testing. Generate sample sales orders to ensure that all data fields are populated correctly and that the layout is as expected. Make any necessary adjustments based on the test results.

6. Deploy the Template: Once testing is complete, upload the template to Oracle ERP using the Template Manager. Configure it as the default template for sales orders, if applicable.

7. Train Users: Provide training to relevant users on how to use the new template. Ensure they understand how to generate sales orders and how to troubleshoot any issues that may arise.

8. Monitor and Maintain: After deployment, monitor the performance of the template. Gather feedback from users and make any necessary updates to improve functionality and usability.

Best Practices for Customizing Sales Order Templates

To ensure that your sales order templates are effective and efficient, consider the following best practices:

1. Maintain Simplicity: Keep the template design simple and easy to read. Avoid cluttering the document with too much information. Focus on including only the most critical details.

2. Ensure Consistency: Maintain consistency in the design of sales order templates across different business units and departments. This helps in creating a unified brand image and avoids confusion among customers.

3. Prioritize Accuracy: Ensure that all data fields are correctly linked to the relevant data sources in Oracle ERP. Regularly review and update the template to reflect any changes in business processes or data structures.

4. Enhance Usability: Design the template in a way that makes it easy for users to generate and interpret sales orders. Use clear labels, organized sections, and intuitive formatting.

5. Incorporate Feedback: Continuously gather feedback from users and stakeholders. Use this feedback to make iterative improvements to the template, ensuring it meets the evolving needs of the business.

6. Stay Compliant: Ensure that the template complies with all relevant legal and regulatory requirements. This may include displaying specific information, adhering to data privacy laws, and including mandatory disclaimers.

7. Leverage Automation: Where possible, leverage automation tools within Oracle ERP to streamline the generation and customization of sales orders. This reduces manual effort and minimizes the risk of errors.

Example of a Customized Sales Order Template

To provide a practical illustration, consider the following example of a customized sales order template for a fictional company, TechGear Inc.:

Header Section:

- Company Logo: TechGear Inc. logo displayed prominently at the top.

- Sales Order Number: Dynamic field displaying the unique sales order number.

- Date: Auto-populated field showing the current date.

- Customer Details: Section displaying customer name, contact information, and billing/shipping addresses.

Line Items Section:

- Item Description: List of products/services with detailed descriptions.

- Quantity: Number of units ordered.

- Unit Price: Price per unit.

- Total Amount: Calculated field showing the total amount for each line item.

Summary Section:

- Subtotal: Sum of all line items.

- Taxes: Auto-calculated field showing applicable taxes.

- Discounts: Any applied discounts.

- Grand Total: Final payable amount.

Footer Section:

- Notes: Customizable section for additional notes or instructions.

- Terms and Conditions: Standard terms and conditions for the sale.

- Signature Lines: Spaces for authorized signatures from the customer and TechGear Inc.

By following the steps and best practices outlined in this section, you can create customized sales order templates in Oracle ERP that are tailored to your business needs, ensuring efficient and effective sales order management.

3.3 Sales Order Approval Workflow

3.3.1 Setting Up Approval Rules for Sales Orders

The sales order approval workflow is a critical component in the sales process, ensuring that all orders are reviewed and authorized before proceeding to fulfillment. This workflow helps maintain accuracy, compliance, and control over the sales process, reducing the risk of errors and unauthorized transactions. Setting up approval rules for sales orders in Oracle ERP involves several steps, each designed to ensure that the approval process is efficient and meets the organization's needs.

Understanding Approval Rules

Approval rules are predefined criteria that sales orders must meet to be approved. These criteria can include order value, customer credit status, product availability, and more. By defining these rules, organizations can automate the approval process, ensuring that only valid and compliant orders proceed to the next stage.

Steps to Set Up Approval Rules

1. Define Approval Criteria

  - Order Value Thresholds: Set limits on order values that require different levels of approval. For example, orders below $5,000 might only need sales manager approval, while those above $20,000 might require executive approval.

  - Customer Credit Status: Ensure that orders from customers with poor credit ratings are flagged for additional review. This helps mitigate the risk of non-payment.

  - Product Availability: Verify that the products in the sales order are available in inventory. Orders for out-of-stock items might need special handling or approval.

  - Discount Levels: Orders with discounts beyond a certain percentage might require additional scrutiny to ensure they comply with company policies.

2. Create Approval Hierarchies

- Approval Levels: Define the different levels of approval required based on the criteria. For example, sales representatives might have the authority to approve small orders, while larger orders require sales manager and finance department approval.

- Approval Chains: Establish the sequence of approvals. For instance, an order might first need sales manager approval, followed by finance approval, and finally, executive approval.

- Role Assignments: Assign specific individuals or roles within the organization to each approval level. This ensures that the right people are responsible for reviewing and approving orders.

3. Configure Oracle ERP Approval Workflow

- Access Approval Management: Navigate to the approval management section in Oracle ERP. This can typically be found under the setup or configuration menu.

- Define Approval Rules: Use the approval management interface to define the approval rules based on the criteria and hierarchies established earlier. This might involve setting up conditional logic to determine which rules apply to specific orders.

- Assign Approvers: Specify the individuals or roles responsible for each approval level. This can be done by selecting users from a list or defining roles within the system.

- Set Notification Preferences: Configure how approvers are notified of pending approvals. This can include email notifications, in-system alerts, or both.

4. Test the Approval Workflow

- Simulate Order Scenarios: Create test orders with different values, customer statuses, and other criteria to ensure that the approval rules work as expected. This helps identify any issues or gaps in the workflow.

- Verify Approval Routing: Check that orders are routed to the correct approvers based on the defined rules. Ensure that notifications are sent and received as expected.

- Resolve Issues: Address any problems identified during testing, such as incorrect routing or missing notifications. Adjust the approval rules and settings as needed.

5. Implement and Monitor the Workflow

- Go Live: Once the approval workflow has been thoroughly tested, implement it in the live system. Ensure that all users are aware of the new process and have received any necessary training.

- Monitor Performance: Continuously monitor the approval workflow to ensure it is functioning as intended. This can involve reviewing approval logs, tracking order approval times, and soliciting feedback from approvers.

- Make Adjustments: Based on monitoring and feedback, make any necessary adjustments to the approval rules or workflow. This might involve fine-tuning criteria, reassigning approvers, or updating notification preferences.

Best Practices for Setting Up Approval Rules

1. Keep it Simple: While it's important to have comprehensive approval rules, overly complex rules can slow down the process and lead to bottlenecks. Aim for simplicity and clarity in your criteria and hierarchies.

2. Involve Key Stakeholders: Ensure that all relevant departments and stakeholders are involved in defining approval rules. This includes sales, finance, legal, and executive teams. Their input will help create a robust and effective workflow.

3. Regularly Review and Update: Business needs and circumstances can change over time. Regularly review and update your approval rules to ensure they remain relevant and effective. This might involve adding new criteria, changing approval levels, or adjusting notification settings.

4. Use Conditional Logic: Leverage conditional logic within Oracle ERP to create dynamic approval rules that adapt to different scenarios. For example, orders from high-risk customers might automatically trigger additional reviews.

5. Train Approvers: Ensure that all individuals involved in the approval process are adequately trained. They should understand the approval criteria, how to review orders, and how to use the Oracle ERP system effectively.

Common Challenges and Solutions

1. Approval Delays

- Challenge: Delays in the approval process can impact order fulfillment and customer satisfaction.

- Solution: Set clear expectations for approval times and use automated reminders to prompt approvers. Consider setting up escalation paths for urgent orders.

2. Misrouted Orders

- Challenge: Orders may be routed to the wrong approvers, causing confusion and delays.

- Solution: Double-check the approval hierarchies and ensure that all rules are correctly configured. Regularly test the workflow to identify and resolve routing issues.

3. Lack of Visibility

- Challenge: Limited visibility into the approval process can make it difficult to track the status of orders.

- Solution: Use Oracle ERP's reporting and dashboard features to provide real-time visibility into the approval workflow. This allows users to track pending approvals, identify bottlenecks, and monitor performance.

4. Insufficient Training

- Challenge: Approvers may not be familiar with the approval process or the Oracle ERP system.

- Solution: Provide comprehensive training and ongoing support to all approvers. This can include training sessions, user guides, and access to a helpdesk.

Conclusion

Setting up approval rules for sales orders in Oracle ERP is a crucial step in ensuring a streamlined and efficient sales process. By defining clear criteria, establishing robust approval hierarchies, and leveraging Oracle ERP's powerful approval management tools, organizations can create a workflow that minimizes errors, ensures compliance, and enhances overall sales performance. Regular monitoring, training, and updates will help maintain the effectiveness of the approval process, ultimately contributing to the organization's success.

3.3.2 Managing Approval Hierarchies

Effective management of approval hierarchies is a crucial aspect of the sales order approval workflow in Oracle ERP's Accounts Receivable module. Approval hierarchies define the structured levels of authority that are responsible for reviewing and approving sales orders before they are processed and fulfilled. This ensures that only authorized personnel can approve significant transactions, thereby reducing the risk of errors and fraud. In this section, we will explore the key concepts, best practices, and detailed steps involved in managing approval hierarchies.

Understanding Approval Hierarchies

Approval hierarchies in Oracle ERP are configured to reflect the organizational structure and decision-making processes of a company. They typically include multiple levels, each representing different roles and responsibilities within the organization. The hierarchy ensures that sales orders pass through appropriate checks and balances, enhancing the accuracy and reliability of the sales order process.

Key Components of Approval Hierarchies:

- Levels of Approval: Each level in the hierarchy corresponds to a specific role or position within the organization. Higher levels have greater authority and are responsible for approving larger or more critical transactions.

- Approval Limits: These are predefined thresholds that determine the maximum amount or value that a particular level of authority can approve. Approval limits help in controlling and monitoring large transactions.

- Delegation of Authority: This feature allows temporary transfer of approval authority to another individual, typically used when the primary approver is unavailable.

- Approval Groups: Groups of users who share the same approval responsibilities. This helps in distributing the workload and ensuring that approvals are not delayed due to the unavailability of a single approver.

Setting Up Approval Hierarchies

Setting up approval hierarchies in Oracle ERP involves several steps, from defining the organizational roles to assigning approval limits and configuring workflow rules. Here's a step-by-step guide:

Step 1: Define Organizational Roles

Begin by mapping out the organizational structure and identifying the roles involved in the sales order approval process. This includes:

- Identifying the different levels of approval required.

- Defining the responsibilities and authority of each role.

Step 2: Establish Approval Limits

Determine the approval limits for each role. These limits should be based on the financial authority and risk management policies of the organization. Consider:

- The maximum transaction amount each role can approve.

- Special conditions or exceptions that might apply to certain transactions.

Step 3: Configure Approval Groups

Create approval groups if multiple individuals share the same approval responsibilities. This ensures that sales orders are processed efficiently, even if one approver is unavailable. Approval groups can be configured to require:

- Any one approver within the group to approve the order.

- All members of the group to approve the order.

Step 4: Set Up Delegation Rules

Configure delegation rules to allow temporary transfer of approval authority. This is particularly useful during periods of absence or leave. Delegation rules should specify:

- The duration of the delegation.

- The specific responsibilities that can be delegated.

- The individuals authorized to receive delegated authority.

Step 5: Implement Workflow Rules

Define the workflow rules that will govern the approval process. Workflow rules determine how sales orders are routed through the approval hierarchy. This includes:

- Sequential approvals where each level must approve the order before it moves to the next.

- Parallel approvals where multiple levels can review the order simultaneously.

- Conditional approvals based on specific criteria such as order value or customer type.

Best Practices for Managing Approval Hierarchies

To ensure the effective management of approval hierarchies, organizations should follow these best practices:

1. Regularly Review and Update Approval Hierarchies

As organizations grow and evolve, their approval hierarchies may need adjustments to reflect changes in structure, roles, and responsibilities. Regular reviews help in:

- Ensuring that the hierarchy remains aligned with the current organizational structure.

- Updating approval limits to reflect changes in financial policies and risk management strategies.

- Adding or removing roles and approval groups as needed.

2. Maintain Clear Documentation

Documenting the approval hierarchy setup and any changes made over time is essential for maintaining clarity and consistency. Documentation should include:

- Detailed descriptions of each role and its responsibilities.

- Approval limits and conditions for each level.

- Workflow rules and exceptions.

- Delegation policies and procedures.

3. Train Users on Approval Processes

Ensure that all users involved in the approval process are adequately trained. This includes:

- Understanding their specific roles and responsibilities within the hierarchy.

- Familiarity with the workflow rules and how to approve or reject sales orders.

- Knowledge of how to handle exceptions and escalate issues when necessary.

4. Utilize Automation and Alerts

Leveraging automation can significantly enhance the efficiency and accuracy of the approval process. Automation tools can:

- Automatically route sales orders to the appropriate approvers based on predefined rules.

- Send alerts and notifications to approvers when action is required.

- Track the status of sales orders in real-time and provide visibility into the approval process.

5. Monitor and Audit Approval Activities

Regular monitoring and auditing of approval activities help in identifying and addressing potential issues before they escalate. This includes:

- Reviewing approval logs and tracking the timeliness of approvals.

- Identifying bottlenecks and delays in the approval process.

- Ensuring compliance with internal policies and regulatory requirements.

Example Scenario: Implementing an Approval Hierarchy

Let's consider a practical example to illustrate the implementation of an approval hierarchy in Oracle ERP:

Company ABC is a mid-sized manufacturing firm with the following approval hierarchy:

- Level 1: Sales Representatives – Can approve sales orders up to $5,000.

- Level 2: Sales Managers – Can approve sales orders up to $25,000.

- Level 3: Finance Manager – Can approve sales orders up to $100,000.

- Level 4: CFO – Must approve any sales orders exceeding $100,000.

Step-by-Step Implementation:

1. Define Roles and Approval Limits:

- Sales Representatives are defined with an approval limit of $5,000.

- Sales Managers have an approval limit of $25,000.

- Finance Manager has an approval limit of $100,000.

- CFO has no limit and must approve all orders above $100,000.

2. Configure Approval Groups:

- Sales Representatives are grouped to allow any one representative to approve orders up to $5,000.

- Sales Managers form another group with similar approval sharing.

3. Set Up Delegation Rules:

- Allow Sales Managers to delegate their authority to Assistant Sales Managers during their absence.

- Define the delegation duration and the scope of responsibilities.

4. Implement Workflow Rules:

- Orders up to $5,000 are routed to Sales Representatives for approval.

- Orders between $5,001 and $25,000 are routed to Sales Managers.

- Orders between $25,001 and $100,000 go to the Finance Manager.

- Orders above $100,000 are routed to the CFO.

5. Train Users:

- Conduct training sessions for all approvers to familiarize them with the new hierarchy and approval process.

- Provide detailed guidelines and documentation.

6. Monitor and Audit:

- Set up regular audits of the approval process to ensure compliance and identify any issues.

- Use Oracle ERP's reporting tools to generate approval activity reports and analyze the data for continuous improvement.

3.3.3 Automating Sales Order Approval Processes

Automating the sales order approval process in Oracle ERP can significantly enhance efficiency, reduce errors, and ensure that sales orders are processed promptly and accurately. Automation not only streamlines the workflow but also integrates with various system components to provide a seamless and efficient approval mechanism. This section delves into the key aspects of automating sales order approval processes, the benefits it offers, and best practices for implementation.

Understanding the Need for Automation

The traditional sales order approval process can be time-consuming and prone to human errors. Manual approvals often involve multiple steps, including data verification, compliance checks, and managerial reviews. This can lead to delays, especially if the approval chain is extensive or if approvers are unavailable. Automation addresses these issues by leveraging technology to expedite the process while maintaining accuracy and compliance.

Key Components of an Automated Approval Process

1. Workflow Configuration

Oracle ERP provides robust tools to configure workflows that align with organizational policies and approval hierarchies. Setting up these workflows involves defining the approval paths, conditions, and actions that will be automated. This includes specifying who needs to approve the sales order at each stage, what criteria must be met for approval, and what actions should be taken upon approval or rejection.

2. Rules and Conditions

Automation relies heavily on predefined rules and conditions. These rules can be based on various factors such as order value, customer credit status, product type, and geographical location. For example, orders exceeding a certain monetary threshold may require approval from senior management, while orders within a predefined limit might be auto-approved if all other conditions are met.

3. Notifications and Alerts

Automated workflows include notification mechanisms to alert relevant stakeholders when an action is required. These notifications can be sent via email, SMS, or in-system alerts, ensuring that approvers are informed promptly. Additionally, reminders can be set up to notify approvers of pending tasks, reducing the likelihood of delays.

4. Integration with Other Modules

An automated approval process in Oracle ERP can be integrated with other modules such as Inventory, Finance, and Shipping. This integration ensures that all necessary checks and balances are performed automatically. For instance, the system can verify stock availability before approving a sales order, or check the customer's credit status with the Accounts Receivable module.

Benefits of Automating Sales Order Approval

1. Increased Efficiency

Automation eliminates manual steps, reducing the time taken to process sales orders. Approvals that previously took days can now be completed in minutes, ensuring faster order fulfillment and improved customer satisfaction.

2. Reduced Errors

By automating repetitive and data-intensive tasks, the likelihood of human error is minimized. The system automatically verifies data accuracy and compliance with predefined rules, ensuring that only valid orders are approved.

3. Consistency and Compliance

Automated workflows ensure that all sales orders are processed consistently according to company policies and regulatory requirements. This standardization helps maintain compliance and reduces the risk of unauthorized approvals.

4. Enhanced Visibility and Tracking

Automation provides real-time visibility into the approval process. Managers can track the status of orders, identify bottlenecks, and generate reports on approval times and patterns. This data can be used to further optimize the workflow and improve performance.

Best Practices for Implementing Automated Approval Processes

1. Define Clear Objectives

Before implementing automation, it is crucial to define clear objectives and understand the specific needs of your organization. Identify the pain points in the current approval process and determine what you aim to achieve with automation, such as reducing approval times, improving accuracy, or enhancing compliance.

2. Involve Stakeholders

Involve key stakeholders from various departments in the planning and implementation process. This includes sales, finance, IT, and management. Their input is valuable in understanding the nuances of the approval process and ensuring that the automated workflow meets all requirements.

3. Customize Workflows

While Oracle ERP provides standard templates for workflows, it is important to customize these to fit your organization's unique needs. Define approval hierarchies, set specific conditions for approvals, and ensure that the workflows are aligned with your business processes.

4. Test Thoroughly

Before going live, conduct thorough testing of the automated workflows. This includes testing various scenarios, such as high-value orders, orders from new customers, and orders requiring multiple approvals. Testing helps identify and resolve any issues that could impact the efficiency and accuracy of the approval process.

5. Train Users

Provide comprehensive training for all users involved in the approval process. This includes approvers, sales staff, and IT personnel. Ensure that they understand how to use the system, how to handle exceptions, and who to contact for support.

6. Monitor and Optimize

After implementation, continuously monitor the performance of the automated workflows. Collect data on approval times, error rates, and user feedback. Use this data to identify areas for improvement and optimize the workflows accordingly.

Real-World Example

Case Study: Streamlining Sales Order Approvals at XYZ Corporation

XYZ Corporation, a multinational company, faced significant delays in its sales order approval process. The manual approval process involved multiple layers of management and frequent back-and-forth communications, leading to delays in order fulfillment and customer dissatisfaction.

To address these challenges, XYZ Corporation implemented an automated sales order approval process using Oracle ERP. The implementation included:

- Defining Approval Rules: Orders above $10,000 required approval from the sales manager and finance director. Orders below this threshold were auto-approved if stock was available and the customer's credit status was satisfactory.

- Setting Up Notifications: Approvers received email notifications for pending approvals, with reminders sent every 24 hours for overdue approvals.

- Integrating with Inventory and Finance: The system automatically checked stock availability and customer credit status before approving orders.

The results were impressive. The average approval time dropped from 48 hours to just 4 hours. The error rate decreased by 30%, and customer satisfaction improved significantly due to faster order processing and delivery.

Conclusion

Automating the sales order approval process in Oracle ERP is a strategic move that can transform your organization's order management efficiency. By leveraging workflow configuration, defining rules and conditions, and integrating with other system components, you can create a streamlined, error-free approval process that enhances productivity and compliance. Adopting best practices and continuously optimizing the workflows will ensure that your automated approval process remains effective and aligned with your business goals.

3.4 Linking Sales Orders to Invoices

Linking sales orders to invoices is a crucial process in the Accounts Receivable module of Oracle ERP. This step ensures that the revenue generated from sales orders is accurately recorded, billed, and tracked. The process involves converting sales orders into invoices, which can then be managed, tracked, and reported within the system. This section will provide a detailed guide on how to convert sales orders to invoices, ensuring accurate and efficient billing practices.

3.4.1 Converting Sales Orders to Invoices

Converting sales orders to invoices involves several steps and considerations to ensure that the invoicing process is accurate and reflects the actual sales transactions. This process not only impacts the financial records but also affects customer satisfaction and cash flow management.

Step-by-Step Guide to Converting Sales Orders to Invoices

1. Access the Sales Order Module

   - To begin the conversion process, navigate to the Sales Order module within Oracle ERP. This module contains all the necessary tools and functionalities to manage and process sales orders.

2. Select the Sales Order to Convert

   - Identify the sales order that needs to be converted into an invoice. This can be done by searching for the sales order number, customer name, or other relevant criteria.

3. Review Sales Order Details

   - Before converting a sales order into an invoice, it is essential to review all the details of the sales order. This includes verifying the quantities, prices, terms, and conditions. Ensure that all the information is accurate and up-to-date.

4. Initiate the Conversion Process

- Once the sales order details have been reviewed and confirmed, initiate the conversion process. This is typically done by selecting an option such as "Convert to Invoice" or "Generate Invoice" within the Sales Order module.

5. Verify Invoice Details

- After initiating the conversion, the system will generate a draft invoice based on the sales order details. Review the draft invoice to ensure that all the information has been accurately transferred. Pay attention to the billing address, item descriptions, quantities, prices, taxes, and any applicable discounts.

6. Make Necessary Adjustments

- If any discrepancies or errors are found during the review, make the necessary adjustments. This may involve correcting item quantities, updating prices, or adjusting tax calculations. Ensure that the final invoice accurately reflects the sales transaction.

7. Finalize and Approve the Invoice

- Once all adjustments have been made, finalize the invoice. This may involve approving the invoice within the system, which can trigger additional workflows such as sending the invoice to the customer or updating the accounts receivable records.

8. Post the Invoice to the General Ledger

- After the invoice has been finalized and approved, it needs to be posted to the general ledger. This step ensures that the financial records are updated to reflect the revenue generated from the sales order.

9. Send the Invoice to the Customer

- The final step in the conversion process is to send the invoice to the customer. This can be done electronically through email, or by generating a physical copy to be mailed. Ensure that the customer receives the invoice promptly to facilitate timely payment.

Key Considerations for Converting Sales Orders to Invoices

- Accuracy of Sales Order Information

- The accuracy of the sales order information is critical to ensure that the invoice generated is correct. Any errors in the sales order will be carried over to the invoice, potentially causing issues with billing and payment.

- Integration with Other Modules

- The Sales Order module should be seamlessly integrated with other modules such as Inventory, Accounts Receivable, and General Ledger. This integration ensures that all relevant data is accurately reflected across the system.

- Handling Partial Shipments

- In cases where sales orders are partially fulfilled, the system should allow for partial conversion of sales orders to invoices. This ensures that customers are billed only for the items that have been shipped.

- Compliance with Tax Regulations

- Ensure that the invoice generation process complies with applicable tax regulations. This includes accurately calculating and applying taxes based on the customer's location and the nature of the goods or services sold.

- Automating the Conversion Process

- Automating the conversion process can improve efficiency and reduce the risk of errors. Oracle ERP provides tools and workflows to automate the generation of invoices from sales orders, streamlining the process and ensuring consistency.

Benefits of Linking Sales Orders to Invoices

- Improved Accuracy

- Linking sales orders to invoices ensures that billing information is accurate and consistent with the sales transaction. This reduces the risk of errors and discrepancies in the invoicing process.

- Enhanced Customer Satisfaction

- Accurate and timely invoicing contributes to enhanced customer satisfaction. Customers appreciate receiving clear and correct invoices, which facilitates prompt payment and reduces disputes.

- Better Cash Flow Management

- Efficiently converting sales orders to invoices ensures that revenue is recognized and recorded promptly. This helps businesses manage their cash flow more effectively, ensuring that funds are available when needed.

- Streamlined Processes

- Automating the conversion of sales orders to invoices streamlines the billing process, reducing manual effort and freeing up resources to focus on other critical tasks.

- Comprehensive Reporting and Analysis

- Linking sales orders to invoices provides comprehensive data for reporting and analysis. Businesses can track sales performance, monitor outstanding invoices, and analyze payment trends to make informed decisions.

Challenges and Solutions

- Handling Complex Sales Orders

- Sales orders with complex pricing structures, multiple items, or special terms can pose challenges during the conversion process. Ensure that the system is configured to handle these complexities accurately.

- Managing Partial Shipments and Backorders

- Converting sales orders to invoices when dealing with partial shipments or backorders requires careful management. Implement workflows that allow for partial invoicing and track outstanding items.

- Ensuring Data Integrity

- Maintaining data integrity across the Sales Order and Accounts Receivable modules is essential. Regularly audit and reconcile data to ensure consistency and accuracy.

- Adapting to Changing Business Requirements

- Businesses may face changing requirements or new regulations that impact the invoicing process. Stay updated with Oracle ERP's features and updates to adapt quickly to these changes.

Conclusion

Converting sales orders to invoices is a fundamental process in managing accounts receivable effectively. By following a structured approach and leveraging the tools and functionalities provided by Oracle ERP, businesses can ensure accurate, efficient, and compliant invoicing. This not only improves financial management but also enhances customer relationships and supports overall business growth.

3.4.2 Tracking Sales Order Fulfillment

Tracking the fulfillment of sales orders is a crucial aspect of the sales order process in the Accounts Receivable module. This section outlines the essential steps and best practices to ensure accurate and efficient tracking of sales orders from creation to fulfillment.

Understanding Sales Order Fulfillment

Sales order fulfillment refers to the process of delivering products or services ordered by a customer. It includes various stages such as order receipt, processing, picking, packing, shipping, and delivery. Accurate tracking of each stage ensures that orders are completed on time, inventory levels are managed effectively, and customer satisfaction is maintained.

Key Components of Sales Order Fulfillment

1. Order Receipt and Acknowledgment:

   - Once a sales order is created and approved, it needs to be acknowledged. This acknowledgment confirms that the order has been received and will be processed.

   - An order acknowledgment email or document is typically sent to the customer, confirming the details of the order and the expected delivery date.

2. Order Processing:

   - The order processing stage involves checking inventory availability, reserving stock, and preparing the order for fulfillment.

   - In Oracle ERP, this stage is managed through the inventory module, which is integrated with the Accounts Receivable module. This integration ensures that stock levels are accurately updated and tracked.

3. Picking and Packing:

- The picking process involves selecting the items from the warehouse that match the sales order. This step is crucial for ensuring that the correct items are shipped to the customer.

- Packing involves securely packaging the picked items to prevent damage during transit. Packing slips and shipping labels are generated during this stage.

4. Shipping:

- Shipping involves dispatching the packed items to the customer. This step includes selecting the appropriate shipping method, coordinating with logistics providers, and updating the shipment status in the system.

- Oracle ERP allows for integration with various shipping carriers, enabling real-time tracking of shipments and automatic updates of shipment status.

5. Delivery Confirmation:

- Delivery confirmation is obtained once the customer receives the shipment. This confirmation can be through delivery receipts, electronic acknowledgment, or confirmation from the shipping carrier.

- Ensuring accurate delivery confirmation helps in closing the sales order and initiating the invoicing process.

Steps to Track Sales Order Fulfillment in Oracle ERP

1. Order Entry and Status Updates:

- Enter the sales order into the Oracle ERP system and update the status at each stage of fulfillment. The system should reflect real-time status updates, including order received, processing, picking, packing, shipped, and delivered.

- Use the order management dashboard to monitor the status of all sales orders and identify any delays or issues in the fulfillment process.

2. Inventory Management Integration:

- Ensure seamless integration between the sales order and inventory modules. This integration allows for real-time tracking of inventory levels, ensuring that items are reserved and picked accurately.

- Regularly update inventory records to reflect the current stock levels and avoid stockouts or overstock situations.

3. Automated Notifications and Alerts:

- Set up automated notifications and alerts for critical stages in the fulfillment process. These notifications can be sent to relevant stakeholders, including sales, warehouse, and logistics teams, as well as customers.

- Alerts can help identify and resolve any issues promptly, ensuring smooth order fulfillment.

4. Shipment Tracking Integration:

- Integrate the Oracle ERP system with shipping carriers to enable real-time tracking of shipments. This integration allows for automatic updates of shipment status, including dispatched, in transit, out for delivery, and delivered.

- Provide customers with shipment tracking information, allowing them to monitor the progress of their orders and anticipate delivery dates.

5. Delivery Confirmation and Closure:

- Confirm delivery with the customer and update the order status in the system. This confirmation can be through delivery receipts, electronic acknowledgment, or feedback from the shipping carrier.

- Once delivery is confirmed, close the sales order and initiate the invoicing process. Ensure that all relevant documentation, such as delivery receipts and packing slips, is attached to the order record.

Best Practices for Tracking Sales Order Fulfillment

1. Maintain Accurate Records:

- Ensure that all order details are accurately recorded in the system, including customer information, order items, quantities, and delivery dates.

- Regularly update records to reflect the current status of each order and maintain a clear audit trail.

2. Monitor Key Performance Indicators (KPIs):

- Track key performance indicators related to sales order fulfillment, such as order processing time, shipping accuracy, on-time delivery rate, and customer satisfaction.

- Use these metrics to identify areas for improvement and optimize the fulfillment process.

3. Implement Quality Control Measures:

- Establish quality control measures at each stage of the fulfillment process, including order processing, picking, packing, and shipping.

- Regularly audit the fulfillment process to ensure that orders are being fulfilled accurately and efficiently.

4. Enhance Communication and Collaboration:

- Foster effective communication and collaboration between sales, warehouse, logistics, and customer service teams. Ensure that all stakeholders are informed of order status and any issues that may arise.

- Use collaboration tools and platforms to streamline communication and share real-time updates.

5. Leverage Technology and Automation:

- Utilize technology and automation tools to streamline the fulfillment process. Automated workflows, real-time tracking, and integration with shipping carriers can significantly enhance efficiency and accuracy.

- Continuously explore new technologies and solutions that can improve the fulfillment process and provide better customer service.

6. Focus on Customer Experience:

- Prioritize customer experience throughout the fulfillment process. Keep customers informed of order status, provide accurate delivery estimates, and offer easy access to shipment tracking information.

- Handle any issues or delays promptly and communicate transparently with customers to maintain their trust and satisfaction.

Challenges in Sales Order Fulfillment and How to Overcome Them

1. Inventory Discrepancies:

- Inventory discrepancies can lead to delays in order fulfillment and customer dissatisfaction. Regularly reconcile inventory records and implement cycle counting to minimize discrepancies.

- Use barcode scanning and RFID technology to improve inventory accuracy and reduce manual errors.

2. Shipping Delays:

- Shipping delays can occur due to various factors, including carrier issues, weather conditions, and supply chain disruptions. Maintain a buffer in delivery timelines to account for potential delays.

- Work with reliable shipping partners and have contingency plans in place for alternative shipping methods.

3. Order Processing Errors:

- Order processing errors, such as incorrect item selection or incomplete order information, can disrupt the fulfillment process. Implement robust order validation and quality control checks to minimize errors.

- Provide training to staff on proper order processing procedures and use automation tools to reduce manual entry errors.

4. Managing High Order Volumes:

- During peak periods, managing high order volumes can strain the fulfillment process. Plan for peak periods by increasing staff, optimizing warehouse layout, and using technology to streamline operations.

- Implement a scalable fulfillment system that can handle increased order volumes without compromising accuracy and efficiency.

By following these steps and best practices, businesses can ensure efficient tracking of sales order fulfillment in the Accounts Receivable module of Oracle ERP. This not only enhances operational efficiency but also improves customer satisfaction by ensuring timely and accurate delivery of orders.

3.4.3 Handling Partial Shipments and Backorders

Introduction to Partial Shipments and Backorders

In the context of sales order processing within Oracle ERP, handling partial shipments and backorders is a crucial aspect of managing customer expectations and maintaining efficient operations. Partial shipments occur when only a portion of the items on a sales order are available for immediate delivery, while backorders refer to the remaining items that are out of stock and will be shipped at a later date. Effective management of these scenarios ensures customer satisfaction, optimizes inventory levels, and streamlines the overall sales order fulfillment process.

Importance of Handling Partial Shipments and Backorders

Partial shipments and backorders are common in many industries, especially those with complex supply chains or fluctuating demand. Properly handling these situations is important for several reasons:

1. Customer Satisfaction: Customers expect timely delivery of their orders. Communicating partial shipments and backorder status transparently helps manage their expectations and maintains trust.

2. Inventory Management: Efficiently managing partial shipments and backorders helps optimize inventory levels, reducing the risk of overstocking or stockouts.

3. Revenue Recognition: Accurate tracking and processing of partial shipments and backorders are essential for correct revenue recognition and financial reporting.

4. Operational Efficiency: Streamlined processes for handling partial shipments and backorders improve overall operational efficiency and reduce administrative overhead.

Configuring Partial Shipments and Backorders in Oracle ERP

Oracle ERP provides robust functionality to handle partial shipments and backorders effectively. Configuring these features involves setting up relevant parameters and rules within the system. Key configuration steps include:

1. Defining Shipment Methods: Specify the methods for handling partial shipments and backorders. This includes setting up rules for splitting shipments, managing backorder queues, and determining priority levels for order fulfillment.

2. Inventory Allocation Rules: Configure inventory allocation rules to prioritize items for shipment based on criteria such as customer priority, order date, and item availability.

3. Backorder Notifications: Set up automated notifications to inform customers about the status of their backordered items. This includes email alerts, order status updates, and estimated delivery times.

4. Shipment and Backorder Policies: Establish clear policies for handling partial shipments and backorders, including guidelines for partial invoicing, shipping charges, and customer communication.

Process Flow for Handling Partial Shipments

The process flow for handling partial shipments in Oracle ERP involves several key steps, from order creation to final delivery:

1. Order Creation: A sales order is created in the system, specifying the items, quantities, and delivery dates. The system checks inventory levels to determine the availability of the ordered items.

2. Inventory Check: Oracle ERP performs an inventory check to identify items that are available for immediate shipment and those that are out of stock. Based on this check, the system generates a partial shipment plan.

3. Partial Shipment Plan: The partial shipment plan outlines the items that will be shipped immediately and those that will be backordered. The plan includes details such as shipment dates, quantities, and shipping methods.

4. Customer Communication: The customer is informed about the partial shipment and backorder status. This communication includes details about the items being shipped, expected delivery dates, and the status of backordered items.

5. Shipment Execution: The available items are picked, packed, and shipped to the customer. The system generates shipment documentation, including packing slips and shipping labels.

6. Invoicing: A partial invoice is generated for the shipped items. The system tracks the remaining items on backorder and updates the order status accordingly.

7. Backorder Fulfillment: Once the backordered items become available, the system generates a backorder fulfillment plan. These items are then picked, packed, and shipped to the customer, completing the order.

Best Practices for Managing Partial Shipments and Backorders

Effective management of partial shipments and backorders requires the implementation of best practices to ensure smooth operations and customer satisfaction:

1. Accurate Inventory Management: Maintain accurate inventory records to minimize the occurrence of backorders. Regularly update inventory levels and perform cycle counts to ensure data accuracy.

2. Clear Communication: Keep customers informed about the status of their orders, including partial shipments and backorders. Provide estimated delivery dates and notify customers of any changes promptly.

3. Efficient Order Processing: Streamline order processing workflows to handle partial shipments and backorders efficiently. Automate tasks such as order splitting, inventory allocation, and customer notifications.

4. Flexible Shipping Options: Offer flexible shipping options to customers, including the ability to split shipments and choose preferred delivery methods. This enhances customer satisfaction and reduces delays.

5. Proactive Backorder Management: Monitor backorder queues regularly and prioritize order fulfillment based on customer requirements and business priorities. Implement backorder mitigation strategies, such as safety stock and alternative sourcing.

6. Customer Service Integration: Integrate customer service processes with sales order management to address customer inquiries and issues related to partial shipments and backorders promptly.

Advanced Features for Handling Partial Shipments and Backorders

Oracle ERP provides advanced features to enhance the management of partial shipments and backorders:

1. Automated Order Splitting: The system can automatically split orders into multiple shipments based on predefined rules and inventory availability. This reduces manual intervention and speeds up order processing.

2. Dynamic Allocation: Oracle ERP supports dynamic allocation of inventory to orders, allowing real-time adjustments based on changing inventory levels and order priorities.

3. Backorder Optimization: Advanced algorithms can optimize backorder fulfillment by considering factors such as lead times, supplier performance, and customer demand patterns.

4. Order Promising: The system can provide accurate order promising dates based on real-time inventory data and supply chain constraints. This helps manage customer expectations effectively.

5. Analytics and Reporting: Comprehensive analytics and reporting tools allow businesses to monitor partial shipments and backorder performance, identify trends, and implement continuous improvement initiatives.

Case Study: Successful Implementation of Partial Shipments and Backorders Management

To illustrate the practical application of handling partial shipments and backorders in Oracle ERP, consider the following case study of a company that successfully implemented these processes:

Company Background: ABC Electronics, a leading distributor of electronic components, faced challenges in managing partial shipments and backorders due to fluctuating demand and complex supply chains.

Challenges:

- High volume of backorders leading to delayed shipments and customer dissatisfaction.

- Inaccurate inventory data resulting in frequent stockouts and overstock situations.

- Inefficient manual processes for handling partial shipments and backorders.

Solution:

- Implemented Oracle ERP with robust inventory management and order processing capabilities.

- Configured automated order splitting and dynamic allocation rules to optimize shipment plans.

- Integrated customer communication tools to provide real-time updates on order status.

Results:

- Reduced backorder volume by 30% through improved inventory accuracy and proactive management.

- Enhanced customer satisfaction with timely communication and accurate order promising.

- Increased operational efficiency by automating partial shipment and backorder processes.

Conclusion

Handling partial shipments and backorders is a critical component of effective sales order management in Oracle ERP. By configuring the system to manage these scenarios, businesses can optimize inventory levels, enhance customer satisfaction, and improve overall operational efficiency. Implementing best practices and leveraging advanced features within Oracle ERP ensures that partial shipments and backorders are handled seamlessly, contributing to a streamlined and responsive supply chain.

3.5 Reporting and Analysis of Sales Orders

3.5.1 Standard Reports for Sales Orders

The ability to generate and analyze reports is crucial for the effective management of sales orders in Oracle ERP's Accounts Receivable module. Standard reports provide insights into various aspects of sales order processing, including order status, fulfillment, revenue, and customer trends. This section will explore the key standard reports available in Oracle ERP for managing sales orders.

1. Sales Order Summary Report

The Sales Order Summary Report provides an overview of all sales orders within a specified period. This report includes key information such as order number, customer name, order date, status, total amount, and fulfillment details. It is useful for managers to quickly assess the overall sales performance and identify any bottlenecks in the order processing pipeline.

2. Sales Order Detail Report

The Sales Order Detail Report offers a more granular view of individual sales orders. It includes detailed information on each line item within an order, such as product descriptions, quantities, unit prices, and delivery dates. This report is essential for ensuring accuracy in order fulfillment and for resolving any discrepancies between orders and shipments.

3. Backorder Report

The Backorder Report identifies sales orders that have not been fully fulfilled due to inventory shortages or other issues. It highlights the items on backorder, the quantities needed, and the expected fulfillment dates. This report helps supply chain managers prioritize inventory replenishment and communicate with customers about delayed shipments.

4. Order Status Report

The Order Status Report tracks the current status of all sales orders, categorizing them as open, fulfilled, partially fulfilled, or canceled. It provides a snapshot of the order processing workflow and helps managers identify any orders that require immediate attention. This report is particularly useful for customer service teams to provide accurate updates to customers regarding their orders.

5. Sales Performance Report

The Sales Performance Report analyzes sales data over time, allowing managers to track sales trends, monitor revenue growth, and assess the performance of sales teams. It includes metrics such as total sales volume, average order value, and sales by product or region. This report is crucial for strategic planning and for setting sales targets.

6. Customer Order History Report

The Customer Order History Report provides a comprehensive view of a customer's order activity, including all past and current orders. It includes details such as order dates, products purchased, quantities, and total amounts. This report is valuable for account managers and sales representatives to understand customer buying patterns and to tailor sales strategies accordingly.

7. Fulfillment Report

The Fulfillment Report tracks the fulfillment status of all sales orders, including the quantities shipped, quantities pending, and any partial shipments. It helps ensure that all orders are processed and delivered in a timely manner and assists in identifying any issues that may be causing delays.

8. Returns and Adjustments Report

The Returns and Adjustments Report details all returned orders and any adjustments made to sales orders, such as refunds or exchanges. This report helps in analyzing the reasons for returns, managing customer dissatisfaction, and ensuring that inventory records are updated accurately.

9. Revenue Recognition Report

The Revenue Recognition Report provides information on recognized revenue from sales orders, ensuring compliance with accounting standards. It tracks revenue based on the fulfillment of orders and delivery of goods, which is essential for accurate financial reporting and auditing purposes.

10. Credit Hold Report

The Credit Hold Report identifies sales orders that are on hold due to credit issues, such as customers exceeding their credit limits or having overdue payments. This report helps credit managers take appropriate actions to release or maintain holds, ensuring that sales are not delayed unnecessarily.

11. Sales Order Aging Report

The Sales Order Aging Report categorizes sales orders based on their age, helping managers identify orders that have been in the system for extended periods. It includes aging buckets, such as 0-30 days, 31-60 days, and over 60 days, which are useful for prioritizing orders and addressing any delays in processing.

12. Exception Reports

Exception Reports highlight any anomalies or issues in the sales order process, such as orders without shipment dates, orders with discrepancies in pricing, or orders missing critical information. These reports are crucial for maintaining data integrity and for proactive issue resolution.

Benefits of Using Standard Reports

Standard reports offer several benefits for the management of sales orders in Oracle ERP:

1. Improved Decision-Making: By providing timely and accurate information, standard reports enable managers to make informed decisions regarding sales strategies, inventory management, and customer service.

2. Operational Efficiency: Reports help identify inefficiencies in the order processing workflow, such as delays in fulfillment or high rates of backorders, allowing for targeted improvements.

3. Enhanced Customer Satisfaction: By tracking order status and fulfillment, reports ensure that customers receive their orders on time and are informed of any delays, improving overall satisfaction.

4. Financial Accuracy: Revenue recognition and credit hold reports ensure that financial records are accurate and compliant with accounting standards, reducing the risk of financial discrepancies.

5. Proactive Issue Resolution: Exception reports highlight potential issues before they escalate, allowing for proactive resolution and minimizing disruptions to the sales process.

Generating Standard Reports in Oracle ERP

Oracle ERP provides a user-friendly interface for generating standard reports. Users can customize report parameters, such as date ranges, customer segments, and product categories, to tailor the reports to their specific needs. The steps to generate a standard report are as follows:

1. Navigate to the Reports Section: Access the Reports section within the Accounts Receivable module.

2. Select the Desired Report: Choose the report you wish to generate from the list of available standard reports.

3. Customize Report Parameters: Input the required parameters, such as date range, customer details, and product information, to customize the report.

4. Generate the Report: Click the generate button to produce the report. Oracle ERP will compile the data and present it in a structured format.

5. Review and Analyze: Review the generated report for insights and analysis. Export the report to various formats, such as PDF or Excel, for further analysis or sharing with stakeholders.

Conclusion

Standard reports in Oracle ERP's Accounts Receivable module play a critical role in managing sales orders effectively. By providing comprehensive insights into order processing, fulfillment, revenue, and customer trends, these reports empower managers to make data-driven decisions, improve operational efficiency, and enhance customer satisfaction. Utilizing these reports ensures that the sales order process is transparent, efficient, and aligned with the overall business objectives.

3.5.2 Analyzing Sales Order Data

Analyzing sales order data is a crucial aspect of managing the sales process within Oracle ERP. Effective analysis helps businesses understand their sales trends, monitor performance, and make informed decisions to improve customer satisfaction and drive revenue growth. This section will delve into the methods, tools, and best practices for analyzing sales order data within the Oracle ERP Accounts Receivable module.

Understanding Sales Order Metrics

To effectively analyze sales order data, it's essential to understand the key metrics and indicators that reflect the performance and efficiency of the sales process. These metrics include:

1. Sales Volume: This metric tracks the total number of sales orders processed within a specific period. It helps in understanding the demand for products or services and identifying trends over time.

2. Order Value: The total monetary value of sales orders provides insights into revenue generation and customer spending patterns.

3. Order Fulfillment Rate: This measures the percentage of orders that are successfully fulfilled within the promised timeframe, indicating the efficiency of the order fulfillment process.

4. Order Cycle Time: The average time taken to process and fulfill a sales order from creation to delivery. Shorter cycle times indicate a more efficient process.

5. Order Accuracy: The percentage of orders processed without errors, such as incorrect quantities, pricing, or shipping details. High order accuracy minimizes customer complaints and returns.

6. Backorder Rate: The proportion of orders that cannot be fulfilled immediately due to stock shortages. A high backorder rate may indicate inventory management issues.

7. Cancellation Rate: The percentage of orders canceled by customers. Analyzing the reasons for cancellations can help identify areas for improvement in the sales process or product offerings.

Data Collection and Preparation

Before analyzing sales order data, it's crucial to ensure that the data is accurate, complete, and up-to-date. This involves:

1. Data Validation: Implementing validation rules to ensure that all sales orders are entered correctly and consistently.

2. Data Cleaning: Regularly reviewing and cleaning the data to remove duplicates, correct errors, and fill in missing information.

3. Data Integration: Ensuring that sales order data is integrated with other relevant data sources, such as inventory, customer, and financial data, for comprehensive analysis.

Tools and Techniques for Sales Order Analysis

Oracle ERP provides various tools and techniques for analyzing sales order data, including:

1. Standard Reports: Oracle ERP offers a range of pre-built reports that provide insights into sales order performance. These reports can be customized to meet specific business needs and include metrics such as sales volume, order value, and fulfillment rates.

2. Ad Hoc Reporting: Users can create custom reports to analyze specific aspects of sales order data. This flexibility allows for in-depth analysis of unique business requirements.

3. Dashboards: Oracle ERP dashboards provide a visual representation of key sales order metrics, enabling users to quickly identify trends, monitor performance, and make informed decisions.

4. Data Visualization Tools: Tools like Oracle BI Publisher and Oracle Analytics Cloud offer advanced data visualization capabilities, allowing users to create interactive charts, graphs, and dashboards for more effective analysis.

5. Data Mining and Predictive Analytics: Advanced data analysis techniques, such as data mining and predictive analytics, can be used to uncover hidden patterns, forecast future trends, and identify opportunities for improvement.

Analyzing Sales Trends and Patterns

Analyzing sales trends and patterns involves examining historical sales data to identify changes in demand, customer preferences, and market conditions. This analysis helps businesses understand:

1. Seasonal Trends: Identifying seasonal variations in sales can help businesses plan for peak periods, optimize inventory levels, and adjust marketing strategies accordingly.

2. Product Performance: Analyzing sales data by product category or SKU can reveal which products are performing well and which may need additional marketing support or discontinuation.

3. Customer Behavior: Understanding customer purchasing patterns, such as frequency of orders and average order value, can help tailor marketing efforts and improve customer retention.

Performance Monitoring and Benchmarking

Performance monitoring involves regularly tracking key sales order metrics to ensure that the sales process is running efficiently and meeting business goals. This includes:

1. KPI Tracking: Establishing key performance indicators (KPIs) for sales order processing and regularly monitoring these KPIs to identify areas for improvement.

2. Benchmarking: Comparing sales order performance against industry standards or competitor data to identify strengths and weaknesses in the sales process.

3. Exception Reporting: Creating reports that highlight exceptions, such as orders that exceed specified thresholds for cycle time or backorder rate, to quickly address potential issues.

Identifying and Addressing Issues

Effective analysis of sales order data can help identify and address issues that may be impacting the sales process. Common issues include:

1. Order Delays: Analyzing cycle time data can help identify bottlenecks in the order processing workflow, such as approval delays or inventory shortages.

2. High Return Rates: Examining return data can reveal common reasons for returns, such as product quality issues or incorrect shipments, allowing businesses to take corrective actions.

3. Customer Complaints: Analyzing customer feedback and complaint data can provide insights into areas where the sales process may be falling short and help prioritize improvements.

Optimizing the Sales Order Process

Using insights gained from sales order analysis, businesses can implement changes to optimize the sales process. This may involve:

1. Process Automation: Identifying manual processes that can be automated to reduce cycle times and improve order accuracy.

2. Workflow Improvements: Streamlining approval workflows and eliminating unnecessary steps to increase efficiency.

3. Inventory Management: Improving inventory forecasting and replenishment processes to reduce backorder rates and ensure timely fulfillment.

4. Customer Communication: Enhancing communication with customers regarding order status, delivery times, and any potential delays to improve customer satisfaction.

Continuous Improvement

Analyzing sales order data is an ongoing process that requires regular review and adjustment to ensure continuous improvement. This involves:

1. Regular Reviews: Conducting regular reviews of sales order performance metrics to identify trends and areas for improvement.

2. Feedback Loops: Implementing feedback loops to gather input from sales teams, customers, and other stakeholders on the effectiveness of changes made to the sales process.

3. Continuous Training: Providing ongoing training and development for sales and customer service teams to ensure they are equipped with the skills and knowledge needed to manage the sales order process effectively.

Leveraging Advanced Analytics

Advanced analytics techniques, such as machine learning and artificial intelligence, can further enhance sales order analysis by providing deeper insights and more accurate predictions. Examples include:

1. Predictive Sales Forecasting: Using historical sales data to predict future demand and identify potential sales opportunities.

2. Customer Segmentation: Segmenting customers based on purchasing behavior and preferences to tailor marketing and sales strategies.

3. Churn Analysis: Identifying patterns that indicate potential customer churn and implementing proactive measures to retain at-risk customers.

In conclusion, analyzing sales order data within Oracle ERP is a critical component of managing the sales process. By understanding key metrics, utilizing advanced tools and techniques, and continuously monitoring and improving performance, businesses can optimize their sales operations, enhance customer satisfaction, and drive revenue growth.

3.5.3 Using Dashboards for Sales Order Management

Dashboards play a crucial role in modern business management by providing a visual representation of key performance indicators (KPIs) and metrics. In the context of sales order management within the Oracle ERP Accounts Receivable module, dashboards offer a powerful tool for monitoring, analyzing, and optimizing sales order processes. This section explores the benefits, key components, and best practices for using dashboards to manage sales orders effectively.

1. Benefits of Using Dashboards for Sales Order Management

Real-Time Insights:

Dashboards provide real-time data, allowing managers and decision-makers to stay updated with the latest sales order information. This immediacy helps in making timely decisions and addressing any issues as they arise.

Enhanced Visibility:

Dashboards consolidate data from various sources into a single view, offering a comprehensive overview of sales order performance. This visibility enables managers to track the progress of sales orders, identify bottlenecks, and ensure that orders are processed efficiently.

Data-Driven Decision Making:

With dashboards, businesses can leverage data to drive decision-making processes. By analyzing trends and patterns, companies can make informed decisions that enhance sales order management and overall business performance.

Improved Communication and Collaboration:

Dashboards can be shared across teams, promoting transparency and facilitating collaboration. Sales, finance, and operations teams can access the same information, ensuring everyone is aligned and working towards common goals.

Performance Tracking:

Dashboards enable businesses to track KPIs related to sales order management, such as order fulfillment rates, order processing times, and revenue generated. Monitoring these KPIs helps in assessing performance and identifying areas for improvement.

2. Key Components of Sales Order Management Dashboards

Order Status and Tracking:

Dashboards should provide a clear view of the status of all sales orders, including pending, in-process, and completed orders. This component allows managers to monitor the progress of orders and ensure timely fulfillment.

Sales Order Volume and Trends:

Visual representations of sales order volumes and trends over time help businesses understand demand patterns and seasonality. This information is crucial for planning inventory, production, and resource allocation.

Customer Insights:

Dashboards should include data on customer orders, such as top customers, order frequency, and average order value. Understanding customer behavior helps in tailoring sales strategies and improving customer satisfaction.

Revenue and Financial Metrics:

Key financial metrics, such as total revenue, average order value, and profit margins, should be prominently displayed on dashboards. These metrics provide insights into the financial health of the sales order process.

Order Fulfillment and Shipping Performance:

Tracking the performance of order fulfillment and shipping processes is essential for ensuring timely delivery. Dashboards should highlight metrics such as on-time delivery rates, shipping costs, and transit times.

Inventory Levels:

Integrating inventory data into sales order management dashboards helps in maintaining optimal stock levels. Businesses can track inventory availability, identify potential stockouts, and plan replenishments effectively.

Exception Management:

Dashboards should highlight any exceptions or issues in the sales order process, such as delayed orders, backorders, or payment disputes. This component enables managers to address problems promptly and maintain smooth operations.

3. Best Practices for Using Dashboards in Sales Order Management

Customizing Dashboards to Fit Business Needs:

Every business has unique requirements, and dashboards should be tailored to meet these needs. Customize dashboards to display relevant metrics and KPIs that align with your sales order management objectives.

Ensuring Data Accuracy and Consistency:

Accurate and consistent data is crucial for reliable insights. Implement robust data validation and cleansing processes to ensure the data displayed on dashboards is accurate and up-to-date.

Regular Monitoring and Updates:

Dashboards should be monitored regularly to keep track of performance and identify any deviations from targets. Schedule regular updates to ensure that the data reflects the latest information.

Leveraging Predictive Analytics:

Advanced dashboards can incorporate predictive analytics to forecast future sales order volumes, identify potential risks, and recommend actions to optimize processes. Utilize predictive analytics to stay ahead of trends and make proactive decisions.

Training and Empowering Users:

Ensure that all relevant stakeholders are trained on how to use dashboards effectively. Empower users to customize their views, generate reports, and leverage the insights provided by dashboards to enhance their decision-making processes.

Integrating with Other Systems:

Dashboards should be integrated with other business systems, such as CRM, ERP, and inventory management, to provide a holistic view of sales order management. Seamless integration ensures that data flows smoothly between systems and enhances overall efficiency.

Visualizing Data Effectively:

Use appropriate visualizations, such as charts, graphs, and gauges, to represent data effectively. Choose visualizations that make it easy to interpret information and highlight key trends and patterns.

4. Implementing Dashboards in Oracle ERP Accounts Receivable

Step 1: Identify Key Metrics and KPIs:

Begin by identifying the key metrics and KPIs that are critical for sales order management. These may include order fulfillment rates, revenue, order processing times, and customer satisfaction scores.

Step 2: Design the Dashboard Layout:

Design a dashboard layout that presents information clearly and logically. Group related metrics together and use intuitive visualizations to represent data.

Step 3: Configure Data Sources:

Connect the dashboard to relevant data sources within the Oracle ERP system. Ensure that data is pulled from reliable sources and is updated in real-time.

Step 4: Customize Visualizations:

Customize visualizations to match the specific needs of your business. Use different types of charts and graphs to represent various metrics and ensure that the visualizations are easy to understand.

Step 5: Set Up Alerts and Notifications:

Configure alerts and notifications for critical metrics. For example, set up alerts for delayed orders, high-value orders, or inventory shortages. These alerts help in proactively managing potential issues.

Step 6: Test and Validate:

Before deploying the dashboard, test it thoroughly to ensure that it functions correctly and displays accurate data. Validate the data against other reports and ensure that the visualizations are clear and meaningful.

Step 7: Train Users:

Provide training to users on how to navigate and use the dashboard. Ensure that users understand how to interpret the data and leverage the insights for decision-making.

Step 8: Monitor and Improve:

Once the dashboard is live, monitor its performance regularly. Gather feedback from users and make continuous improvements to enhance its effectiveness.

5. Examples of Sales Order Management Dashboards

Example 1: Executive Summary Dashboard:

An executive summary dashboard provides a high-level overview of sales order performance. Key metrics may include total sales, order fulfillment rates, average order value, and top-performing products. This dashboard helps executives understand the overall health of the sales order process and make strategic decisions.

Example 2: Order Fulfillment Dashboard:

An order fulfillment dashboard focuses on tracking the progress of sales orders through the fulfillment process. Metrics may include order status, shipping times, delivery performance, and exceptions. This dashboard helps operations teams ensure timely and accurate order fulfillment.

Example 3: Customer Insights Dashboard:

A customer insights dashboard provides detailed information about customer orders and behavior. Metrics may include top customers, order frequency, order value, and customer satisfaction scores. This dashboard helps sales and marketing teams tailor their strategies to meet customer needs and drive sales.

Example 4: Financial Performance Dashboard:

A financial performance dashboard tracks key financial metrics related to sales orders, such as total revenue, profit margins, and payment status. This dashboard helps finance teams monitor financial performance and manage cash flow effectively.

Conclusion

Using dashboards for sales order management in Oracle ERP Accounts Receivable offers significant advantages in terms of visibility, efficiency, and data-driven decision-making. By implementing best practices and leveraging the power of real-time data, businesses can optimize their sales order processes, enhance customer satisfaction, and achieve their financial goals. As technology continues to evolve, the role of dashboards in business management will only become more critical, making it essential for organizations to invest in robust dashboard solutions.

CHAPTER IV
Managing Customer Invoices

4.1 Creating Customer Invoices

4.1.1 Steps to Create an Invoice

Creating customer invoices is a critical process within the Accounts Receivable module of Oracle ERP. Properly generated invoices ensure accurate billing, facilitate timely payments, and contribute to the financial health of the organization. This section provides a comprehensive guide to the steps involved in creating an invoice, from the initial setup to the final posting.

Step 1: Access the Invoicing Module

To begin the invoice creation process, navigate to the Accounts Receivable module within Oracle ERP. The invoicing functions can typically be found under the "Transactions" menu. Select the "Invoices" option to access the invoicing workspace.

Step 2: Initiate a New Invoice

Once in the invoicing workspace, initiate a new invoice by clicking on the "Create Invoice" button. This action will open a new invoice form where you will enter all necessary information.

Step 3: Enter Customer Information

The first section of the invoice form requires you to enter customer details. These include:

- Customer Name or ID: Select the customer from the drop-down list or enter their ID.

- Customer Address: Verify the billing address, which should auto-populate based on the customer selection.

- Contact Information: Ensure the correct contact person and contact details are associated with the invoice.

Step 4: Specify Invoice Date and Number

Next, input the invoice date. This is the date the invoice is issued, which could be the current date or a backdated one if applicable. The invoice number might be auto-generated based on your company's numbering conventions, but ensure it follows the sequence and format required by your organization's policies.

Step 5: Define Payment Terms

Select the appropriate payment terms for the invoice. Payment terms dictate when the payment is due and may include:

- Net 30, Net 60, etc.: Indicates the number of days the customer has to pay the invoice.

- Discount Terms: If early payment discounts are offered, specify the terms (e.g., 2% discount if paid within 10 days).

Step 6: Add Line Items

The core of the invoice consists of the line items that detail the products or services being billed. For each line item, provide the following information:

- Item Description: A detailed description of the product or service.

- Quantity: The number of units being billed.

- Unit Price: The price per unit of the product or service.

- Total Amount: Automatically calculated based on quantity and unit price.

- Tax Codes: Apply relevant tax codes if applicable.

Step 7: Apply Discounts and Adjustments

If there are any applicable discounts or adjustments, apply them at this stage. This can include volume discounts, promotional discounts, or adjustments for previous overcharges or undercharges.

Step 8: Verify Tax Calculations

Ensure that all tax calculations are accurate. This includes sales tax, VAT, or any other applicable taxes. Verify that the tax rates are correct and that the total tax amount is properly calculated.

Step 9: Review Shipping Information

If the invoice includes physical products that need shipping, enter the shipping details. This includes:

- Shipping Method: The method used to ship the products (e.g., standard, express).

- Shipping Address: Confirm or enter the address where the products will be delivered.

- Shipping Charges: Add any shipping charges to the invoice total.

Step 10: Add Additional Charges or Fees

Include any additional charges or fees that may apply. This can range from handling fees, service fees, or other miscellaneous charges.

Step 11: Review and Validate the Invoice

Before finalizing the invoice, review all entered information for accuracy. Check that:

- All line items are correct.

- Payment terms are clearly stated.

- Discounts and adjustments are properly applied.

- Tax calculations are accurate.

- Shipping and additional charges are included.

Step 12: Save and Submit the Invoice

Once the invoice has been reviewed and all information is accurate, save the invoice. Depending on the system's configuration, you may need to submit the invoice for approval.

Step 13: Approval Workflow

If your organization uses an approval workflow, the invoice will be routed to the appropriate personnel for review and approval. The approver will check for accuracy, compliance with company policies, and ensure all necessary documentation is attached. Once approved, the invoice can be finalized.

Step 14: Finalize and Post the Invoice

After approval, finalize the invoice by posting it to the general ledger. Posting the invoice records the transaction in the accounting system, making it part of the company's financial records.

Step 15: Distribute the Invoice to the Customer

The final step is distributing the invoice to the customer. This can be done electronically via email, through an online portal, or by traditional mail. Ensure the invoice is sent promptly to facilitate timely payment.

Best Practices for Creating Customer Invoices

Creating accurate and detailed invoices is vital for effective accounts receivable management. Here are some best practices to consider:

- Automation: Utilize automation features within Oracle ERP to streamline the invoice creation process. Automated workflows can reduce errors and save time.

- Templates: Use standardized invoice templates to ensure consistency and compliance with company policies.

- Training: Ensure that all staff involved in the invoicing process are well-trained and understand the importance of accuracy and completeness.

- Validation Checks: Implement validation checks within the ERP system to catch common errors before the invoice is finalized.

- Customer Communication: Maintain clear communication with customers regarding their invoices, payment terms, and any disputes or discrepancies.

Conclusion

Creating customer invoices in Oracle ERP involves a series of detailed steps that ensure accuracy, compliance, and efficiency. By following the outlined steps and adhering to best practices, organizations can streamline their invoicing processes, improve cash flow, and enhance customer satisfaction. Properly managed invoicing is a cornerstone of effective accounts receivable management and overall financial health.

4.1.2 Mandatory Fields and Information

Creating customer invoices in Oracle ERP is a critical process that requires careful attention to detail. Ensuring all mandatory fields are correctly filled in is essential for accurate billing and financial reporting. This section will cover the key fields and information required to create a customer invoice successfully.

4.1.2.1 Customer Information

The first and foremost information required on a customer invoice is the customer's details. This includes:

Customer Name: The legal name of the customer or company being billed.

Customer Address: The billing address of the customer. This can include street address, city, state, postal code, and country.

Customer Contact Information: Contact details such as phone number and email address. This information is crucial for any follow-up communication or resolving queries related to the invoice.

4.1.2.2 Invoice Number

Every invoice must have a unique invoice number. This number is essential for tracking and referencing the invoice in future transactions. Invoice numbers typically follow a sequential pattern, but they can also include prefixes or other identifiers to distinguish different types of transactions or departments within the company.

4.1.2.3 Invoice Date

The invoice date is the date when the invoice is created. This date is crucial as it determines the payment due date and can also affect financial reporting periods. It is essential to ensure the invoice date is accurate and reflects the actual date the invoice was issued.

4.1.2.4 Purchase Order Number

If the invoice is linked to a purchase order (PO), the PO number must be included. The purchase order number helps in matching the invoice to the corresponding purchase order, ensuring that the goods or services billed have been requested and approved by the customer.

4.1.2.5 Description of Goods or Services

A detailed description of the goods or services provided is necessary for the invoice. This includes:

Item Description: A clear and concise description of each item or service provided.

Quantity: The quantity of each item or the extent of each service provided.

Unit Price: The price per unit of each item or service.

Total Price: The total price for each line item (quantity multiplied by unit price).

Providing a detailed description helps the customer understand what they are being billed for and can prevent disputes or queries about the invoice.

4.1.2.6 Tax Information

Depending on the jurisdiction and the nature of the goods or services provided, tax information must be included on the invoice. This includes:

Tax Rate: The applicable tax rate for each item or service.

Tax Amount: The total tax amount for each line item.

Total Tax: The total tax amount for the entire invoice.

Accurate tax information is crucial for compliance with local tax laws and for the customer to claim any applicable tax credits.

4.1.2.7 Payment Terms

The payment terms outline the conditions under which the payment should be made. This includes:

Due Date: The date by which the payment must be made.

Payment Method: Accepted payment methods (e.g., bank transfer, credit card, check).

Early Payment Discounts: Any discounts offered for early payment.

Late Payment Penalties: Any penalties or interest charges for late payment.

Clear payment terms help ensure timely payments and can improve cash flow management.

4.1.2.8 Currency

The currency in which the invoice is issued must be clearly specified. This is particularly important for international transactions. The currency code (e.g., USD, EUR, JPY) should be included to avoid any confusion about the amount to be paid.

4.1.2.9 Total Amount Due

The total amount due is the sum of all line items and applicable taxes. This amount should be prominently displayed on the invoice to ensure it is easily identifiable.

4.1.2.10 Terms and Conditions

Including any additional terms and conditions on the invoice can help prevent misunderstandings or disputes. This might include:

Return Policy: Conditions under which goods can be returned.

Warranty Information: Any warranties provided with the goods or services.

Dispute Resolution: Procedures for resolving any disputes related to the invoice.

4.1.2.11 Authorized Signatory

Including the name and signature of the authorized person issuing the invoice adds a level of authenticity and formality. This can also help in verifying the invoice's legitimacy in case of any disputes.

4.1.2.12 Invoice Footer Information

The footer of the invoice can include additional information such as:

Company Details: The company's registered address, contact information, and tax identification number.

Bank Details: Bank account information for payments, including account number and routing number.

Legal Disclaimers: Any legal disclaimers or notices required by law.

Detailed Walkthrough of Creating an Invoice

Creating a customer invoice in Oracle ERP involves navigating through several steps to ensure all mandatory fields and information are correctly entered. Below is a detailed walkthrough of the process:

Step 1: Accessing the Invoicing Module

1. Log in to Oracle ERP: Start by logging into the Oracle ERP system with the appropriate user credentials.

2. Navigate to Accounts Receivable: From the main menu, navigate to the Accounts Receivable module.

3. Open the Invoicing Section: Within Accounts Receivable, select the option to create a new invoice.

Step 2: Entering Customer Information

1. Select Customer: Choose the customer from the customer database. If the customer is new, create a new customer record with all necessary details.

2. Verify Customer Details: Ensure all customer information, such as name, address, and contact details, are accurate and up to date.

Step 3: Entering Invoice Details

1. Generate Invoice Number: The system will typically generate an invoice number automatically. Verify that the number is correct.

2. Enter Invoice Date: The invoice date should be set to the current date, but it can be adjusted if necessary.

3. Enter Purchase Order Number: If applicable, enter the purchase order number provided by the customer.

Step 4: Adding Line Items

1. Add Item Description: For each item or service, enter a detailed description.

2. Enter Quantity and Unit Price: Specify the quantity and unit price for each item.

3. Calculate Total Price: The system will automatically calculate the total price for each line item.

Step 5: Applying Tax Information

1. Select Tax Codes: Choose the appropriate tax codes for each line item.

2. Verify Tax Amounts: Ensure the tax amounts are correctly calculated based on the selected tax rates.

Step 6: Reviewing Payment Terms

1. Specify Due Date: Enter the payment due date based on the agreed payment terms.

2. Select Payment Method: Specify the accepted payment methods.

3. Enter Early Payment Discounts: If applicable, enter any discounts for early payment.

4. Enter Late Payment Penalties: Specify any penalties for late payment.

Step 7: Finalizing the Invoice

1. Review Total Amount Due: Ensure the total amount due, including all line items and taxes, is correct.

2. Add Terms and Conditions: Include any additional terms and conditions relevant to the invoice.

3. Add Authorized Signatory: Enter the name and signature of the authorized person issuing the invoice.

Step 8: Saving and Sending the Invoice

1. Save the Invoice: Save the invoice in the system.

2. Send the Invoice: Choose the option to send the invoice to the customer via email or print it for physical mailing.

Best Practices for Creating Customer Invoices

To ensure the invoicing process is efficient and error-free, consider the following best practices:

1. Standardize Invoice Templates

Using standardized invoice templates can help ensure consistency and accuracy. Templates should include all mandatory fields and be customizable to meet specific customer requirements.

2. Automate Invoice Creation

Automating the invoice creation process can reduce errors and save time. Use Oracle ERP's automation features to generate invoices based on predefined rules and templates.

3. Verify Customer Information

Regularly update and verify customer information to prevent billing issues. Ensure that customer records are accurate and complete before creating invoices.

4. Review Payment Terms

Clearly communicate payment terms to customers and ensure they are included on every invoice. This helps set expectations and can improve cash flow management.

5. Monitor Invoice Status

Track the status of invoices to ensure they are sent, received, and paid on time. Use Oracle ERP's tracking features to monitor outstanding invoices and follow up on overdue payments.

6. Train Staff

Provide training to staff responsible for creating and managing invoices. Ensure they are familiar with Oracle ERP's invoicing features and understand the importance of accurate invoicing.

7. Conduct Regular Audits

Regularly audit the invoicing process to identify and address any issues. This can help ensure compliance with financial regulations and improve the overall efficiency of the invoicing process.

By following these best practices and ensuring all mandatory fields and information are accurately entered, organizations can streamline their invoicing process, reduce errors, and improve financial management.

4.1.3 Customizing Invoice Templates

Customizing invoice templates in Oracle ERP is a critical aspect of managing customer invoices effectively. It ensures that the invoices reflect your company's branding, comply with legal requirements, and provide clear, relevant information to your customers. This section will guide you through the process of customizing invoice templates, highlighting best practices and common customization scenarios.

Understanding the Importance of Customization

Invoice templates are more than just a tool for billing; they are a reflection of your company's professionalism and attention to detail. Customizing them allows you to:

- Enhance Brand Identity: Include your company logo, colors, and fonts to make invoices immediately recognizable.

- Ensure Compliance: Incorporate necessary legal and tax information specific to your business and jurisdiction.

- Improve Clarity: Format invoices in a way that makes it easy for customers to understand charges, due dates, and payment instructions.

- Increase Efficiency: Tailor templates to include all required fields, reducing the need for manual adjustments.

Steps to Customize Invoice Templates

1. Accessing the Template Management Module

  - Navigate to the 'Accounts Receivable' section in Oracle ERP.

  - Select 'Setup' and then 'Templates'.

  - Choose 'Invoice Templates' from the list of available template types.

2. Choosing a Base Template

  - Oracle ERP provides several default templates. Select one that closely matches your requirements.

  - Open the template in the template editor to begin customization.

3. Customizing the Header and Footer

  - Header: Add your company logo, name, address, and contact information.

  - Footer: Include additional information such as terms and conditions, legal disclaimers, and contact details for payment inquiries.

4. Modifying the Body of the Invoice

  - Invoice Details: Ensure the inclusion of invoice number, date, and due date.

  - Customer Information: Include the customer's name, address, and contact details.

  - Line Items: Customize the layout and information for each line item. Ensure clarity in description, quantity, unit price, and total amount.

5. Adding Custom Fields

- Oracle ERP allows the addition of custom fields to capture specific information relevant to your business.

- Examples include purchase order numbers, project codes, or special discount details.

6. Setting Up Conditional Formatting

- Use conditional formatting to highlight important information, such as overdue invoices or early payment discounts.

- Set rules to change the appearance of fields based on their values (e.g., red text for overdue amounts).

7. Testing the Template

- Before finalizing, generate sample invoices using the new template.

- Review them for accuracy, completeness, and visual appeal. Ensure all necessary information is correctly displayed.

8. Finalizing and Saving the Template

- Save the customized template with a unique name for easy identification.

- Set the new template as the default if it will be used for most transactions.

Best Practices for Customizing Invoice Templates

1. Consistency in Design

- Maintain a consistent design across all customer-facing documents. This helps reinforce brand recognition and professionalism.

2. Legal and Regulatory Compliance

- Ensure that your invoice template complies with local laws and regulations, including tax codes, payment terms, and invoice numbering requirements.

3. Clear and Concise Information

- Avoid cluttering the invoice with unnecessary information. Keep it clear and concise to ensure customers can easily find what they need.

4. Customer-Specific Customization

- For key customers, consider creating customized templates that cater to their specific needs or preferences. This can enhance customer satisfaction and loyalty.

5. Use of Technology

- Leverage Oracle ERP's capabilities for automation and dynamic data insertion. Use placeholders and variables to automatically fill in customer-specific details.

Common Customization Scenarios

1. Industry-Specific Requirements

- Different industries may have unique invoicing requirements. For example, construction companies might need to include project codes, while retail businesses might require SKU numbers and barcodes.

2. International Transactions

- Customize templates to include multi-currency support, language translations, and international tax information for global customers.

3. Early Payment Discounts

- Highlight early payment discounts clearly on the invoice. Include the discount amount, deadline for payment to avail of the discount, and the net amount after the discount.

4. Electronic Invoicing

- Prepare templates for electronic invoicing by including digital signatures, QR codes, and links for online payment portals.

5. Customer Loyalty Programs

- If your business offers loyalty programs, customize invoices to show points earned from the transaction or redeemable discounts.

Example of a Customized Invoice Template

To illustrate, consider a sample invoice template for a software development company. The template includes:

- Header: Company logo, name, and contact details.

- Body:

  - Invoice Information: Invoice number, date, and due date.

  - Customer Information: Customer name, address, and contact person.

  - Line Items: Each line item includes a description of the service (e.g., "Development of Custom Software Module"), hours worked, hourly rate, and total cost.

  - Summary: Subtotal, applicable taxes, and total amount due.

- Footer: Payment instructions, terms and conditions, and a thank you note.

Conclusion

Customizing invoice templates in Oracle ERP is a vital step in managing customer invoices efficiently. It ensures that invoices are not only functional and compliant but also serve as a professional touchpoint with your customers. By following the steps and best practices outlined in this section, you can create invoice templates that enhance your business operations and customer relationships.

4.2 Invoice Approval Workflow

4.2.1 Setting Up Approval Rules

Setting up approval rules for invoices in the Oracle ERP Accounts Receivable module is a critical step to ensure the accuracy, compliance, and efficiency of the invoicing process. Properly configured approval rules help maintain control over financial transactions, reduce errors, and prevent fraudulent activities. This section will cover the key aspects of setting up approval rules, including defining the approval process, establishing criteria for approval, configuring approval hierarchies, and automating the workflow.

Defining the Approval Process

The approval process in the Accounts Receivable module begins with the creation of an invoice and ends with the final approval or rejection. The process can involve multiple steps and participants, depending on the complexity and requirements of the organization. The typical steps in the approval process include:

1. Invoice Creation: The process starts with the creation of an invoice by an authorized user. This includes entering all necessary details such as customer information, invoice amount, and due date.

2. Initial Review: The invoice is then reviewed by the initial approver, who checks for completeness and accuracy.

3. Approval Hierarchy: The invoice is routed through a predefined approval hierarchy, which may involve multiple levels of approvers.

4. Final Approval: Once all required approvals are obtained, the invoice is marked as approved.

5. Notification: The approval or rejection of the invoice is communicated to the relevant stakeholders.

Establishing Criteria for Approval

To set up effective approval rules, it is essential to establish clear criteria for when and how invoices should be approved. These criteria can vary based on the organization's policies and the nature of the transactions. Common criteria include:

- Invoice Amount: Different approval levels may be required for invoices of varying amounts. For example, invoices below a certain threshold may require only a single approval, while higher amounts may need multiple approvals.

- Customer Category: Invoices from certain categories of customers, such as high-value or high-risk customers, may require additional scrutiny and approval.

- Type of Service or Product: Specific services or products may have unique approval requirements due to their nature or regulatory considerations.

- Geographical Location: Invoices generated for customers in certain regions may require approval from regional managers or compliance officers.

- Payment Terms: Invoices with non-standard payment terms may need additional approval to ensure they comply with company policies.

Configuring Approval Hierarchies

An approval hierarchy is a structured system that defines the levels of approval required for an invoice based on the established criteria. In Oracle ERP, configuring an approval hierarchy involves the following steps:

1. Identify Approvers: Determine who within the organization has the authority to approve invoices at different levels. This may include roles such as departmental managers, financial controllers, and senior executives.

2. Define Approval Levels: Establish the levels of approval required based on the criteria. For example, invoices up to $10,000 may require approval from a departmental manager, while those above $50,000 may need approval from a senior executive.

3. Assign Approvers to Levels: Assign the identified approvers to the corresponding approval levels. This ensures that invoices are routed to the correct individuals based on the established criteria.

4. Configure Escalation Rules: Set up escalation rules to handle situations where an approver is unavailable or does not respond within a specified time frame. This ensures that invoices are not delayed unnecessarily.

Automating the Approval Workflow

Automating the approval workflow in Oracle ERP helps streamline the process, reduce manual intervention, and ensure compliance with the established approval rules. Automation involves configuring the system to automatically route invoices through the approval hierarchy based on predefined criteria. Key steps in automating the workflow include:

1. Workflow Configuration: Use the Oracle ERP workflow management tools to define the approval process. This includes setting up the steps, conditions, and actions required for the workflow.

2. Define Routing Rules: Configure the system to automatically route invoices to the appropriate approvers based on the criteria. This may involve setting up routing rules based on invoice amount, customer category, or other relevant factors.

3. Set Up Notifications: Configure automated notifications to alert approvers when an invoice requires their attention. Notifications can be sent via email, system alerts, or other communication channels.

4. Track Approvals: Use the system's tracking and reporting features to monitor the status of invoices in the approval process. This helps ensure that invoices are approved in a timely manner and allows for quick identification of any bottlenecks or issues.

5. Implement Exception Handling: Set up exception handling rules to manage situations where an invoice does not meet the standard approval criteria. This may involve routing the invoice to a designated approver for manual review.

Ensuring Compliance and Auditability

One of the key benefits of setting up approval rules in Oracle ERP is the ability to ensure compliance with organizational policies and regulatory requirements. To achieve this, it is important to:

1. Document Approval Policies: Clearly document the approval policies and criteria used to set up the approval rules. This documentation should be easily accessible to all relevant stakeholders.

2. Regularly Review and Update Rules: Periodically review the approval rules and criteria to ensure they remain aligned with the organization's policies and any changes in regulatory requirements.

3. Audit Trail: Maintain a detailed audit trail of all approval actions within the system. This includes recording who approved or rejected an invoice, the date and time of the action, and any comments or notes added by the approvers.

4. Conduct Regular Audits: Perform regular audits of the approval process to verify compliance with the documented policies and to identify any areas for improvement. This can help uncover any potential issues or discrepancies in the approval workflow.

Best Practices for Setting Up Approval Rules

To maximize the effectiveness of the approval rules and workflow, consider the following best practices:

1. Involve Key Stakeholders: Engage key stakeholders, including finance, compliance, and departmental managers, in the process of defining approval rules and criteria. Their input can help ensure the rules are comprehensive and aligned with organizational goals.

2. Simplify the Process: Avoid overly complex approval hierarchies that can slow down the process. Aim for a balance between control and efficiency by limiting the number of approval levels to what is necessary.

3. Leverage Technology: Utilize the full capabilities of the Oracle ERP system to automate and streamline the approval workflow. This includes using features such as automated routing, notifications, and tracking.

4. Train Users: Provide thorough training for all users involved in the approval process. This includes understanding how to use the system, the importance of timely approvals, and the criteria for approval.

5. Monitor Performance: Continuously monitor the performance of the approval workflow using system reports and metrics. Identify any bottlenecks or delays and take corrective actions as needed.

Conclusion

Setting up approval rules for invoices in the Oracle ERP Accounts Receivable module is a critical component of effective financial management. By defining a clear approval process, establishing criteria, configuring approval hierarchies, and automating the workflow, organizations can ensure accuracy, compliance, and efficiency in their invoicing operations. Following best practices and regularly reviewing the approval rules can further enhance the effectiveness of the approval process and support the overall financial health of the organization.

4.2.2 Managing Approval Hierarchies

Managing approval hierarchies is a critical aspect of the invoice approval workflow in Oracle ERP's Accounts Receivable (AR) module. This section delves into the importance, setup, and management of approval hierarchies to ensure efficient and accurate invoice processing. An approval hierarchy defines the chain of command through which invoices must pass for approval before they can be processed further. Properly managed approval hierarchies not only streamline operations but also help maintain compliance and control over financial transactions.

Importance of Approval Hierarchies

Approval hierarchies serve several essential functions within an organization:

- Control and Compliance: They ensure that all invoices are reviewed and approved by appropriate personnel, maintaining compliance with internal policies and external regulations.

- Risk Management: By defining clear approval paths, organizations can mitigate risks associated with unauthorized or erroneous transactions.

- Efficiency: Automated approval workflows reduce manual intervention, speeding up the invoice processing time.

- Transparency and Accountability: Clearly defined roles and responsibilities within the hierarchy enhance transparency and accountability, as every action taken on an invoice is recorded and traceable.

Setting Up Approval Hierarchies

The process of setting up approval hierarchies in Oracle ERP involves several steps, including defining roles, establishing approval levels, and configuring the workflow rules. Here is a detailed guide:

1. Define Roles and Responsibilities:

   - Identify all the roles involved in the invoice approval process. These roles might include Accounts Payable Clerks, Supervisors, Managers, and Finance Directors.

   - Clearly outline the responsibilities of each role to avoid confusion and overlap. For instance, clerks might be responsible for initial invoice entry, while supervisors handle the first level of approval, and managers or directors give the final sign-off.

2. Establish Approval Levels:

   - Determine the number of approval levels required based on the organization's structure and the complexity of transactions.

   - For instance, a three-tier approval hierarchy might involve initial approval by a clerk, second-level approval by a supervisor, and final approval by a manager or director.

3. Set Approval Limits:

   - Define monetary thresholds for each approval level. For example, clerks might approve invoices up to $1,000, supervisors up to $10,000, and managers or directors for amounts above $10,000.

   - These limits help ensure that higher-value transactions receive the necessary scrutiny.

4. Configure Workflow Rules:

   - Utilize Oracle ERP's workflow configuration tools to set up the approval rules. This involves mapping out the approval path and specifying the conditions under which each level of approval is required.

   - Workflow rules can include criteria such as invoice amount, department, vendor, and type of expense.

5. Automate the Workflow:

   - Leverage Oracle ERP's automation capabilities to route invoices through the predefined approval hierarchy automatically.

- Automation reduces manual errors and ensures that invoices move seamlessly from one approval stage to the next.

Managing Approval Hierarchies

Once the approval hierarchy is set up, ongoing management is crucial to ensure it continues to function effectively. This involves monitoring the workflow, making necessary adjustments, and training employees.

1. Monitoring the Workflow:

   - Regularly review the workflow performance to identify bottlenecks or delays in the approval process.

   - Utilize Oracle ERP's reporting and analytics tools to track key metrics such as approval times, pending approvals, and exceptions.

2. Adjusting the Hierarchy:

   - Periodically reassess the approval hierarchy to accommodate organizational changes, such as new roles, departments, or changes in approval limits.

   - Update the workflow rules and approval paths as needed to reflect these changes.

3. Training and Communication:

   - Ensure that all employees involved in the approval process are adequately trained on their roles and responsibilities.

   - Provide regular updates and refresher courses to keep everyone informed about any changes to the approval hierarchy or workflow rules.

4. Handling Exceptions:

   - Define a clear process for handling exceptions, such as urgent invoices that require expedited approval or invoices that fall outside the standard workflow.

   - Implement override mechanisms that allow for manual intervention when necessary, while ensuring that these exceptions are properly documented and approved.

Best Practices for Managing Approval Hierarchies

To maximize the effectiveness of your approval hierarchies, consider the following best practices:

1. Standardization:

   - Standardize the approval process across the organization to ensure consistency and fairness.

   - Use predefined templates and forms to streamline the workflow and reduce customization efforts.

2. Segregation of Duties:

   - Maintain a clear segregation of duties within the approval process to prevent conflicts of interest and fraud.

   - Ensure that no single individual has control over all aspects of the invoice processing and approval.

3. Continuous Improvement:

   - Continuously evaluate and improve the approval process based on feedback and performance metrics.

   - Encourage employees to suggest improvements and address any issues promptly.

4. Documentation and Audit Trails:

   - Maintain thorough documentation of the approval hierarchy and workflow rules.

   - Ensure that all actions taken during the approval process are logged, creating a robust audit trail for compliance and review.

5. Technology Integration:

   - Integrate the approval workflow with other ERP modules and financial systems to ensure a seamless flow of information.

   - Utilize advanced technologies such as artificial intelligence and machine learning to enhance the efficiency and accuracy of the approval process.

Common Challenges and Solutions

While managing approval hierarchies can significantly improve invoice processing, organizations may encounter several challenges. Here are some common issues and potential solutions:

1. Resistance to Change:

   - Employees might resist changes to the approval process, especially if it involves adopting new technologies or workflows.

   - Solution: Provide comprehensive training and emphasize the benefits of the new system, such as improved efficiency and reduced errors.

2. Complexity of Workflow:

   - Complex approval hierarchies can lead to confusion and delays.

   - Solution: Simplify the workflow wherever possible and ensure that roles and responsibilities are clearly defined.

3. Bottlenecks and Delays:

   - Invoices may get stuck at certain approval levels, causing delays in processing.

   - Solution: Monitor the workflow regularly to identify bottlenecks and take corrective actions, such as redistributing workload or adjusting approval limits.

4. Lack of Visibility:

   - Limited visibility into the approval process can hinder effective management.

   - Solution: Utilize Oracle ERP's reporting and analytics tools to gain real-time insights into the workflow and make data-driven decisions.

By effectively managing approval hierarchies, organizations can ensure that their invoice approval processes are efficient, compliant, and transparent. This not only enhances the overall performance of the Accounts Receivable module but also contributes to better financial management and control.

4.2.3 Automating Invoice Approval Processes

Automation of the invoice approval process in Oracle ERP's Accounts Receivable module can significantly streamline operations, reduce human errors, and improve efficiency. Implementing automated workflows for invoice approvals involves setting up rules and conditions that guide the system to perform specific actions when certain criteria are met. This section details the steps and considerations for automating invoice approval processes, including setting up workflows, defining rules, and monitoring the automated processes.

1. Understanding the Need for Automation

Automating the invoice approval process addresses several key challenges:

- Efficiency: Manual approval processes are time-consuming. Automation reduces the time needed for approvals by routing invoices through predefined workflows.

- Accuracy: Automation minimizes human errors that often occur during manual processing.

- Compliance: Automated workflows ensure that all invoices are processed according to the company's policies and regulatory requirements.

- Visibility and Control: Automation provides real-time tracking and reporting capabilities, enhancing control over the approval process.

2. Setting Up Automated Workflows

Setting up an automated workflow in Oracle ERP involves several steps. The process starts with defining the approval rules and conditions that will trigger specific actions. Here's a step-by-step guide:

Step 1: Define Approval Rules and Conditions

- Identify Approval Criteria: Determine the criteria that will trigger the approval process. This could include invoice amount, type of purchase, vendor, or any other relevant factor.

- Set Conditions: Specify the conditions under which each rule applies. For example, invoices over a certain amount might require higher-level approval.

Step 2: Configure Workflow in Oracle ERP

- Access Workflow Configuration: Navigate to the workflow configuration section within the Accounts Receivable module.

- Create New Workflow: Select the option to create a new workflow and assign it a name that clearly describes its purpose (e.g., "High-Value Invoice Approval Workflow").

- Define Steps and Actions: Outline the steps involved in the workflow, including who needs to approve each step. Assign specific actions to each step, such as sending an email notification or updating the invoice status.

Step 3: Assign Approval Roles

- Define Roles and Responsibilities: Assign roles to different users or user groups responsible for approving invoices. Ensure that each role has the appropriate permissions.

- Set Approval Hierarchies: Establish hierarchies that determine the sequence of approvals. For example, a supervisor might approve invoices before they are sent to a manager for final approval.

Step 4: Integrate Notifications

- Configure Email Notifications: Set up email notifications to alert approvers when an invoice requires their attention. Notifications should include relevant invoice details and a link to the invoice within the system.

- Escalation Procedures: Define escalation procedures for invoices that are not approved within a specified time frame. This ensures that invoices do not get stuck in the approval process.

Step 5: Test the Workflow

- Simulate Approval Scenarios: Conduct tests to simulate various approval scenarios and ensure that the workflow behaves as expected. Address any issues or inconsistencies that arise during testing.

- Adjust and Optimize: Based on test results, fine-tune the workflow to optimize efficiency and accuracy.

3. Implementing Automated Approval Processes

Once the workflows are configured, the implementation phase involves rolling out the automated processes to end-users and monitoring their effectiveness.

Training and Onboarding

- User Training: Provide comprehensive training to all users involved in the approval process. Training should cover how to use the automated workflows, respond to notifications, and approve invoices.

- Documentation: Create detailed documentation outlining the workflow steps, roles, and responsibilities. This serves as a reference for users and helps ensure consistent adherence to the process.

Monitoring and Evaluation

- Real-Time Tracking: Utilize the tracking features within Oracle ERP to monitor the progress of invoices through the approval workflow. Real-time tracking provides visibility into the status of each invoice and highlights any bottlenecks.

- Performance Metrics: Establish key performance indicators (KPIs) to measure the effectiveness of the automated approval process. KPIs might include the average time to approve an invoice, the number of invoices processed per period, and the percentage of invoices approved without manual intervention.

- Feedback Loop: Implement a feedback loop where users can report issues or suggest improvements. Regularly review this feedback to make necessary adjustments to the workflow.

4. Best Practices for Automating Invoice Approval Processes

Adopting best practices ensures that the automated approval process is efficient, compliant, and user-friendly. Here are some recommended practices:

Standardize Approval Criteria

- Consistent Criteria: Ensure that approval criteria are standardized across the organization. This reduces confusion and ensures that all invoices are subject to the same approval standards.

- Document Criteria: Clearly document the criteria and conditions for approvals. Make this documentation accessible to all users involved in the approval process.

Leverage Data Analytics

- Analyze Approval Data: Use data analytics to analyze approval patterns and identify areas for improvement. For example, if certain types of invoices frequently encounter delays, investigate the root cause and address it.

- Continuous Improvement: Regularly review and refine the automated workflow based on insights gained from data analytics. This continuous improvement approach helps maintain an efficient and effective approval process.

Ensure Compliance

- Regulatory Compliance: Ensure that the automated approval process complies with all relevant regulations and standards. Regular audits and reviews can help maintain compliance.

- Policy Adherence: Verify that the workflow enforces the organization's policies and procedures. Automated checks and validations can help ensure adherence to these policies.

Foster User Adoption

- User-Friendly Interface: Design the workflow interface to be intuitive and user-friendly. Simplified navigation and clear instructions can enhance user adoption.

- Support and Assistance: Provide ongoing support to users, including a helpdesk or support team to address any issues or questions. This support can improve user satisfaction and ensure smooth operation of the workflow.

5. Advanced Features and Customization

Oracle ERP offers advanced features and customization options to enhance the automated approval process. Leveraging these features can further optimize efficiency and control.

Custom Approval Paths

- Conditional Paths: Configure conditional approval paths that change based on specific criteria. For example, high-value invoices might follow a different approval path than low-value ones.

- Dynamic Routing: Implement dynamic routing to automatically assign invoices to approvers based on workload, availability, or expertise.

Integration with Other Modules

- Seamless Integration: Ensure that the automated approval process integrates seamlessly with other ERP modules, such as Procurement, Finance, and Inventory. This integration facilitates a smooth flow of information and reduces manual data entry.

- Cross-Module Workflows: Create cross-module workflows that span multiple areas of the ERP system. For example, a workflow might start in Procurement and continue through Accounts Receivable.

Mobile Approvals

- Mobile Access: Enable mobile access to the approval workflow, allowing approvers to review and approve invoices on the go. Mobile approvals increase flexibility and reduce delays.

- Push Notifications: Implement push notifications to alert approvers of pending approvals. Notifications should include key invoice details and action buttons for quick approval or rejection.

Audit Trails and Security

- Detailed Audit Trails: Maintain detailed audit trails of all approval actions. Audit trails should record who approved each invoice, when it was approved, and any changes made during the process.

- Security Measures: Implement robust security measures to protect sensitive information. This includes role-based access controls, encryption, and regular security audits.

Conclusion

Automating the invoice approval process in Oracle ERP's Accounts Receivable module offers numerous benefits, including increased efficiency, reduced errors, and enhanced compliance. By carefully setting up and configuring automated workflows, organizations can streamline their operations and improve financial management. Following best practices and leveraging advanced features ensures that the automated process is robust, user-friendly, and adaptable to changing business needs. Through continuous monitoring and improvement, the automated approval workflow can remain an integral part of an efficient and effective Accounts Receivable process.

4.3 Posting and Adjusting Invoices

4.3.1 Posting Invoices to the General Ledger

The process of posting invoices to the General Ledger (GL) in Oracle ERP is a critical step in ensuring accurate financial records and reporting. This section will guide you through the detailed steps required to post invoices effectively, ensuring that all financial transactions are properly recorded and that the integrity of your financial data is maintained.

Overview of General Ledger Posting

The General Ledger serves as the central repository for all financial transactions within your organization. Posting invoices to the GL ensures that revenue and receivables are accurately captured, facilitating accurate financial reporting and analysis. This process involves several key steps, including creating accounting entries, validating them, and finally posting them to the GL.

Steps to Create and Post Invoices to the General Ledger

Step 1: Accessing the Accounts Receivable Module

Begin by logging into your Oracle ERP system and navigating to the Accounts Receivable module. This module is where you manage all activities related to customer invoicing, receipts, and adjustments.

Step 2: Creating an Invoice

To create an invoice, follow these steps:

1. Navigate to the Invoice Workbench: In the Accounts Receivable module, locate the Invoice Workbench. This interface allows you to create, review, and manage customer invoices.

2. Enter Invoice Information: Click on the 'Create Invoice' button to begin entering invoice details. This includes:

- Customer Information: Select the customer from the dropdown menu or search for the customer using their name or customer number.

- Invoice Date: Enter the date of the invoice. This is typically the date the goods were shipped or the services were rendered.

- Invoice Number: Assign a unique invoice number, either manually or through an automated numbering system.

- Invoice Amount: Enter the total amount due for the invoice, including any applicable taxes and discounts.

3. Add Line Items: For each product or service sold, add a line item to the invoice. This involves:

- Item Description: Provide a description of the product or service.

- Quantity and Unit Price: Enter the quantity sold and the unit price.

- Tax and Discounts: Apply any relevant taxes and discounts.

4. Save and Validate: Once all required information is entered, save the invoice. The system will perform a validation check to ensure that all mandatory fields are completed and that there are no errors.

Step 3: Generating Accounting Entries

After creating the invoice, the next step is to generate the accounting entries that will be posted to the General Ledger. This involves the following:

1. Navigate to the Accounting Entries Interface: In the Accounts Receivable module, locate the interface for generating accounting entries.

2. Select the Invoice: Choose the invoice for which you want to generate accounting entries. This can be done by searching for the invoice number or selecting it from a list of pending invoices.

3. Generate Entries: Click on the 'Generate Accounting Entries' button. The system will automatically create the necessary debit and credit entries based on the invoice details. Typically, this involves:

- Debit to Accounts Receivable: This entry increases the receivables balance, indicating that the customer owes the amount.

- Credit to Revenue: This entry records the revenue earned from the sale of goods or services.

- Tax Entries: If applicable, tax amounts will be recorded in the appropriate tax accounts.

4. Review and Approve: Once the entries are generated, review them for accuracy. Ensure that the amounts and accounts are correct. If everything is in order, approve the entries.

Step 4: Validating Accounting Entries

Before posting the accounting entries to the General Ledger, it's crucial to validate them. This ensures that all data is accurate and that there are no discrepancies. Follow these steps to validate the entries:

1. Run the Validation Program: In the Accounts Receivable module, run the accounting validation program. This program checks the integrity of the accounting entries and ensures that all mandatory information is included.

2. Review Validation Results: After the validation program completes, review the results. Look for any errors or warnings. Common validation issues include missing account numbers, incorrect amounts, and incomplete information.

3. Resolve Errors: If any errors are found, resolve them before proceeding. This may involve correcting data in the invoice or updating account mappings.

Step 5: Posting to the General Ledger

Once the accounting entries are validated and approved, they are ready to be posted to the General Ledger. Posting transfers the entries from the Accounts Receivable subledger to the General Ledger, where they become part of the official financial records. Follow these steps to post the entries:

1. Navigate to the Posting Interface: In the Accounts Receivable module, locate the interface for posting accounting entries to the General Ledger.

2. Select Entries to Post: Choose the validated and approved accounting entries that you want to post. You can select individual entries or post them in batches.

3. Initiate Posting: Click on the 'Post to General Ledger' button. The system will transfer the selected entries to the General Ledger.

4. Review Posting Results: After the posting process completes, review the results. Ensure that all entries were successfully posted and that there are no errors. If any issues arise, investigate and resolve them promptly.

Step 6: Verifying Posted Entries in the General Ledger

To ensure that the posting process was successful, it's important to verify the entries in the General Ledger. This involves:

1. Accessing the General Ledger Module: Navigate to the General Ledger module in Oracle ERP.

2. Query Posted Entries: Use the query functionality to search for the entries that were posted from Accounts Receivable. You can search by date, account number, or transaction type.

3. Review and Reconcile: Review the posted entries to ensure they match the original invoice details. Reconcile the entries with the Accounts Receivable subledger to confirm accuracy.

Step 7: Reporting and Analysis

After posting invoices to the General Ledger, leverage Oracle ERP's reporting and analysis tools to monitor and manage your financial data. This involves:

1. Generating Standard Reports: Use predefined reports to view posted invoices, accounts receivable balances, and revenue details.

2. Customizing Reports: Customize reports to meet your specific business needs. This may include adding filters, modifying layouts, and creating new report templates.

3. Analyzing Data: Use analytical tools to analyze financial data, identify trends, and make informed decisions. This includes monitoring key performance indicators (KPIs) such as days sales outstanding (DSO) and aging of receivables.

Best Practices for Posting Invoices

1. Regular Reconciliation: Regularly reconcile the Accounts Receivable subledger with the General Ledger to ensure data accuracy and consistency.

2. Automating Processes: Implement automation tools to streamline the creation, validation, and posting of invoices. This reduces manual effort and minimizes errors.

3. Training and Documentation: Provide comprehensive training to staff involved in the invoicing and posting process. Maintain detailed documentation of procedures and best practices.

4. Continuous Monitoring: Continuously monitor the posting process and address any issues promptly. Use dashboards and alerts to stay informed about the status of financial transactions.

By following these detailed steps and best practices, you can ensure accurate and efficient posting of invoices to the General Ledger in Oracle ERP, maintaining the integrity of your financial records and supporting effective financial management.

4.3.2 Making Invoice Adjustments and Corrections

Making invoice adjustments and corrections in Oracle ERP is a critical process to ensure that the financial records accurately reflect the transactions of the business. Adjustments and corrections can arise from various scenarios, such as pricing errors, incorrect quantities, or misapplied discounts. This section will provide a detailed guide on how to effectively make these adjustments and corrections within the Accounts Receivable (AR) module of Oracle ERP.

Understanding Invoice Adjustments

Invoice adjustments are modifications made to an existing invoice to correct any errors or discrepancies. These adjustments can include changes to the amount due, the quantity of goods or services, the tax amount, or any other aspect of the invoice that needs correction. It's essential to document the reason for each adjustment to maintain a clear audit trail.

Types of Invoice Adjustments

1. Price Adjustments: Correcting pricing errors due to incorrect unit prices or applied discounts.

2. Quantity Adjustments: Modifying the number of items or services billed.

3. Tax Adjustments: Adjusting the tax amount due to incorrect tax rates or tax codes.

4. Discount Adjustments: Correcting errors related to discounts applied to the invoice.

5. Terms Adjustments: Changes to payment terms that may affect the invoice due date or payment schedule.

6. Charge Adjustments: Adding or removing charges such as shipping fees or handling charges.

Steps to Make Invoice Adjustments

Step 1: Identify the Invoice Needing Adjustment

1. Access the AR Module: Log in to Oracle ERP and navigate to the Accounts Receivable module.

2. Search for the Invoice: Use the search functionality to locate the specific invoice that requires adjustment. You can search by invoice number, customer name, date, or other relevant criteria.

3. Review the Invoice Details: Open the invoice and review all the details to identify the specific areas that need correction.

Step 2: Determine the Adjustment Type

1. Assess the Error: Determine the nature of the error that needs correction. Is it a pricing error, quantity error, tax error, etc.?

2. Select the Adjustment Type: Choose the appropriate adjustment type based on the nature of the error.

Step 3: Create the Adjustment

1. Initiate the Adjustment Process: In the invoice screen, select the option to create an adjustment. This may be labeled as "Adjust Invoice," "Invoice Correction," or similar.

2. Enter Adjustment Details: Input the necessary details for the adjustment:

  - Adjustment Type: Select the type of adjustment from a dropdown menu or list.

- Adjustment Amount: Enter the amount to be adjusted. This could be a positive or negative amount depending on whether you are increasing or decreasing the invoice total.

- Reason for Adjustment: Provide a reason for the adjustment. This is crucial for audit purposes.

- Supporting Documentation: Attach any supporting documentation that justifies the adjustment, such as corrected pricing information, revised purchase orders, or communication with the customer.

Step 4: Review and Approve the Adjustment

1. Review the Adjustment: Carefully review the details of the adjustment to ensure accuracy.

2. Submit for Approval: If your organization requires approval for invoice adjustments, submit the adjustment for approval. The approval workflow will vary based on your organization's settings in Oracle ERP.

3. Approval Process: The designated approvers will review the adjustment details. Once approved, the adjustment will be applied to the invoice.

Step 5: Apply the Adjustment to the Invoice

1. Post the Adjustment: Once approved, the adjustment needs to be posted to the general ledger. This step updates the financial records to reflect the adjustment.

2. Verify the Updated Invoice: After posting, verify the invoice to ensure that the adjustment has been correctly applied and the invoice details are accurate.

3. Notify the Customer: If necessary, notify the customer about the adjustment. This could be through an updated invoice, a credit memo, or direct communication.

Common Scenarios for Invoice Adjustments

1. Pricing Errors:

- Scenario: A customer was overcharged due to an incorrect unit price.

- Solution: Create a price adjustment to reduce the invoice amount by the overcharged amount. Document the correct pricing and provide the justification for the adjustment.

2. Quantity Errors:

  - Scenario: The quantity of goods billed does not match the quantity delivered.

  - Solution: Adjust the quantity on the invoice to match the actual quantity delivered. This may involve increasing or decreasing the total amount due.

3. Tax Errors:

  - Scenario: Incorrect tax rate applied to the invoice.

  - Solution: Adjust the tax amount to reflect the correct tax rate. Ensure that the correct tax code is used for future invoices.

4. Discount Errors:

  - Scenario: A discount was not applied to the invoice.

  - Solution: Create a discount adjustment to apply the correct discount amount. Update the invoice total accordingly.

5. Terms Adjustments:

  - Scenario: The payment terms were incorrectly entered, affecting the due date.

  - Solution: Adjust the payment terms to reflect the agreed-upon terms. Ensure that this change is communicated to the customer.

Best Practices for Making Invoice Adjustments

1. Maintain Clear Documentation: Always document the reason for the adjustment and keep records of any supporting documentation.

2. Ensure Proper Authorization: Follow your organization's approval workflow for adjustments to ensure that all changes are authorized and properly documented.

3. Communicate with Customers: Keep customers informed about any adjustments that affect their invoices. Clear communication helps maintain good customer relationships.

4. Regularly Review Invoices: Regularly review invoices for accuracy to catch errors early and minimize the need for adjustments.

5. Use Automation Tools: Utilize Oracle ERP's automation tools to streamline the adjustment process and reduce the risk of human error.

Conclusion

Making invoice adjustments and corrections in Oracle ERP's Accounts Receivable module is a crucial process that ensures the accuracy and integrity of your financial records. By following the detailed steps outlined in this section, you can effectively manage and correct any discrepancies in your invoices, maintain clear documentation, and uphold strong financial controls. Implementing these best practices will help your organization achieve accurate billing, efficient cash flow management, and robust financial reporting.

4.3.3 Handling Disputed Invoices

Disputed invoices are a common occurrence in business transactions, often arising from discrepancies or disagreements between the supplier and the customer regarding goods delivered, services rendered, or billing terms. Effectively managing disputed invoices is crucial for maintaining strong customer relationships and ensuring timely resolution of financial discrepancies. This section will delve into the detailed process of handling disputed invoices within the Oracle ERP Accounts Receivable module.

Understanding Disputed Invoices

Before diving into the resolution process, it's essential to understand the nature of disputed invoices. Disputes can arise due to various reasons, including:

- Goods or Services Not Received: The customer claims they did not receive the goods or services as per the invoice.

- Quality or Quantity Issues: There might be discrepancies in the quality or quantity of goods delivered.

- Pricing or Billing Discrepancies: Differences in pricing, discounts, or billing terms could lead to disputes.

- Contractual Issues: Disputes related to contractual obligations or terms agreed upon between the supplier and the customer.

Each disputed invoice requires thorough investigation and documentation to resolve the issue promptly and accurately.

Steps to Handle Disputed Invoices

Step 1: Identification and Notification

1. Identify Disputed Invoices: Monitor incoming communications, such as emails or calls from customers indicating a dispute.

2. Notification: Upon identification of a disputed invoice, acknowledge receipt of the dispute and initiate the resolution process promptly. Communicate with the customer to understand the nature of the dispute and gather necessary details.

Step 2: Investigation and Documentation

1. Review Documentation: Gather all relevant documents related to the disputed transaction, including sales orders, delivery receipts, contracts, and correspondence with the customer.

2. Investigate: Verify the details of the disputed invoice against the documented information. Investigate the reasons for the dispute thoroughly to determine its validity.

3. Internal Review: Engage relevant departments (e.g., sales, shipping, finance) to gather insights and clarify any discrepancies.

Step 3: Resolution and Adjustment

1. Negotiation: Initiate discussions with the customer to resolve the dispute amicably. Understand their perspective and negotiate a mutually agreeable solution.

2. Adjustment: If the dispute is valid, adjust the invoice accordingly. This may involve issuing credit notes, adjusting the invoice amount, or revising payment terms as per the negotiated agreement.

Step 4: Documentation and Approval

1. Document Resolution: Maintain detailed records of the dispute resolution process, including any agreements reached with the customer.

2. Approval: Obtain necessary approvals for any adjustments made to the invoice. Ensure compliance with internal financial policies and procedures.

Step 5: System Update and Communication

1. Update ERP System: Enter adjustments or corrections into the Oracle ERP Accounts Receivable module. Ensure accurate recording of changes to maintain financial integrity.

2. Customer Communication: Communicate the resolution to the customer formally, providing documentation of adjustments made and confirming next steps, such as revised payment schedules or credit notes.

Best Practices for Handling Disputed Invoices

- Prompt Response: Address disputed invoices promptly to prevent escalation and maintain customer satisfaction.

- Thorough Documentation: Maintain comprehensive records of all communications, investigations, and resolutions related to disputed invoices.

- Cross-functional Collaboration: Engage relevant departments to facilitate a holistic resolution process.

- Clear Communication: Keep the customer informed throughout the resolution process, ensuring transparency and clarity.

Conclusion

Effectively managing disputed invoices requires a structured approach, combining diligent investigation, effective communication, and accurate documentation. By following these steps within the Oracle ERP Accounts Receivable module, businesses can mitigate financial risks, preserve customer relationships, and uphold operational efficiency.

CHAPTER V
Managing Receipts and Payments

5.1 Recording Customer Receipts

5.1.1 Different Methods for Recording Receipts

Recording customer receipts accurately and efficiently is a critical process in managing accounts receivable. It ensures that the cash inflows are properly accounted for, which in turn helps maintain accurate financial records and improves cash flow management. Oracle ERP provides several methods for recording receipts to accommodate different business needs and preferences. This section will detail the various methods for recording receipts in Oracle ERP, including manual entry, electronic receipts, and automated processes.

1. Manual Entry of Receipts

Manual entry of receipts is the traditional method where accounts receivable staff manually input receipt details into the system. This method is often used for small businesses or organizations that handle a low volume of transactions.

Steps to Record Receipts Manually:

- Step 1: Access the Receipts Workbench

 Navigate to the Accounts Receivable module and select the Receipts Workbench. This is the central hub where all receipt activities are managed.

- Step 2: Enter Receipt Information

Click on the 'New Receipt' button to open the receipt entry form. Fill in the necessary details such as receipt number, date, amount, currency, and payment method. The source of the receipt (e.g., customer payment, bank deposit) should also be specified.

- Step 3: Assign to Customer Account

Link the receipt to the relevant customer account by selecting the customer from the customer list. Ensure that the customer information is accurate to avoid misallocations.

- Step 4: Match Receipts to Invoices

Once the customer account is selected, match the receipt to the appropriate open invoices. This step ensures that the payment is applied to the correct outstanding invoices, reducing the accounts receivable balance accordingly.

- Step 5: Save and Post the Receipt

After verifying all the details, save the receipt entry and post it to the general ledger. Posting the receipt updates the financial records and reflects the receipt in the customer's account.

Advantages:

- Flexibility in handling diverse payment sources.

- Detailed control over receipt entry.

Disadvantages:

- Time-consuming and labor-intensive.

- Higher risk of human errors.

2. Electronic Receipts

Electronic receipts involve the use of electronic payment systems and bank integrations to automatically record receipts in Oracle ERP. This method is increasingly popular due to its efficiency and accuracy.

Steps to Record Electronic Receipts:

- Step 1: Set Up Electronic Payment Channels

Configure electronic payment channels such as ACH (Automated Clearing House), wire transfers, and credit card processing within Oracle ERP. Ensure that the system is integrated with your bank and payment processors.

- Step 2: Import Electronic Payment Files

Import electronic payment files received from banks or payment processors into Oracle ERP. These files typically contain details of all transactions processed through electronic channels.

- Step 3: Auto-Apply Receipts to Invoices

Use the auto-apply feature to automatically match electronic receipts to open invoices. The system uses predefined rules and customer identifiers to link payments to the correct invoices.

- Step 4: Review and Confirm

Review the auto-applied receipts to ensure that all matches are accurate. Make any necessary adjustments manually if the system fails to match certain receipts.

- Step 5: Post Receipts

Once confirmed, post the receipts to update the financial records and customer accounts.

Advantages:

- Increased efficiency and reduced manual effort.

- Lower risk of errors and discrepancies.

- Faster processing of high volumes of transactions.

Disadvantages:

- Requires setup and maintenance of electronic payment channels.

- Initial setup can be complex and time-consuming.

3. Lockbox Processing

Lockbox processing is a service provided by banks where customer payments are sent directly to a special post office box (lockbox). The bank collects and processes these payments, then transmits the details to the organization for recording in Oracle ERP.

Steps to Record Receipts via Lockbox Processing:

- Step 1: Set Up Lockbox Service with Bank

 Establish a lockbox service with your bank. The bank will provide a lockbox number and collect payments sent to this address.

- Step 2: Configure Lockbox in Oracle ERP

 Set up the lockbox configuration in Oracle ERP by defining the lockbox number, transmission formats, and processing rules. Ensure that the lockbox is linked to the correct customer accounts and bank accounts.

- Step 3: Import Lockbox Transmission Files

 The bank will send transmission files containing payment details. Import these files into Oracle ERP using the lockbox interface.

- Step 4: Validate and Process Receipts

 Validate the imported data to ensure that it is accurate and complete. Process the receipts by matching them to the corresponding invoices based on customer identifiers and payment amounts.

- Step 5: Post Receipts

 After successful validation and processing, post the receipts to update the general ledger and customer accounts.

Advantages:

- Reduces manual handling of payments.

- Streamlines the payment collection process.

- Enhances accuracy and efficiency in recording receipts.

Disadvantages:

- Requires coordination with the bank.

- Initial setup can be complex and involves ongoing management.

4. Automated Clearing House (ACH) Receipts

ACH receipts involve the electronic transfer of funds between banks and the automated recording of these transactions in Oracle ERP.

Steps to Record ACH Receipts:

- Step 1: Set Up ACH Payments

  Configure ACH payment options in Oracle ERP. Ensure that the system is integrated with your bank to facilitate ACH transactions.

- Step 2: Initiate ACH Transactions

  When customers make payments via ACH, these transactions are processed by the bank and the details are transmitted to your system.

- Step 3: Import ACH Files

  Import ACH payment files into Oracle ERP. These files contain the details of each ACH transaction, including customer identifiers and payment amounts.

- Step 4: Auto-Apply and Review Receipts

  Use the auto-apply feature to match ACH receipts to open invoices. Review the matches to ensure accuracy and make any necessary adjustments.

- Step 5: Post Receipts

  Post the ACH receipts to update the financial records and customer accounts.

Advantages:

- Efficient and secure method for processing payments.

- Reduces manual intervention and errors.

- Facilitates faster clearing and settlement of funds.

Disadvantages:

- Requires ACH setup and bank integration.

- Dependent on customers opting for ACH payments.

5. Credit Card Receipts

Credit card receipts involve recording payments made by customers using credit cards. This method is common in businesses that offer online sales or in-person credit card transactions.

Steps to Record Credit Card Receipts:

- Step 1: Set Up Credit Card Processing

  Configure credit card processing options in Oracle ERP. Integrate with payment gateways and processors to handle credit card transactions.

- Step 2: Process Credit Card Payments

  When customers make credit card payments, these transactions are processed by the payment gateway and the details are transmitted to your system.

- Step 3: Import Credit Card Transaction Files

  Import the credit card transaction files into Oracle ERP. These files contain details of each credit card payment, including customer information and payment amounts.

- Step 4: Match and Apply Receipts

  Match the imported credit card receipts to open invoices using the auto-apply feature. Review the matches to ensure accuracy and make adjustments as needed.

- Step 5: Post Receipts

  Post the credit card receipts to update the financial records and customer accounts.

Advantages:

- Convenient for customers and improves sales.

- Reduces manual processing and errors.

- Enhances cash flow with faster payment processing.

Disadvantages:

- Requires setup and integration with credit card processors.

- Involves transaction fees and processing costs.

Conclusion

Oracle ERP offers multiple methods for recording customer receipts, each with its own advantages and challenges. Choosing the appropriate method depends on the specific needs of your organization, the volume of transactions, and the preferred payment methods of your customers. By leveraging these methods effectively, businesses can ensure accurate and efficient recording of receipts, which is crucial for maintaining healthy cash flow and accurate financial records.

5.1.2 Matching Receipts to Invoices

Introduction

Matching receipts to invoices is a fundamental task in the accounts receivable process. Ensuring that customer payments are accurately matched to their corresponding invoices is crucial for maintaining financial accuracy and customer satisfaction. This section delves into the detailed procedures for matching receipts to invoices within Oracle ERP, providing step-by-step instructions and best practices to streamline the process.

Importance of Matching Receipts to Invoices

Accurate matching of receipts to invoices ensures that the company's financial records reflect the correct state of customer payments. This process helps in:

- Reducing discrepancies in financial statements.

- Ensuring timely and accurate financial reporting.

- Enhancing customer satisfaction by providing precise account statements.

- Improving cash flow management by accurately tracking outstanding receivables.

Step-by-Step Process for Matching Receipts to Invoices

1. Access the Receipts Workbench

   - Navigate to the Receipts Workbench within Oracle ERP.

   - Select the appropriate operating unit and navigate to the Receipts Workbench form.

2. Query Receipts

   - Use the query functionality to locate the receipt you need to match to an invoice.

   - You can search by receipt number, customer name, or date range to find the specific receipt.

3. Open the Receipt Details

   - Once the receipt is located, open its details to view the payment information.

   - Ensure that the receipt details match the customer's payment information, including the amount and payment method.

4. Initiate the Match Process

   - Click on the 'Apply' button to start the matching process.

   - The system will display a list of open invoices for the customer associated with the receipt.

5. Select Invoices to Match

   - From the list of open invoices, select the invoices that correspond to the payment.

   - Ensure the total amount of the selected invoices matches the receipt amount. If the receipt amount is higher than the invoice amount, the remaining balance can be applied to other invoices or left as unapplied.

6. Apply the Receipt

- Click on 'Apply' to match the selected invoices with the receipt.

- The system will automatically update the invoice status to 'Paid' or 'Partially Paid' based on the receipt amount.

7. Review and Confirm

  - Review the matching details to ensure accuracy.

  - Confirm the application of the receipt to the invoices.

Handling Partial Payments

When a customer makes a partial payment, the matching process requires careful attention to detail:

1. Identify Partial Payment Receipts

  - Locate the receipt indicating a partial payment.

  - Note the receipt amount and the total amount due for the invoice.

2. Select Invoice for Partial Payment

  - Choose the invoice to which the partial payment will be applied.

  - Enter the amount to be applied from the receipt.

3. Apply Partial Payment

  - Click on 'Apply' to record the partial payment against the selected invoice.

  - The system will update the invoice status to 'Partially Paid' and reflect the remaining balance.

4. Track Outstanding Balance

  - Monitor the outstanding balance for the partially paid invoice.

  - Ensure that subsequent payments are matched to this invoice until it is fully paid.

Handling Overpayments

In cases where the customer pays more than the invoice amount:

1. Identify Overpayment Receipts

  - Locate the receipt indicating an overpayment.

  - Note the overpayment amount and the total amount due for the invoice.

2. Select Invoice for Overpayment

  - Choose the invoice to which the overpayment will be applied.

  - Enter the total amount due for the invoice.

3. Apply Overpayment

  - Click on 'Apply' to record the payment against the selected invoice.

  - The system will update the invoice status to 'Paid' and reflect the overpayment as unapplied or available credit.

4. Handle Remaining Balance

  - Monitor the remaining overpayment amount.

  - Apply the balance to other open invoices or leave it as an unapplied credit for future transactions.

Best Practices for Matching Receipts to Invoices

1. Regular Reconciliation

  - Conduct regular reconciliation of receipts and invoices to ensure accuracy.

  - This helps in identifying discrepancies early and resolving them promptly.

2. Clear Communication with Customers

  - Maintain clear communication with customers regarding payment details.

  - Provide accurate and timely invoices to facilitate easier matching of receipts.

3. Utilize Automation Tools

  - Leverage automation tools within Oracle ERP to streamline the matching process.

- Automated matching reduces manual effort and increases accuracy.

4. Implement Internal Controls

  - Establish internal controls to ensure that receipts are matched accurately and promptly.

  - Regular audits and reviews can help in maintaining the integrity of the accounts receivable process.

5. Training and Development

  - Provide training to accounts receivable staff on the matching process and best practices.

  - Regular updates and refreshers on Oracle ERP functionalities can enhance efficiency.

Common Issues and Troubleshooting

1. Unmatched Receipts

  - Issue: Receipt remains unmatched due to missing or incorrect invoice information.

  - Solution: Verify the customer and invoice details. Use the query functionality to locate the correct invoice and apply the receipt.

2. Duplicate Invoices

  - Issue: Multiple invoices for the same transaction lead to confusion during matching.

  - Solution: Review the invoices and consolidate duplicate entries. Ensure that only one invoice is matched with the receipt.

3. Discrepancies in Payment Amounts

  - Issue: Payment amount does not match the invoice amount due to partial or overpayments.

  - Solution: Follow the procedures for handling partial and overpayments as detailed above. Ensure accurate application of receipt amounts.

4. System Errors

  - Issue: Technical issues within Oracle ERP affecting the matching process.

  - Solution: Report system errors to the IT support team for resolution. Use manual processes as a temporary measure to ensure continuity.

Conclusion

Matching receipts to invoices is a critical task in managing accounts receivable efficiently. By following the detailed procedures outlined in this section, organizations can ensure accurate financial records, enhance customer satisfaction, and improve cash flow management. Implementing best practices and leveraging automation tools within Oracle ERP further streamlines the process, reducing manual effort and increasing accuracy. Regular training and development for accounts receivable staff ensure that they are well-equipped to handle the matching process effectively, contributing to the overall financial health of the organization.

5.1.3 Handling Partial Payments and Overpayments

Handling partial payments and overpayments is a crucial aspect of managing customer receipts in the Accounts Receivable (AR) module of Oracle ERP. This section will cover the following key areas:

- Understanding Partial Payments and Overpayments

- Recording Partial Payments

- Recording Overpayments

- Managing Unapplied Amounts

- Reporting and Reconciliation

Understanding Partial Payments and Overpayments

Partial Payments occur when a customer pays less than the full amount of an invoice. This could be due to disputes, payment agreements, or cash flow issues on the customer's side. Effective management of partial payments ensures that the customer's account remains accurate and up-to-date, reflecting outstanding balances correctly.

Overpayments happen when a customer pays more than the invoice amount. This can occur due to errors, advance payments, or customer mistakes. Proper handling of overpayments is essential to maintain correct account balances and ensure customer satisfaction.

Recording Partial Payments

Recording partial payments involves the following steps:

1. Access the Receipts Workbench:

  - Navigate to the Receipts Workbench in the Oracle Accounts Receivable module.

  - Select the option to create a new receipt.

2. Enter Receipt Information:

  - Input the basic receipt details such as receipt number, receipt date, and amount received.

  - Select the payment method (e.g., cash, check, electronic transfer).

3. Apply Partial Payment to an Invoice:

  - In the application section, search for the customer by name or account number.

  - Locate the specific invoice to which the partial payment will be applied.

  - Enter the amount being paid against the invoice. The system will automatically calculate the remaining balance.

  - Save the receipt application.

4. Review and Confirm:

  - Review the receipt and application details for accuracy.

  - Confirm and post the receipt to update the customer's account and the General Ledger.

Recording Overpayments

Handling overpayments follows a similar process with additional steps for managing the excess amount:

1. Access the Receipts Workbench:

  - Navigate to the Receipts Workbench.

  - Select the option to create a new receipt.

2. Enter Receipt Information:

  - Input the receipt number, date, and the total amount received.

  - Select the payment method.

3. Apply Overpayment to an Invoice:

  - Search for the customer and locate the relevant invoice.

  - Enter the full invoice amount in the application section.

  - The system will identify the overpayment and display the unapplied amount.

4. Manage Unapplied Amount:

  - Decide how to handle the overpayment. Options include:

    - Applying the excess amount to another open invoice.

    - Leaving it as an unapplied receipt for future use.

    - Issuing a refund to the customer.

  - Document the decision and apply it accordingly in the system.

5. Review and Confirm:

  - Review all details for accuracy.

  - Confirm and post the receipt.

Managing Unapplied Amounts

Unapplied amounts occur when payments do not fully match any outstanding invoices. These amounts need careful management to ensure they are correctly applied or refunded:

1. Track Unapplied Receipts:

  - Regularly review unapplied receipt reports to track these amounts.

- Investigate the reasons for unapplied receipts, such as customer errors or pending invoices.

2. Apply Unapplied Receipts:

- As new invoices are generated, apply unapplied amounts to reduce the outstanding balance.

- Use the Receipts Workbench to manually apply unapplied receipts when appropriate.

3. Issue Refunds for Overpayments:

- For significant overpayments, contact the customer to confirm whether they prefer a refund.

- Process refunds through the Oracle ERP system by creating a credit memo and issuing a payment.

Reporting and Reconciliation

Effective reporting and reconciliation are crucial for managing partial payments and overpayments:

1. Generate Detailed Reports:

- Utilize standard and customized reports in Oracle ERP to monitor partial and overpayments.

- Reports should include information on unapplied receipts, customer balances, and aging analysis.

2. Reconcile Accounts Regularly:

- Conduct regular reconciliations of the Accounts Receivable subledger with the General Ledger.

- Ensure that all partial payments and overpayments are accurately recorded and reflected in financial statements.

3. Audit and Compliance:

- Implement audit trails to track all receipt applications and adjustments.

- Ensure compliance with accounting standards and organizational policies regarding handling customer payments.

Best Practices for Managing Partial Payments and Overpayments

1. Customer Communication:

 - Maintain clear communication with customers regarding their payment status and any discrepancies.

 - Send regular account statements and reminders to customers with outstanding balances.

2. Automation and Workflow:

 - Leverage automation tools within Oracle ERP to streamline receipt processing and application.

 - Set up approval workflows for handling overpayments and issuing refunds.

3. Training and Documentation:

 - Provide comprehensive training to AR staff on managing partial payments and overpayments.

 - Develop and maintain detailed process documentation to ensure consistency and accuracy.

4. Continuous Improvement:

 - Regularly review and refine processes for handling partial payments and overpayments.

 - Gather feedback from customers and staff to identify areas for improvement.

Example Scenario: Handling a Partial Payment

Scenario: A customer has an outstanding invoice of $1,000 but makes a partial payment of $600 due to temporary cash flow issues.

1. Recording the Payment:

 - Access the Receipts Workbench and create a new receipt for $600.

- Search for the customer and locate the $1,000 invoice.

- Apply $600 to the invoice, leaving a remaining balance of $400.

2. Customer Communication:

- Send an updated account statement to the customer, showing the partial payment and outstanding balance.

- Contact the customer to discuss the remaining balance and agree on a payment plan if necessary.

3. Monitoring and Follow-Up:

- Set a reminder to follow up with the customer regarding the outstanding balance.

- Regularly review the aging report to monitor overdue balances and take appropriate actions.

Example Scenario: Handling an Overpayment

Scenario: A customer mistakenly pays $1,200 for an invoice of $1,000, resulting in an overpayment of $200.

1. Recording the Payment:

- Create a new receipt for $1,200 in the Receipts Workbench.

- Locate the $1,000 invoice and apply the full amount, leaving $200 as an unapplied receipt.

2. Managing the Overpayment:

- Contact the customer to inform them of the overpayment and discuss options:

- Apply the $200 to a future invoice.

- Issue a refund for the $200.

- Document the customer's preference and take the necessary action in Oracle ERP.

3. Adjusting Account Balances:

  - If issuing a refund, create a credit memo and process the refund payment.

  - Update the customer's account to reflect the adjustment and ensure accurate reporting.

By following these detailed procedures and best practices, organizations can effectively manage partial payments and overpayments, ensuring accurate financial records and maintaining strong customer relationship.

5.2 Applying and Unapplying Receipts

5.2.1 Applying Receipts to Customer Invoices

In the Oracle ERP Accounts Receivable module, applying receipts to customer invoices is a fundamental process. It involves linking customer payments to the corresponding invoices to update the customer's outstanding balance and accurately reflect the company's receivables. This process ensures that the financial records are accurate and up-to-date, facilitating effective cash flow management.

Understanding the Importance of Applying Receipts

Applying receipts to customer invoices is crucial for several reasons:

- Accurate Financial Records: It ensures that the company's financial statements accurately reflect the payments received and the outstanding balances.

- Customer Account Management: It helps in maintaining precise customer accounts, allowing for better credit management and customer relationship management.

- Cash Flow Management: Proper application of receipts aids in monitoring cash inflows, which is vital for managing the company's cash flow effectively.

- Compliance and Reporting: Accurate application of receipts ensures compliance with accounting standards and provides reliable data for financial reporting and audits.

Steps to Apply Receipts to Customer Invoices

Applying receipts to customer invoices in Oracle ERP involves several steps, which can be categorized into preparation, application, and validation. Here's a detailed guide to the process:

Preparation

1. Gather Necessary Information:

   - Customer Details: Ensure you have the correct customer information, including customer ID, name, and contact details.

- Invoice Details: Collect all relevant invoices for which the receipts will be applied. This includes invoice numbers, dates, amounts, and due dates.

- Payment Details: Have the payment information ready, such as payment date, amount, payment method, and reference numbers.

2. Access the Receipts Workbench:

- Navigate to the Receipts Workbench in the Oracle ERP Accounts Receivable module. This is the primary interface for managing receipts.

3. Create a Receipt Batch:

- If handling multiple receipts, create a receipt batch to organize them. This helps in managing and applying receipts efficiently.

Application

1. Enter Receipt Information:

- Receipt Date: Enter the date when the payment was received.

- Receipt Number: Assign a unique identifier for the receipt. This can be auto-generated or manually entered.

- Payment Method: Select the payment method used by the customer, such as check, wire transfer, credit card, or cash.

- Amount: Enter the total amount received from the customer.

2. Select the Customer:

- Customer Search: Use the customer search function to locate the customer who made the payment. You can search by customer ID, name, or other relevant criteria.

- Customer Selection: Select the correct customer from the search results to ensure the receipt is applied to the right account.

3. Match Receipt to Invoices:

- Invoice Search: Search for the outstanding invoices of the selected customer. You can filter invoices by date, amount, status, or other parameters.

- Select Invoices: Choose the invoices to which the receipt will be applied. Ensure the total of the selected invoices matches the receipt amount. If not, decide how to distribute the payment across multiple invoices.

4. Apply the Receipt:

- Full Payment: If the receipt amount matches the invoice amount exactly, apply the receipt as a full payment to the invoice.

- Partial Payment: If the receipt amount is less than the invoice amount, apply the receipt as a partial payment. The remaining balance will be tracked as outstanding.

- Overpayment: If the receipt amount exceeds the invoice amount, you can apply the excess amount to other invoices or keep it as an unapplied amount for future invoices.

5. Handling Discounts and Adjustments:

- Discounts: Apply any applicable early payment discounts if the customer has paid within the discount period.

- Adjustments: Make necessary adjustments for discrepancies, such as small underpayments or overpayments, based on company policies.

Validation

1. Review and Confirm:

- Review Entries: Carefully review all entries to ensure accuracy. Verify that the correct invoices have been selected and that the payment amounts are accurate.

- Confirm Application: Confirm the application of the receipt to finalize the process. This updates the customer's account and the general ledger.

2. Generate Receipts Report:

- Receipts Report: Generate a receipts report to document the applied receipts. This report can be used for internal review and auditing purposes.

- Save and Print: Save a digital copy of the report and print it if necessary for record-keeping.

3. Follow Up on Unapplied Amounts:

- Unapplied Receipts: If there are any unapplied amounts, make a note to follow up with the customer or apply them to future invoices.

- Customer Communication: Communicate with the customer regarding any unapplied amounts or discrepancies to ensure mutual understanding and agreement.

Best Practices for Applying Receipts

To ensure the process of applying receipts to customer invoices is efficient and accurate, consider the following best practices:

1. Automate Where Possible:

- Use automation tools available in Oracle ERP to streamline the receipt application process. Automated matching and application can save time and reduce errors.

2. Regular Reconciliation:

- Regularly reconcile the Accounts Receivable ledger with bank statements and other financial records to ensure all receipts are accounted for and accurately applied.

3. Maintain Clear Communication:

- Maintain clear and consistent communication with customers regarding their payments. Provide them with regular statements and updates on their account status.

4. Train Your Team:

- Ensure that the Accounts Receivable team is well-trained in using the Oracle ERP system. Regular training sessions can help keep the team updated on best practices and system updates.

5. Monitor and Review:

- Regularly monitor and review the receipt application process. Identify any recurring issues or discrepancies and take corrective actions promptly.

Troubleshooting Common Issues

While applying receipts to customer invoices, you may encounter various issues. Here are some common problems and how to troubleshoot them:

1. Receipt Amount Mismatch:

  - Issue: The receipt amount does not match any outstanding invoices.

  - Solution: Verify the payment details with the customer. Check for possible errors in the recorded amount or look for partial payments.

2. Incorrect Customer Selection:

  - Issue: The receipt is applied to the wrong customer account.

  - Solution: Use the customer search function carefully and double-check the selected customer before applying the receipt.

3. Duplicate Receipts:

  - Issue: The same payment is recorded and applied multiple times.

  - Solution: Implement a verification process to check for duplicate receipts before application. Use unique receipt numbers to identify and avoid duplicates.

4. Unapplied Amounts:

  - Issue: Part of the receipt remains unapplied.

  - Solution: Follow up with the customer to determine how the unapplied amount should be handled. Apply it to future invoices or issue a refund if necessary.

5. System Errors:

  - Issue: Technical issues or errors in the Oracle ERP system prevent the application of receipts.

  - Solution: Contact your IT support team or Oracle support for assistance in resolving system errors. Regular system maintenance and updates can help prevent such issues.

Conclusion

Applying receipts to customer invoices in the Oracle ERP Accounts Receivable module is a critical task that requires attention to detail and accuracy. By following the outlined steps and best practices, you can ensure that customer payments are correctly recorded and applied, leading to accurate financial records and efficient cash flow management. Regular monitoring, reconciliation, and clear communication with customers are essential for maintaining a smooth and error-free receipt application process.

5.2.2 Unapplying and Reapplying Receipts

Unapplying and reapplying receipts in Oracle ERP's Accounts Receivable module is a crucial aspect of managing customer payments. This process allows for adjustments to be made when receipts have been applied incorrectly, ensuring accurate financial records and customer account balances. This section will provide a comprehensive guide on how to unapply and reapply receipts, including step-by-step instructions, best practices, and common scenarios where these actions are necessary.

Unapplying Receipts

Unapplying a receipt involves removing the application of a payment from a specific invoice or set of invoices. This action may be necessary if a payment was applied to the wrong invoice, if a payment needs to be redistributed among multiple invoices, or if an overpayment was made.

Step-by-Step Guide to Unapply Receipts

1. Navigating to the Receipts Workbench:

   - Log in to Oracle ERP and navigate to the Accounts Receivable module.

   - Select the "Receipts" menu and choose "Receipts Workbench."

2. Query the Receipt:

   - In the Receipts Workbench, enter the receipt number or other relevant criteria (such as customer name or date) to find the specific receipt you need to unapply.

   - Click "Find" to retrieve the receipt details.

3. Open the Receipt:

   - Once the receipt appears in the search results, double-click on it to open the receipt details.

4. Navigate to Applications:

- In the receipt details window, go to the "Applications" tab to view the list of invoices the receipt is applied to.

5. Unapply the Receipt:

  - Select the invoice(s) from which you want to unapply the receipt.

  - Click on the "Unapply" button or choose "Unapply" from the actions menu.

  - Confirm the unapplication in the prompt that appears.

6. Review Unapplied Amount:

  - After unapplying, check the unapplied amount of the receipt to ensure it reflects the correct balance.

  - Save the changes to finalize the unapplication process.

Best Practices for Unapplying Receipts

- Verification Before Unapplying: Always verify the details of the receipt and the associated invoices before unapplying to avoid unnecessary adjustments and potential errors.

- Documentation: Maintain proper documentation of why the receipt was unapplied, including relevant notes in the system for future reference.

- Reconciliation: After unapplying a receipt, reconcile the customer account to ensure that the unapplied amount is correctly reflected and no discrepancies exist.

Common Scenarios for Unapplying Receipts

- Incorrect Invoice Application: If a payment was mistakenly applied to the wrong invoice, unapplying the receipt allows for the correction.

- Overpayment: If a customer overpaid, unapplying the receipt can help redistribute the excess amount or prepare it for a refund.

- Invoice Adjustment: In cases where an invoice needs adjustment (e.g., due to errors in the billed amount), unapplying the receipt facilitates the necessary corrections.

Reapplying Receipts

Reapplying a receipt involves applying an unapplied payment to one or more invoices. This action is essential when redistributing payments or correcting previous application errors.

Step-by-Step Guide to Reapply Receipts

1. Navigating to the Receipts Workbench:

   - Log in to Oracle ERP and navigate to the Accounts Receivable module.

   - Select the "Receipts" menu and choose "Receipts Workbench."

2. Query the Receipt:

   - In the Receipts Workbench, enter the receipt number or other relevant criteria to find the unapplied receipt.

   - Click "Find" to retrieve the receipt details.

3. Open the Receipt:

   - Once the receipt appears in the search results, double-click on it to open the receipt details.

4. Navigate to Applications:

   - In the receipt details window, go to the "Applications" tab to view the list of unapplied amounts.

5. Select Invoices for Reapplication:

   - Choose the invoices to which you want to reapply the receipt. Ensure the selected invoices are correct and reflect the intended application.

6. Apply the Receipt:

   - Enter the amount to be applied to each selected invoice. The total applied amount should not exceed the unapplied balance of the receipt.

   - Click on the "Apply" button or choose "Apply" from the actions menu.

   - Save the changes to finalize the reapplication process.

Best Practices for Reapplying Receipts

- Review Customer Account: Before reapplying a receipt, review the customer's account to identify the correct invoices and ensure proper allocation of the payment.

- Partial Payments: When reapplying receipts as partial payments to multiple invoices, carefully distribute the amounts to avoid any imbalances.

- Documentation: Document the reason for reapplying the receipt and any notes regarding the customer's payment preferences or agreements.

Common Scenarios for Reapplying Receipts

- Redistribution of Payments: If a payment was unapplied due to initial misallocation, reapplying allows for the correct distribution across the intended invoices.

- Settling Multiple Invoices: When a customer makes a bulk payment intended for multiple invoices, reapplying the receipt ensures each invoice is appropriately settled.

- Correcting Previous Errors: If an error occurred in the initial application, reapplying the receipt to the correct invoices rectifies the mistake.

Troubleshooting Unapplying and Reapplying Receipts

- Mismatch in Amounts: If the unapplied or reapplied amounts do not match the expected balances, double-check the receipt and invoice details for any discrepancies.

- System Errors: Occasionally, system issues may prevent unapplying or reapplying receipts. In such cases, contact Oracle support for assistance.

- Audit Trails: Ensure that all actions taken during the unapplying and reapplying processes are logged and documented for audit purposes.

Conclusion

Unapplying and reapplying receipts are critical processes within the Oracle ERP Accounts Receivable module. These actions allow for flexibility in managing customer payments and ensure the accuracy of financial records. By following the detailed steps and best practices outlined in this section, users can effectively handle these tasks, maintain accurate customer accounts, and support overall financial management.

5.2.3 Managing Receipt Write-Offs

Managing receipt write-offs is a critical process in the Accounts Receivable (AR) module of Oracle ERP. It involves handling the accounting for amounts that are not collectible from customers and need to be written off from the receivables ledger. This section will delve into the details of managing receipt write-offs, including the steps to perform write-offs, the implications of these write-offs on financial statements, and best practices to ensure accuracy and compliance.

Understanding Receipt Write-Offs

Receipt write-offs occur when a portion or the entirety of a receivable amount is deemed uncollectible and needs to be removed from the books. This can happen due to various reasons such as customer bankruptcy, disputed amounts, or simply inability to collect after extensive efforts. The write-off process ensures that the company's financial statements accurately reflect the true financial position and do not overstate receivables.

Steps to Manage Receipt Write-Offs

1. Identify the Amount to be Written Off:

   - The first step in managing receipt write-offs is to identify the specific amounts that need to be written off. This could be part of an invoice, a full invoice, or an overpayment that cannot be refunded or adjusted.

   - Regularly review the aging report of receivables to identify potential write-offs. Look for amounts that are significantly past due and have had no recent collection activity.

2. Approval Process:

   - Before proceeding with a write-off, it is crucial to follow the company's approval process. This typically involves obtaining authorization from the finance manager or another senior authority within the organization.

- Document the reasons for the write-off and keep a record of the approvals. This documentation is important for audit trails and future reference.

3. Recording the Write-Off in Oracle ERP:

  - Navigate to the Accounts Receivable module and select the option to manage receipts.

  - Locate the specific receipt that needs to be adjusted. This can be done using the search functionality by entering relevant details such as customer name, invoice number, or receipt number.

  - Select the receipt and choose the option to apply/unapply.

  - Enter the amount to be written off and select the write-off reason from the predefined list. This ensures consistency and helps in reporting and analysis.

  - Confirm the write-off by saving the transaction. The system will automatically adjust the receivables ledger and update the financial statements accordingly.

4. Impact on Financial Statements:

  - When a receipt is written off, it reduces the Accounts Receivable balance on the balance sheet. This reflects a more accurate picture of the company's financial position.

  - The write-off amount is recorded as an expense in the income statement, usually under bad debt expense. This impacts the company's profitability.

5. Reversing a Write-Off:

  - In some cases, it may be necessary to reverse a write-off if the customer makes a payment after the write-off has been recorded.

  - To reverse a write-off, navigate to the transaction and select the option to reverse. The system will prompt for the reason and require appropriate authorization.

  - Once reversed, the receivable amount will be reinstated, and the bad debt expense will be adjusted accordingly.

Best Practices for Managing Receipt Write-Offs

1. Regular Monitoring and Review:

- Regularly monitor receivables and review aging reports to identify potential write-offs early. This proactive approach helps in timely decision-making and maintaining accurate financial records.

2. Documentation and Approval:

- Ensure that all write-offs are well-documented with clear reasons and approvals. This documentation is crucial for audits and internal reviews.

3. Consistent Write-Off Policies:

- Develop and adhere to consistent policies for writing off receivables. This includes defining thresholds for write-offs, approval hierarchies, and documentation requirements.

4. Training and Awareness:

- Provide regular training to AR staff on the procedures and policies for managing write-offs. This ensures that the team is aware of the correct steps and the importance of accurate record-keeping.

5. Audit and Compliance:

- Conduct periodic audits of write-offs to ensure compliance with company policies and accounting standards. This helps in identifying any discrepancies or areas for improvement.

Case Study: Managing Write-Offs at XYZ Corporation

XYZ Corporation, a mid-sized manufacturing company, faced challenges in managing their receivables and write-offs. They implemented the following strategies to streamline their processes:

1. Enhanced Monitoring:

- XYZ Corporation introduced monthly reviews of aging reports. They set up a dedicated team to focus on receivables that were over 90 days past due.

- This team was responsible for contacting customers, negotiating payment plans, and identifying potential write-offs early.

2. Improved Documentation:

- The company established a standardized template for documenting write-offs. This included details such as customer information, invoice details, reasons for write-off, and approval signatures.

- They also introduced a digital approval workflow within Oracle ERP, which streamlined the process and ensured that all write-offs were properly authorized.

3. Training and Awareness Programs:

- Regular training sessions were conducted for the AR team, focusing on best practices for managing receivables and write-offs.

- The training emphasized the importance of accurate documentation and compliance with company policies.

4. Policy Revisions:

- XYZ Corporation reviewed and updated their write-off policies. They defined clear thresholds for write-offs based on the amount and the age of the receivable.

- They also established a hierarchy of approvals, ensuring that larger write-offs required higher levels of authorization.

5. Audit and Feedback:

- Periodic audits were conducted to review write-offs and ensure compliance with policies. The audit findings were used to further refine processes and address any gaps.

- Feedback from the audit process was incorporated into training sessions and policy updates.

As a result of these strategies, XYZ Corporation was able to reduce the number of outstanding receivables and improve the accuracy of their financial statements. The enhanced processes also ensured better compliance and provided a clear audit trail for all write-offs.

Conclusion

Managing receipt write-offs is a crucial aspect of the Accounts Receivable module in Oracle ERP. By following a structured approach, companies can ensure that their financial records are accurate and reflect the true state of their receivables. Implementing best practices, regular monitoring, and adhering to company policies are essential to effectively manage write-offs and maintain financial integrity.

5.3 Managing Customer Refunds

Managing customer refunds efficiently is critical for maintaining customer satisfaction and ensuring accurate financial records. This section will cover the detailed steps involved in issuing refunds to customers, processing refund requests, and recording refund transactions in Oracle ERP's Accounts Receivable module.

5.3.1 Issuing Refunds to Customers

Issuing refunds to customers can be complex, involving multiple steps and considerations to ensure that the process is both accurate and efficient. This section will provide a comprehensive guide on how to issue refunds to customers using Oracle ERP's Accounts Receivable module.

Overview of the Refund Process

Refunds can be issued for various reasons, including overpayments, returns, and billing errors. The process generally involves the following steps:

1. Identifying the Need for a Refund: Determine why a refund is necessary.

2. Validating the Refund Request: Ensure the refund request is legitimate and complies with company policies.

3. Calculating the Refund Amount: Accurately calculate the amount to be refunded.

4. Processing the Refund: Use Oracle ERP to issue the refund.

5. Notifying the Customer: Inform the customer about the refund.

6. Recording the Refund Transaction: Ensure the refund is properly recorded in the financial system.

Step-by-Step Guide to Issuing Refunds

1. Identifying the Need for a Refund

The first step is to identify the reason for the refund. Common reasons include:

- Overpayments: Customers may accidentally overpay their invoices.

- Returns: Customers return goods or services that were previously paid for.

- Billing Errors: Incorrect billing may require a refund.

Use Oracle ERP to review the customer's account and identify any overpayments, returns, or errors that justify a refund.

2. Validating the Refund Request

Before processing a refund, validate the request to ensure it meets company policies and procedures. This may involve:

- Reviewing the Customer's Account: Check the customer's account history for any previous refunds or issues.

- Verifying Documentation: Ensure all necessary documentation, such as return receipts or overpayment proofs, is available.

- Approval Process: Some refunds may require approval from a manager or finance department.

3. Calculating the Refund Amount

Calculate the refund amount accurately. Consider any applicable deductions or adjustments. Use Oracle ERP to verify the original payment and any related transactions.

4. Processing the Refund in Oracle ERP

Use the following steps to process the refund in Oracle ERP:

- Navigate to the Accounts Receivable Module: Access the module from the Oracle ERP main menu.

- Locate the Customer Account: Use the customer search function to find the customer's account.

- Create a Credit Memo: A credit memo is used to record the refund transaction.

  - Select the option to create a new credit memo.

  - Enter the customer details and the reason for the refund.

- Specify the refund amount and any applicable tax adjustments.

- Save the credit memo.

- Generate a Refund Request: Once the credit memo is approved, generate a refund request.

- Select the option to create a new refund request.

- Link the refund request to the credit memo.

- Confirm the refund amount and the payment method (e.g., bank transfer, check).

- Submit the refund request for approval.

- Approval and Processing: Follow the approval workflow defined in Oracle ERP.

- The request may need approval from multiple levels, depending on the company's policies.

- Once approved, the refund is processed and the payment is issued to the customer.

5. Notifying the Customer

After processing the refund, inform the customer about the status and details of the refund. This can be done through:

- Email Notification: Send an email detailing the refund amount, reason, and payment method.

- Customer Portal: If available, update the customer's account on the portal with the refund details.

- Phone Call: In some cases, a direct phone call may be appropriate, especially for high-value refunds.

6. Recording the Refund Transaction

Ensure the refund transaction is accurately recorded in the financial system. Use Oracle ERP to:

- Update the Customer's Account: Adjust the account balance to reflect the refund.

- Post the Refund to the General Ledger: Record the refund in the general ledger to maintain accurate financial records.

- Reconcile the Refund: Reconcile the refund with the original payment and any related transactions.

Best Practices for Issuing Refunds

To ensure the refund process is efficient and accurate, follow these best practices:

1. Standardize the Refund Process: Develop a standardized process for issuing refunds, including clear policies and procedures.

2. Training and Education: Ensure staff are trained on how to handle refunds in Oracle ERP.

3. Regular Audits: Conduct regular audits of refund transactions to identify any discrepancies or issues.

4. Customer Communication: Maintain clear and transparent communication with customers regarding refunds.

5. Documentation: Keep detailed records of all refund transactions for audit and compliance purposes.

Troubleshooting Common Issues

Despite best efforts, issues may arise during the refund process. Here are some common issues and how to troubleshoot them:

1. Discrepancies in Refund Amounts

   - Review Transaction History: Verify all related transactions to identify discrepancies.

   - Recalculate Refunds: Double-check calculations and adjust if necessary.

2. Delayed Refund Approvals

   - Follow Up with Approvers: Ensure timely follow-up with approvers to expedite the process.

   - Streamline Approval Workflow: Consider simplifying the approval process if delays are common.

3. Customer Complaints

- Address Complaints Promptly: Investigate and resolve complaints quickly to maintain customer satisfaction.

- Provide Clear Explanations: Ensure customers understand the reason for any delays or issues with their refunds.

Conclusion

Issuing refunds to customers is an essential part of managing the Accounts Receivable module in Oracle ERP. By following the detailed steps and best practices outlined above, companies can ensure refunds are handled efficiently and accurately, maintaining customer satisfaction and financial integrity. Proper training, standardized procedures, and effective use of Oracle ERP features are key to managing customer refunds successfully.

5.3.2 Processing Refund Requests

Managing customer refunds efficiently is crucial for maintaining strong customer relationships and ensuring the financial integrity of the organization. Processing refund requests involves several steps, from receiving the request to issuing the refund and recording the transaction. Here, we will explore the detailed process of handling refund requests in Oracle ERP's Accounts Receivable module.

Step 1: Receiving the Refund Request

The refund process begins when a customer submits a request for a refund. This can happen through various channels, such as customer service, sales representatives, or directly through an online portal. The request should include relevant details such as:

- Customer name and contact information

- Invoice number related to the refund

- Reason for the refund request

- Amount to be refunded

In Oracle ERP, refund requests can be logged into the system using the Customer Service module or directly within the Accounts Receivable module. Ensuring that all necessary details are captured at this stage is critical for the smooth processing of the refund.

Step 2: Verifying the Refund Request

Once the refund request is received, the next step is to verify its validity. This involves checking several aspects:

- Invoice Verification: Confirm that the invoice number provided by the customer exists in the system and matches the details of the transaction in question.

- Payment Verification: Ensure that the payment for the invoice has been received and correctly recorded. This includes checking for any partial payments or overpayments that might impact the refund amount.

- Reason for Refund: Assess the reason for the refund request. Common reasons include product returns, overpayment, service issues, or billing errors. Verification of the reason ensures that the refund is justified and adheres to company policies.

In Oracle ERP, this verification can be done using standard reports and queries to pull up invoice and payment details, ensuring that the request is legitimate and accurate.

Step 3: Approval Process

After verifying the refund request, it often needs to go through an approval process, especially for large amounts or for reasons that require higher authorization. The approval workflow in Oracle ERP can be configured to route the request through the necessary channels based on predefined rules. This might include:

- Initial Approval: The request is first reviewed by the Accounts Receivable team or customer service representative who verifies the initial details.

- Managerial Approval: If the refund amount exceeds a certain threshold, the request might need managerial approval. The system can be set up to automatically escalate such requests.

- Final Approval: For very large refunds or special cases, final approval might be required from higher management or the finance department.

Oracle ERP's workflow automation features ensure that each step of the approval process is documented and traceable, reducing the risk of errors and ensuring compliance with company policies.

Step 4: Issuing the Refund

Once the refund request is approved, the next step is to issue the refund. This can be done through various methods depending on the company's policies and the customer's preference:

- Check Refunds: A common method where a refund check is issued to the customer. The Accounts Payable module in Oracle ERP can be used to generate and print the check.

- Credit Card Refunds: For transactions initially made through credit cards, refunds can be processed back to the same card. Oracle ERP can interface with payment gateways to handle this seamlessly.

- Bank Transfers: For customers who prefer direct bank transfers, refunds can be processed through electronic funds transfer (EFT). The bank details can be securely managed in the system.

- Store Credit: Some companies might offer store credit instead of a direct refund. This can be managed by creating a credit memo in the system that the customer can use for future purchases.

Each method involves creating a refund transaction in the system, which ensures that the financial records are updated accordingly.

Step 5: Recording the Refund Transaction

Recording the refund transaction accurately is crucial for maintaining correct financial records. In Oracle ERP, this involves several steps:

- Creating a Credit Memo: A credit memo is created in the Accounts Receivable module to reverse the original invoice amount. This ensures that the customer's account reflects the refund.

- Journal Entries: The system automatically generates the necessary journal entries to reflect the refund in the general ledger. This includes debiting the sales revenue account and crediting the accounts receivable.

- Updating Customer Balance: The customer's balance is updated to reflect the refund. This ensures that their account accurately shows the current amount due or credit available.

- Reporting: Standard reports can be generated to track refunds processed, ensuring that all transactions are accounted for and discrepancies are avoided.

Step 6: Communicating with the Customer

Effective communication with the customer is vital throughout the refund process. Keeping the customer informed ensures transparency and builds trust. Steps include:

- Acknowledgment: Send an acknowledgment email or notification to the customer when the refund request is received.

- Status Updates: Provide updates during the verification and approval stages, especially if there are delays or additional information is needed.

- Confirmation: Once the refund is issued, send a confirmation to the customer, including details of the refund amount, method, and expected time frame for receiving the funds.

Oracle ERP can automate much of this communication through the Customer Relationship Management (CRM) module, ensuring timely and consistent updates.

Best Practices for Processing Refund Requests

1. Standardize Procedures: Establish standardized procedures for processing refunds to ensure consistency and efficiency. This includes clear guidelines for verification, approval, and recording steps.

2. Use Automation: Leverage Oracle ERP's automation capabilities to streamline the refund process, reduce manual errors, and ensure timely processing.

3. Monitor and Audit: Regularly monitor refund transactions and conduct audits to ensure compliance with company policies and identify any discrepancies or fraudulent activities.

4. Customer Feedback: Gather feedback from customers on the refund process to identify areas for improvement and enhance the customer experience.

5. Training and Development: Provide regular training for staff involved in processing refunds to ensure they are familiar with the latest procedures and system functionalities.

Conclusion

Processing refund requests efficiently is a critical aspect of managing accounts receivable in Oracle ERP. By following the detailed steps outlined above, organizations can ensure that refunds are handled accurately, promptly, and in compliance with company policies. This not only helps maintain strong customer relationships but also ensures the integrity of the financial records.

5.3.3 Recording Refund Transactions

Introduction

Recording refund transactions accurately in Oracle ERP ensures that your financial statements reflect the true state of your accounts and that customers receive their refunds promptly. This process involves several steps, from verifying the refund details to posting the refund in the system. Below, we will explore each step in detail, including best practices and common pitfalls to avoid.

Step-by-Step Guide to Recording Refund Transactions

Step 1: Verify Refund Details

Before recording a refund transaction, it is essential to verify the details of the refund request. This verification process includes:

- Confirming the Reason for the Refund: Ensure that the reason for the refund is valid and documented. Common reasons include overpayment, duplicate payments, returned goods, or service cancellations.

- Reviewing the Original Invoice: Check the original invoice or payment receipt to confirm the amount paid and the payment method used.

- Validating Customer Information: Ensure that the customer's information, such as name, account number, and contact details, is accurate and up-to-date.

Step 2: Initiate the Refund Process in Oracle ERP

Once the refund details are verified, the next step is to initiate the refund process in Oracle ERP. This involves creating a refund transaction in the Accounts Receivable module:

- Navigate to the Refunds Section: Access the Accounts Receivable module and navigate to the refunds section.

- Create a New Refund Transaction: Select the option to create a new refund transaction. This will open a form where you can enter the refund details.

Step 3: Enter Refund Details

In the refund transaction form, you will need to enter specific details about the refund:

- Customer Information: Enter the customer's name, account number, and contact details.

- Refund Amount: Specify the amount to be refunded. Ensure that this amount matches the verified refund amount.

- Reason for Refund: Select the reason for the refund from a predefined list. If necessary, provide additional notes to explain the reason in detail.

- Original Invoice or Receipt Number: Enter the number of the original invoice or payment receipt related to the refund.

- Payment Method: Specify the payment method for the refund (e.g., check, bank transfer, credit card reversal).

Step 4: Review and Approve the Refund Transaction

After entering the refund details, the next step is to review and approve the refund transaction:

- Review the Transaction: Carefully review all the details entered in the refund transaction form. Verify that the customer information, refund amount, reason for the refund, and payment method are correct.

- Approval Workflow: If your organization has an approval workflow for refunds, submit the transaction for approval. The approval process ensures that refunds are authorized by the appropriate personnel and helps prevent fraud.

Step 5: Record the Refund in the General Ledger

Once the refund transaction is approved, it needs to be recorded in the General Ledger (GL) to update your financial records:

- Post the Refund Transaction: Post the refund transaction to the GL. This step updates the customer's account and reduces the accounts receivable balance by the refund amount.

- Verify GL Entries: After posting, verify the GL entries to ensure that the refund has been recorded correctly. The refund should be reflected as a debit to the accounts receivable account and a credit to the cash or bank account used for the refund.

Step 6: Issue the Refund to the Customer

With the refund transaction recorded in Oracle ERP, the next step is to issue the refund to the customer:

- Process the Refund Payment: Depending on the payment method specified, process the refund payment. For example, if the refund is issued via check, generate and mail the check to the customer. If it is a bank transfer, initiate the transfer through your banking system.

- Notify the Customer: Send a notification to the customer to inform them that the refund has been processed. Include details such as the refund amount, payment method, and expected time for the refund to be received.

Step 7: Update Customer Records

Finally, update the customer records to reflect the refund:

- Adjust Customer Account Balance: Ensure that the customer's account balance is updated to reflect the refunded amount.

- Document the Refund: Attach any relevant documentation, such as the refund request, approval, and payment confirmation, to the customer's record for future reference.

Best Practices for Recording Refund Transactions

To ensure accuracy and efficiency in recording refund transactions, consider the following best practices:

- Use Standardized Procedures: Implement standardized procedures for verifying, processing, and recording refunds to maintain consistency and accuracy.

- Automate Where Possible: Utilize Oracle ERP's automation features to streamline the refund process, reduce manual errors, and save time.

- Regular Audits: Conduct regular audits of refund transactions to identify and address any discrepancies or issues promptly.

- Training and Documentation: Provide training to staff involved in the refund process and maintain up-to-date documentation on procedures and best practices.

Common Pitfalls and How to Avoid Them

Recording refund transactions can be prone to errors if not managed carefully. Here are some common pitfalls and tips on how to avoid them:

- Inaccurate Data Entry: Double-check all data entered into the refund transaction form to prevent errors.

- Missing Approvals: Ensure that all refund transactions go through the necessary approval workflows to prevent unauthorized refunds.

- Delayed Refund Processing: Set up reminders and alerts to ensure refunds are processed promptly and customers are notified in a timely manner.

Conclusion

Recording refund transactions accurately in Oracle ERP is essential for maintaining financial integrity and customer satisfaction. By following the steps outlined above and adhering to best practices, you can ensure that refunds are processed efficiently and reflected correctly in your financial records. Regular audits and continuous process improvements will further enhance the accuracy and effectiveness of your refund management process.

CHAPTER VI
Collections and Credit Management

6.1 Exploring Real-Time Data Use Cases

6.1.1 Defining Collection Policies

Collections strategies are essential to maintaining a healthy cash flow and ensuring that outstanding receivables are collected promptly. A well-defined collection policy is the foundation of an effective collections strategy. It provides clear guidelines and procedures for managing the collections process, ensuring consistency, and improving the efficiency of the accounts receivable function.

1. Understanding the Importance of Collection Policies

Collection policies are crucial for several reasons:

- Cash Flow Management: Effective collection policies help maintain a steady cash flow, ensuring that the business has the necessary funds to meet its obligations.

- Minimizing Bad Debts: By following a structured approach to collections, companies can minimize the risk of bad debts and write-offs.

- Customer Relationships: Clear policies help manage customer expectations and maintain positive relationships by setting transparent terms for payments and collections.

- Compliance: Well-documented policies ensure compliance with regulatory requirements and internal controls.

2. Components of a Collection Policy

A comprehensive collection policy typically includes the following components:

- Credit Terms and Conditions: Define the standard credit terms offered to customers, such as net 30, net 60, or cash on delivery (COD). Specify the conditions under which credit is extended, including credit limits and approval processes.

- Billing Procedures: Outline the process for generating and sending invoices, including the timing and frequency of billing cycles. Ensure that invoices are clear, accurate, and contain all necessary information.

- Payment Methods: Specify the acceptable methods of payment, such as checks, electronic funds transfer (EFT), credit cards, and online payment platforms. Provide details on how payments should be made and any associated fees.

- Due Dates and Grace Periods: Clearly state the due dates for payments and any applicable grace periods. Define the consequences of late payments, including late fees and interest charges.

- Collection Steps and Timeline: Outline the steps to be taken when a payment is overdue, including reminders, follow-up calls, and escalation procedures. Specify the timeline for each step to ensure timely action.

- Dispute Resolution: Provide a process for handling disputes or discrepancies in invoices. Define how customers can raise concerns and the steps to resolve them.

- Write-Off Procedures: Establish criteria for writing off uncollectible debts and the approval process for write-offs. Define how write-offs are documented and reported.

3. Developing a Collection Policy

To develop an effective collection policy, follow these steps:

Step 1: Assess the Current Situation

- Analyze Current Practices: Review existing collection practices and identify areas for improvement. Assess the effectiveness of current policies and procedures.

- Gather Data: Collect data on past due accounts, average collection periods, and the effectiveness of different collection methods. Use this data to inform policy decisions.

Step 2: Define Objectives

- Set Clear Goals: Define the objectives of the collection policy, such as reducing the average collection period, minimizing bad debts, or improving cash flow. Ensure that goals are specific, measurable, achievable, relevant, and time-bound (SMART).

- Align with Business Strategy: Ensure that the collection policy aligns with the overall business strategy and financial goals. Consider the impact on customer relationships and brand reputation.

Step 3: Involve Stakeholders

- Engage Key Stakeholders: Involve key stakeholders, including finance, sales, and customer service teams, in the development of the policy. Seek input and feedback to ensure that the policy is practical and comprehensive.

- Customer Insights: Consider feedback from customers to understand their payment preferences and challenges. Use this information to create customer-friendly policies.

Step 4: Draft the Policy

- Document Policies and Procedures: Clearly document all aspects of the collection policy, including credit terms, billing procedures, payment methods, due dates, collection steps, dispute resolution, and write-off procedures.

- Use Clear Language: Ensure that the policy is written in clear, concise language that is easy to understand. Avoid jargon and technical terms that may confuse readers.

Step 5: Review and Revise

- Internal Review: Conduct an internal review of the draft policy with key stakeholders to identify any gaps or areas for improvement. Make necessary revisions based on feedback.

- Legal and Compliance Review: Ensure that the policy complies with relevant laws and regulations. Seek input from legal and compliance teams to address any potential issues.

Step 6: Communicate the Policy

- Internal Communication: Communicate the collection policy to all relevant internal teams, including finance, sales, and customer service. Provide training and resources to ensure that everyone understands and follows the policy.

- Customer Communication: Inform customers about the collection policy, including payment terms, due dates, and consequences of late payments. Provide clear and concise information through invoices, statements, and communication channels.

Step 7: Monitor and Evaluate

- Track Performance: Monitor the effectiveness of the collection policy by tracking key performance indicators (KPIs), such as days sales outstanding (DSO), collection rates, and bad debt levels.

- Regular Review: Regularly review and update the collection policy to address changing business needs, customer feedback, and regulatory requirements. Make adjustments as necessary to ensure continued effectiveness.

4. Implementing Collection Policies in Oracle ERP

Oracle ERP provides robust tools and features to support the implementation of collection policies. Follow these steps to implement collection policies in Oracle ERP:

Step 1: Configure Credit Terms

- Define Credit Terms: Set up standard credit terms in the Oracle ERP system, including net 30, net 60, and other terms as defined in the collection policy.

- Assign Credit Terms: Assign the appropriate credit terms to customer accounts based on their payment history and creditworthiness.

Step 2: Set Up Billing and Invoicing

- Automate Invoicing: Use Oracle ERP's automated invoicing features to generate and send invoices promptly. Ensure that invoices include all necessary information, such as due dates, payment methods, and contact details.

- Schedule Billing Cycles: Set up billing cycles in Oracle ERP to ensure timely and consistent invoicing. Schedule billing runs based on the defined billing procedures in the collection policy.

Step 3: Define Payment Methods

- Configure Payment Options: Set up acceptable payment methods in Oracle ERP, including EFT, credit cards, and online payment platforms. Ensure that the system can handle multiple payment methods and process transactions efficiently.

- Provide Payment Instructions: Include clear payment instructions on invoices and statements to guide customers on how to make payments.

Step 4: Implement Collection Steps and Timeline

- Set Up Reminders and Alerts: Use Oracle ERP's reminder and alert features to automate the collection steps outlined in the policy. Set up reminders for upcoming due dates, overdue invoices, and follow-up actions.

- Create Collection Workflows: Define collection workflows in Oracle ERP to ensure that the appropriate steps are taken at each stage of the collections process. Automate follow-up calls, escalation procedures, and other collection actions.

Step 5: Manage Disputes and Write-Offs

- Track Disputes: Use Oracle ERP to track and manage customer disputes. Record dispute details, resolution steps, and outcomes to ensure transparency and accountability.

- Automate Write-Offs: Set up criteria for write-offs in Oracle ERP and automate the approval process. Ensure that write-offs are documented and reported accurately.

Conclusion

Defining collection policies is a critical step in setting up an effective collections strategy in Oracle ERP. By establishing clear guidelines and procedures, businesses can improve cash flow, minimize bad debts, and maintain positive customer relationships. Implementing these policies in Oracle ERP ensures consistency, efficiency, and compliance, supporting the overall financial health of the organization.

6.1.2 Implementing Collection Strategies

Implementing effective collection strategies is essential for managing accounts receivable efficiently and ensuring that your organization maintains a healthy cash flow. Collections strategies involve systematic approaches to recover outstanding debts while maintaining positive relationships with customers. This section will explore the key components and best practices for implementing robust collection strategies in Oracle ERP's Accounts Receivable module.

1. Defining Clear Objectives

The first step in implementing collection strategies is to define clear and measurable objectives. These objectives should align with the organization's overall financial goals and should be communicated effectively to the collections team. Typical objectives include:

- Reducing the average collection period.

- Minimizing bad debts.

- Improving cash flow predictability.

- Maintaining positive customer relationships.

By setting specific targets, such as reducing the days sales outstanding (DSO) or increasing the percentage of current receivables, the collections team can focus their efforts on achieving these goals.

2. Segmenting Customers

Customer segmentation is crucial for tailoring collection strategies to different customer groups. Not all customers are the same, and their payment behaviors and risk profiles can vary significantly. Segmenting customers based on factors such as payment history, credit risk, and purchase volume allows for more targeted and effective collection efforts. Common segmentation criteria include:

- High-risk vs. low-risk customers.

- Large accounts vs. small accounts.

- Domestic vs. international customers.

By categorizing customers into segments, you can develop specific strategies and allocate resources more effectively.

3. Developing a Collection Policy

A comprehensive collection policy serves as the foundation for all collection activities. This policy should outline the procedures and guidelines for handling overdue accounts, including:

- Payment terms and conditions.

- Timelines for follow-up actions.

- Communication protocols.

- Escalation procedures.

- Consequences for non-payment.

The collection policy should be clear, consistent, and aligned with legal and regulatory requirements. It should also be flexible enough to accommodate different customer situations and market conditions.

4. Automating Collection Processes

Automation plays a vital role in implementing efficient collection strategies. Oracle ERP's Accounts Receivable module offers various automation tools and features that streamline the collections process, reduce manual effort, and improve accuracy. Key automation features include:

- Automated reminders: Sending automated payment reminders to customers based on predefined schedules helps ensure timely follow-ups.

- Workflow automation: Automating approval workflows for collection actions, such as escalations and write-offs, enhances efficiency and reduces delays.

- Predictive analytics: Using predictive analytics to identify at-risk accounts and prioritize collection efforts based on probability of payment.

By leveraging automation, the collections team can focus on higher-value tasks and improve overall productivity.

5. Setting Up a Dunning Process

The dunning process involves systematically reminding customers of their overdue payments through a series of escalating communications. Oracle ERP supports the creation and management of dunning letters, which are sent at predefined intervals. Key steps in setting up a dunning process include:

- Defining dunning levels: Establishing multiple levels of dunning letters with increasing urgency and tone.

- Scheduling reminders: Setting up a schedule for sending dunning letters based on the aging of receivables.

- Customizing templates: Creating customized dunning letter templates that include relevant account information and payment instructions.

- Tracking responses: Monitoring customer responses to dunning letters and adjusting follow-up actions accordingly.

A well-structured dunning process ensures consistent and timely communication with customers, encouraging prompt payment and reducing overdue receivables.

6. Training and Empowering the Collections Team

The success of any collection strategy relies heavily on the skills and dedication of the collections team. Providing comprehensive training and empowering the team with the right tools and information is essential. Key training topics include:

- Understanding the collection policy and procedures.

- Effective communication techniques for different customer scenarios.

- Using Oracle ERP's collections features and automation tools.

- Negotiation and conflict resolution skills.

Regular training sessions, performance reviews, and feedback mechanisms help ensure that the collections team remains motivated and aligned with the organization's goals.

7. Monitoring and Analyzing Collection Performance

Continuous monitoring and analysis of collection performance are critical for identifying areas for improvement and making data-driven decisions. Oracle ERP provides various reporting and analytics tools that offer insights into key metrics, such as:

- Days sales outstanding (DSO).

- Aging of receivables.

- Collection effectiveness index (CEI).

- Percentage of current vs. overdue receivables.

By regularly reviewing these metrics, the collections team can identify trends, assess the effectiveness of their strategies, and make necessary adjustments to optimize performance.

8. Managing Disputed Invoices

Disputed invoices can pose significant challenges to the collections process. Addressing disputes promptly and effectively is crucial for maintaining positive customer relationships and ensuring timely resolution. Key steps in managing disputed invoices include:

- Identifying disputes: Establishing processes for customers to raise disputes and ensuring that these are logged and tracked in Oracle ERP.

- Investigating disputes: Assigning responsible team members to investigate disputes, gather relevant information, and communicate with customers.

- Resolving disputes: Developing resolution strategies, such as offering discounts, issuing credit memos, or adjusting invoices.

- Escalating unresolved disputes: Implementing escalation procedures for disputes that cannot be resolved at the initial level.

Effective dispute management minimizes delays in collections and enhances customer satisfaction.

9. Implementing Customer Communication Strategies

Effective communication is a cornerstone of successful collections. Developing customer communication strategies that are consistent, professional, and customer-centric helps foster positive relationships and encourages timely payments. Key communication strategies include:

- Personalizing communications: Addressing customers by name and referencing specific account details in all communications.

- Maintaining professionalism: Ensuring that all communications are polite, respectful, and adhere to the organization's brand and tone.

- Providing multiple contact channels: Offering customers various ways to reach the collections team, such as phone, email, and online portals.

- Following up consistently: Ensuring that follow-up actions are carried out as per the collection policy and that customers are kept informed of the status of their accounts.

10. Utilizing Customer Portals for Self-Service

Customer portals provide a convenient platform for customers to view their account status, make payments, and communicate with the collections team. Oracle ERP supports the implementation of customer portals, which can significantly enhance the collections process by:

- Providing real-time account information: Allowing customers to view their outstanding balances, payment history, and due dates.

- Enabling online payments: Offering secure online payment options that facilitate quick and easy payments.

- Streamlining communication: Providing a centralized platform for customers to raise queries, dispute invoices, and receive updates.

By empowering customers with self-service options, organizations can reduce the burden on the collections team and improve the overall customer experience.

11. Reviewing and Updating Collection Strategies

The collections landscape is dynamic, and strategies must be reviewed and updated regularly to remain effective. Key steps in this ongoing process include:

- Conducting periodic reviews: Scheduling regular reviews of collection strategies to assess their effectiveness and identify areas for improvement.

- Gathering feedback: Soliciting feedback from the collections team, customers, and other stakeholders to gain insights into potential enhancements.

- Staying informed: Keeping abreast of industry trends, regulatory changes, and best practices in collections management.

- Implementing changes: Making necessary adjustments to the collection policy, procedures, and automation tools based on review findings.

By continuously refining collection strategies, organizations can adapt to changing conditions and maintain high levels of efficiency and effectiveness.

Conclusion

Implementing effective collection strategies in Oracle ERP's Accounts Receivable module involves a combination of clear objectives, customer segmentation, comprehensive policies, automation, and continuous improvement. By following the best practices outlined in this section, organizations can enhance their collections process, reduce overdue receivables, and improve overall financial health. Maintaining positive customer relationships while ensuring timely payments is a delicate balance, but with the right strategies in place, it is achievable and sustainable.

6.1.3 Monitoring Collection Performance

Monitoring collection performance is a critical aspect of managing the Accounts Receivable (AR) process. Effective monitoring ensures that collection strategies are working as intended, highlights areas needing improvement, and helps maintain healthy cash flow. This section delves into the key components and best practices for monitoring collection performance within Oracle ERP.

Understanding Key Performance Indicators (KPIs)

Key Performance Indicators (KPIs) are essential metrics used to evaluate the effectiveness of collection strategies. Common KPIs for monitoring collection performance include:

1. Days Sales Outstanding (DSO):

  - Definition: The average number of days it takes to collect payment after a sale has been made.

  - Calculation: (Total Accounts Receivable / Total Credit Sales) x Number of Days

  - Importance: A lower DSO indicates that the company is collecting receivables more quickly, improving cash flow.

2. Collection Effectiveness Index (CEI):

  - Definition: A measure of the effectiveness of the collections process over a specific period.

  - Calculation: (Total Receivables Collected / Total Receivables Available for Collection) x 100

  - Importance: CEI provides insight into how effectively the collections team is converting receivables into cash.

3. Aging of Accounts Receivable:

  - Definition: Categorizes receivables based on the length of time they have been outstanding.

  - Importance: Helps identify overdue accounts and prioritize collection efforts.

4. Bad Debt Ratio:

  - Definition: The proportion of receivables deemed uncollectible.

  - Calculation: (Total Bad Debts / Total Credit Sales) x 100

  - Importance: Indicates the level of risk associated with credit sales and the effectiveness of credit policies.

5. Dispute Resolution Time:

  - Definition: The average time taken to resolve disputes with customers.

  - Importance: Timely resolution of disputes is crucial for maintaining customer relationships and ensuring prompt payments.

Setting Up Dashboards and Reports

Oracle ERP provides powerful tools for setting up dashboards and generating reports that offer real-time insights into collection performance. Here's how to effectively use these tools:

1. Dashboards:

  - Customization: Customize dashboards to display relevant KPIs and metrics. Include visual aids such as charts and graphs for easy interpretation.

  - Real-Time Data: Ensure dashboards are configured to display real-time data for up-to-date monitoring.

  - User Access: Provide access to relevant team members, ensuring they have the information needed to make informed decisions.

2. Reports:

  - Standard Reports: Utilize standard reports available in Oracle ERP, such as aging reports, collection effectiveness reports, and DSO reports.

  - Custom Reports: Develop custom reports tailored to specific business needs. These reports can focus on particular aspects of the collections process, such as region-specific performance or product-specific collections.

  - Scheduled Reports: Set up scheduled reports to be automatically generated and distributed to stakeholders. This ensures regular updates on collection performance.

Conducting Regular Performance Reviews

Regular performance reviews are essential to ensure collection strategies are effective and to make necessary adjustments. Key steps in conducting performance reviews include:

1. Review Meetings:

  - Frequency: Schedule regular meetings (e.g., monthly or quarterly) to review collection performance.

  - Participants: Include key stakeholders such as the collections team, finance managers, and senior management.

- Agenda: Focus on reviewing KPIs, identifying trends, and discussing challenges and opportunities.

2. Analyzing Trends:

- Historical Data: Analyze historical data to identify trends and patterns in collection performance.

- Comparative Analysis: Compare current performance against previous periods and industry benchmarks to gauge effectiveness.

3. Identifying Issues:

- Root Cause Analysis: Conduct root cause analysis to identify underlying issues affecting collection performance, such as process bottlenecks or systemic issues.

- Customer Feedback: Gather feedback from customers to understand any issues from their perspective that may be affecting timely payments.

Implementing Corrective Actions

When performance issues are identified, implementing corrective actions is crucial to improving collection efficiency. Steps to take include:

1. Process Improvement:

- Streamlining Processes: Identify and eliminate inefficiencies in the collections process. This may involve automating manual tasks or reconfiguring workflows.

- Training and Development: Provide additional training for the collections team to enhance their skills and knowledge.

2. Policy Adjustments:

- Credit Policies: Review and adjust credit policies to ensure they align with business objectives and market conditions.

- Payment Terms: Reevaluate payment terms offered to customers, considering shorter terms for high-risk accounts.

3. Technology Enhancements:

- Automation Tools: Invest in automation tools to improve the efficiency and accuracy of the collections process.

- Integration: Ensure seamless integration between the Accounts Receivable module and other Oracle ERP modules to enhance data flow and process consistency.

Leveraging Predictive Analytics

Predictive analytics can provide valuable insights into future collection performance and potential issues. Oracle ERP offers advanced analytics tools that can help:

1. Predictive Models:

- Develop Models: Develop predictive models to forecast collection performance based on historical data and trends.

- Scenario Analysis: Use scenario analysis to understand the impact of different strategies and decisions on collection performance.

2. Risk Assessment:

- Customer Risk Profiles: Assess the risk profiles of customers to identify those who may be more likely to default on payments.

- Proactive Measures: Implement proactive measures for high-risk accounts, such as stricter credit terms or increased monitoring.

Communicating Performance to Stakeholders

Effective communication of collection performance to stakeholders ensures transparency and alignment with business objectives. Best practices include:

1. Regular Updates:

- Frequency: Provide regular updates on collection performance, aligning with reporting cycles (e.g., monthly, quarterly).

- Format: Use clear and concise formats, such as executive summaries or visual dashboards, to present performance data.

2. Stakeholder Engagement:

- Key Stakeholders: Engage with key stakeholders, including senior management, sales teams, and finance departments, to keep them informed and involved.

- Feedback Loop: Establish a feedback loop to gather input from stakeholders and make necessary adjustments to collection strategies.

Continuous Improvement and Adaptation

The business environment is dynamic, and collection strategies must evolve to keep pace with changes. Emphasize continuous improvement and adaptation by:

1. Monitoring Market Trends:

- Industry Benchmarks: Stay informed about industry benchmarks and best practices in collections management.

- Economic Indicators: Monitor economic indicators that may impact customers' ability to pay.

2. Adapting Strategies:

- Flexibility: Maintain flexibility in collection strategies to adapt to changing market conditions and customer behaviors.

- Innovation: Encourage innovation in the collections process, leveraging new technologies and methodologies to enhance performance.

Conclusion

Monitoring collection performance is a vital component of effective Accounts Receivable management. By leveraging KPIs, dashboards, and reports, conducting regular performance reviews, implementing corrective actions, utilizing predictive analytics, and communicating with stakeholders, businesses can ensure their collections strategies are optimized. Continuous improvement and adaptation are essential to maintaining a healthy cash flow and achieving long-term financial stability.

6.2 Managing Customer Credit

Managing customer credit is a critical aspect of the accounts receivable process in Oracle ERP. Proper credit management helps businesses minimize risk, maintain healthy cash flow, and ensure that customers meet their payment obligations on time. This section covers the steps and best practices for establishing and managing customer credit limits within the Oracle ERP Accounts Receivable module.

6.2.1 Establishing Credit Limits

Establishing credit limits for customers is the first step in effective credit management. Credit limits define the maximum amount of credit that a company is willing to extend to a customer at any given time. Setting appropriate credit limits helps mitigate the risk of non-payment and ensures that the company's cash flow remains stable.

Understanding Credit Limits

A credit limit is the maximum outstanding balance that a customer is allowed to have with the company. This limit is determined based on various factors, including the customer's financial stability, payment history, credit rating, and the nature of the business relationship. Credit limits can be set at different levels, such as overall company credit limit, individual customer credit limit, or specific transaction credit limit.

Steps to Establish Credit Limits

1. Customer Assessment:

   - Before setting a credit limit, conduct a thorough assessment of the customer's financial health. This includes reviewing their credit history, payment behavior, and financial statements. Use external credit rating agencies and financial reports to gather relevant information.

- Assess the customer's industry and market conditions to understand potential risks. Some industries may have higher default rates or longer payment cycles, which should be factored into the credit limit decision.

2. Define Credit Policies:

- Establish clear credit policies that outline the criteria for setting credit limits. These policies should consider the customer's creditworthiness, the company's risk tolerance, and the strategic importance of the customer relationship.

- Define the approval process for setting and adjusting credit limits. Specify who has the authority to approve credit limits and under what circumstances adjustments can be made.

3. Calculate Credit Limit:

- Use the information gathered during the customer assessment to calculate an appropriate credit limit. This calculation should consider the customer's average monthly purchases, payment terms, and any seasonal variations in their business.

- Apply a credit scoring model to standardize the credit limit determination process. This model can assign scores based on various factors, such as payment history, financial ratios, and credit ratings, and translate these scores into recommended credit limits.

4. Document Credit Limits:

- Once the credit limit is determined, document it in the Oracle ERP system. This involves entering the credit limit information into the customer's account profile within the Accounts Receivable module.

- Ensure that all relevant stakeholders, such as sales, finance, and customer service teams, are informed of the established credit limits. This helps maintain consistency and prevents unauthorized credit extensions.

Implementing Credit Limits in Oracle ERP

Oracle ERP provides robust functionality for managing customer credit limits. The Accounts Receivable module allows businesses to define, monitor, and enforce credit limits effectively. Here are the steps to implement credit limits in Oracle ERP:

1. Define Credit Profiles:

- Create credit profiles in Oracle ERP to categorize customers based on their creditworthiness. These profiles can include predefined credit limits, credit terms, and risk classifications.

- Assign customers to appropriate credit profiles based on the results of their credit assessments. This helps streamline the credit management process and ensures consistency in credit limit application.

2. Set Credit Limits in Customer Profiles:

- Navigate to the customer profile section in the Accounts Receivable module and enter the credit limit information. This includes specifying the overall credit limit, individual transaction limits, and any specific conditions or exceptions.

- Oracle ERP allows for flexibility in setting credit limits. Businesses can define credit limits in multiple currencies, set different limits for different types of transactions, and apply credit limits at the account or site level.

3. Monitor Credit Utilization:

- Use Oracle ERP's reporting and analytics capabilities to monitor credit utilization in real time. This includes tracking outstanding balances, overdue invoices, and credit limit breaches.

- Set up automated alerts and notifications to inform relevant stakeholders when customers approach or exceed their credit limits. This enables proactive credit management and timely intervention.

4. Enforce Credit Limits:

- Configure Oracle ERP to enforce credit limits automatically during the order-to-cash process. This ensures that orders are placed on hold or rejected if they exceed the customer's credit limit.

- Implement approval workflows for credit limit exceptions. This allows authorized personnel to review and approve orders that exceed credit limits based on predefined criteria.

Best Practices for Establishing Credit Limits

1. Regularly Review Credit Limits:

 - Periodically review and update credit limits based on changes in the customer's financial condition, payment behavior, and business environment. Regular reviews help ensure that credit limits remain appropriate and reflect current risks.

 - Establish a schedule for credit limit reviews, such as quarterly or annually, and involve cross-functional teams in the review process.

2. Use Data-Driven Decision Making:

 - Leverage data analytics and credit scoring models to make informed decisions about credit limits. Use historical data, industry benchmarks, and predictive analytics to assess credit risk accurately.

 - Continuously refine credit scoring models based on feedback and new information. This helps improve the accuracy and reliability of credit limit recommendations.

3. Communicate Clearly with Customers:

 - Clearly communicate credit limits and payment terms to customers during the onboarding process. Ensure that customers understand their credit terms and any implications of exceeding their credit limits.

 - Maintain open communication with customers regarding their credit status, payment expectations, and any changes to their credit limits.

4. Balance Risk and Reward:

 - Consider the strategic importance of the customer relationship when setting credit limits. While it's essential to mitigate risk, it's also important to support business growth by extending appropriate credit to valuable customers.

 - Balance risk and reward by setting credit limits that align with the customer's potential for future business and profitability.

5. Implement Strong Internal Controls:

- Establish strong internal controls to prevent unauthorized changes to credit limits. Use role-based access controls in Oracle ERP to ensure that only authorized personnel can modify credit limit information.

- Conduct regular audits of credit limit management processes to identify and address any discrepancies or control weaknesses.

Challenges and Solutions in Establishing Credit Limits

1. Dealing with Incomplete Information:

   - Challenge: Sometimes, complete financial information may not be available for new or small customers, making it difficult to assess creditworthiness accurately.

   - Solution: Use alternative sources of information, such as trade references, industry reports, and third-party credit assessments. Consider starting with a lower credit limit and gradually increasing it based on the customer's payment behavior.

2. Managing High-Risk Customers:

   - Challenge: High-risk customers, such as those with a history of late payments or financial instability, pose a significant credit risk.

   - Solution: Implement stricter credit policies and closer monitoring for high-risk customers. Consider requiring advance payments, letters of credit, or collateral to mitigate risk.

3. Balancing Credit Limits with Sales Goals:

   - Challenge: Sales teams may push for higher credit limits to meet sales targets, potentially increasing the company's credit risk.

   - Solution: Foster collaboration between sales and finance teams to balance sales goals with risk management. Use data-driven credit assessments to support credit limit decisions and ensure alignment with the company's risk tolerance.

4. Adapting to Market Changes:

   - Challenge: Economic and market conditions can change rapidly, affecting the creditworthiness of customers and industries.

- Solution: Stay informed about market trends and adjust credit policies and limits accordingly. Use real-time data and analytics to identify emerging risks and opportunities.

By following these best practices and leveraging Oracle ERP's robust credit management capabilities, businesses can effectively establish and manage customer credit limits. This not only minimizes credit risk but also supports healthy customer relationships and sustainable business growth.

6.2.2 Credit Approval Processes

Managing customer credit effectively requires a robust and well-defined credit approval process. This process ensures that the credit extended to customers is within acceptable risk levels and aligns with the company's financial goals. In Oracle ERP, the credit approval process is an integral part of the Accounts Receivable module, providing a systematic approach to evaluate, approve, and monitor customer creditworthiness. This section delves into the key steps and best practices for setting up and managing credit approval processes within Oracle ERP.

Understanding the Credit Approval Workflow

The credit approval process in Oracle ERP typically involves multiple stages, each designed to assess and mitigate the risks associated with extending credit to customers. The workflow generally includes:

1. Credit Application Submission: Customers submit a credit application, providing essential financial and business information.

2. Initial Credit Assessment: An initial evaluation of the customer's creditworthiness based on the provided information.

3. Credit Scoring and Rating: Using predefined criteria and scoring models to assign a credit rating to the customer.

4. Credit Limit Proposal: Proposing an appropriate credit limit based on the customer's credit rating and business needs.

5. Credit Committee Review: A review by a credit committee or designated approvers to validate the proposed credit limit.

6. Approval or Rejection: The final decision to approve or reject the credit application.

7. Communication and Documentation: Communicating the decision to the customer and documenting the approval process.

Step-by-Step Credit Approval Process

Step 1: Credit Application Submission

The process begins with the customer submitting a credit application. This application should include:

- Business name and contact details

- Financial statements (balance sheet, income statement, cash flow statement)

- Trade references and credit history

- Bank references

- Business plan and projections

Oracle ERP can be configured to capture all necessary information through an online form or a manual entry process. This ensures that all required data is collected systematically.

Step 2: Initial Credit Assessment

Once the credit application is submitted, an initial assessment is conducted. This involves:

- Verifying the accuracy and completeness of the submitted information

- Checking the customer's credit history and payment behavior with other suppliers

- Evaluating the financial health of the customer using financial ratios (e.g., liquidity ratios, profitability ratios, debt ratios)

Oracle ERP offers tools to automate parts of this assessment, such as integrating with credit reporting agencies to fetch real-time credit reports and scores.

Step 3: Credit Scoring and Rating

The next step is to score and rate the customer's creditworthiness. This involves:

- Establishing a credit scoring model that considers various factors like payment history, financial strength, industry risk, and business stability

- Assigning weights to each factor based on its importance

- Calculating a composite credit score that reflects the overall risk

In Oracle ERP, you can configure credit scoring models and automate the scoring process. The system can generate a credit rating (e.g., excellent, good, fair, poor) based on the calculated score.

Step 4: Credit Limit Proposal

Based on the customer's credit rating, a credit limit is proposed. This involves:

- Determining the maximum amount of credit the company is willing to extend

- Considering the customer's purchasing history and projected sales

- Balancing the potential revenue with the associated credit risk

Oracle ERP can automate this step by setting rules and guidelines for credit limit proposals. For example, a customer with an excellent rating might be eligible for a higher credit limit compared to a customer with a fair rating.

Step 5: Credit Committee Review

The proposed credit limit is then reviewed by a credit committee or designated approvers. This step includes:

- Reviewing the credit assessment and scoring results

- Discussing any potential concerns or red flags

- Making adjustments to the proposed credit limit if necessary

In Oracle ERP, this review process can be managed through workflow automation, ensuring that the credit application moves seamlessly through the approval stages. Approvers can provide their inputs and approvals electronically.

Step 6: Approval or Rejection

After the review, a final decision is made to approve or reject the credit application. This decision is based on:

- The customer's credit rating and proposed credit limit

- Input from the credit committee or approvers

- The company's credit policy and risk appetite

Oracle ERP provides tools to document the decision-making process and ensure that all approvals are recorded for future reference. If the application is approved, the customer's credit limit is updated in the system.

Step 7: Communication and Documentation

The final step is to communicate the decision to the customer and document the approval process. This involves:

- Sending an approval or rejection notification to the customer

- Providing reasons for the decision if necessary

- Documenting the entire credit approval process for audit and compliance purposes

Oracle ERP can automate the communication process, sending out customized email notifications to customers. All documentation related to the credit approval process is stored in the system, ensuring compliance and easy retrieval during audits.

Best Practices for Effective Credit Approval Processes

To ensure the effectiveness of the credit approval process, consider the following best practices:

1. Establish Clear Credit Policies: Define clear and consistent credit policies that outline the criteria for credit approval, scoring models, and decision-making guidelines. Ensure these policies are communicated to all relevant stakeholders.

2. Automate Where Possible: Leverage Oracle ERP's automation capabilities to streamline the credit approval process. This includes automating data collection, credit scoring, workflow management, and communication.

3. Regularly Review and Update Credit Limits: Periodically review and adjust customer credit limits based on their payment behavior, financial health, and business needs. This helps manage credit risk more effectively.

4. Maintain Accurate and Up-to-Date Information: Ensure that customer information, including financial data and credit history, is accurate and up-to-date. Use Oracle ERP's integration capabilities to fetch real-time data from external sources.

5. Monitor Credit Performance: Continuously monitor the performance of customers with approved credit limits. Use Oracle ERP's reporting and analytics tools to track payment behavior, outstanding balances, and potential red flags.

6. Ensure Compliance: Adhere to regulatory requirements and industry standards related to credit management. Oracle ERP's compliance features help ensure that your credit approval processes meet legal and regulatory standards.

7. Provide Training and Support: Offer regular training and support to staff involved in the credit approval process. Ensure they are familiar with Oracle ERP's features and best practices for credit management.

By following these steps and best practices, companies can effectively manage customer credit, minimize risks, and enhance their overall financial health. Oracle ERP's robust features and automation capabilities provide a solid foundation for implementing and maintaining efficient credit approval processes.

6.2.3 Monitoring and Adjusting Credit Limits

Monitoring Credit Limits

Monitoring credit limits is a continuous process that helps businesses stay informed about their customers' credit status and make informed decisions regarding credit extensions and collections. Here are the key steps and best practices for monitoring credit limits:

1. Regular Review of Credit Reports:

  - Utilize credit reporting tools within Oracle ERP to generate regular reports on customer credit status.

  - Schedule periodic reviews, such as monthly or quarterly, to assess the creditworthiness of each customer.

  - Analyze credit scores, payment history, and outstanding balances to identify potential credit risks.

2. Setting Up Credit Alerts:

  - Configure alerts within Oracle ERP to notify relevant personnel when a customer's credit limit is approaching its threshold.

  - Use automated notifications to ensure timely action is taken before the credit limit is exceeded.

  - Implement escalation procedures for high-risk accounts, ensuring that management is aware of potential issues.

3. Tracking Payment Behavior:

  - Monitor payment behavior to detect any changes in a customer's financial stability.

- Look for patterns such as late payments, partial payments, or increased frequency of credit limit requests.

- Use this information to adjust credit limits proactively and mitigate risk.

4. Conducting Financial Health Checks:

- Perform periodic financial health checks on key customers to assess their ongoing viability.

- Utilize financial statements, industry reports, and market analysis to gain insights into a customer's financial condition.

- Integrate this information into the credit management process to ensure credit limits reflect current risk levels.

5. Utilizing Customer Credit Histories:

- Maintain comprehensive records of each customer's credit history within the AR module.

- Use historical data to predict future payment behavior and adjust credit limits accordingly.

- Consider both positive and negative trends to create a balanced credit policy.

Adjusting Credit Limits

Adjusting credit limits based on ongoing monitoring is essential to maintain a dynamic and responsive credit management strategy. Here are the steps to adjust credit limits effectively:

1. Reviewing Credit Limit Requests:

- Establish a standardized process for customers to request changes to their credit limits.

- Require customers to provide financial documentation and justification for the requested increase.

- Evaluate requests based on the customer's credit history, payment behavior, and overall financial health.

2. Evaluating Credit Risk:

  - Assess the credit risk associated with each customer before adjusting their credit limits.

  - Use risk assessment tools within Oracle ERP to calculate risk scores and potential exposure.

  - Consider factors such as the customer's industry, market conditions, and historical payment performance.

3. Approving or Declining Adjustments:

  - Implement a structured approval process for credit limit adjustments.

  - Involve multiple stakeholders, including sales, finance, and senior management, in the decision-making process.

  - Document the rationale for approval or decline to maintain transparency and consistency.

4. Updating Credit Limits in Oracle ERP:

  - Once approved, update the customer's credit limit within the AR module.

  - Ensure that all relevant fields are updated to reflect the new credit limit accurately.

  - Notify the customer of the change and provide updated credit terms if necessary.

5. Communicating Changes to Internal Teams:

  - Inform internal teams, including sales, collections, and customer service, of any changes to credit limits.

  - Ensure that all teams are aware of the new limits to avoid confusion and maintain a unified approach.

  - Use internal communication tools and meetings to keep everyone updated on significant changes.

Best Practices for Monitoring and Adjusting Credit Limits

To ensure an effective credit management process, businesses should adopt the following best practices:

1. Leverage Technology:

- Use advanced features within Oracle ERP to automate credit monitoring and adjustment processes.

- Implement predictive analytics and machine learning to identify credit risks early and take proactive measures.

- Utilize dashboards and real-time reporting to stay informed about credit status and trends.

2. Establish Clear Policies:

- Develop and document clear policies for credit monitoring and adjustments.

- Ensure that all employees involved in credit management understand and adhere to these policies.

- Regularly review and update policies to reflect changes in business strategy and market conditions.

3. Maintain Customer Relationships:

- Foster strong relationships with customers to gain insights into their financial health and credit needs.

- Communicate regularly with customers to address any concerns and negotiate credit terms.

- Use customer feedback to improve the credit management process and enhance customer satisfaction.

4. Train and Educate Staff:

- Provide ongoing training and education for employees involved in credit management.

- Ensure that staff members are proficient in using Oracle ERP tools and understanding credit policies.

- Encourage continuous learning and professional development to keep up with industry best practices.

5. Monitor Market Conditions:

- Stay informed about market conditions and economic trends that could impact customers' creditworthiness.

- Use external data sources, such as industry reports and economic forecasts, to supplement internal credit assessments.

- Adjust credit policies and limits based on changes in the market to mitigate potential risks.

Case Study: Successful Credit Limit Adjustment

To illustrate the importance and impact of effective credit limit monitoring and adjustment, consider the following case study:

Company Background:

A mid-sized manufacturing company, XYZ Corp., has a diverse customer base and relies heavily on extending credit to its customers to drive sales. The company uses Oracle ERP to manage its accounts receivable processes.

Challenge:

XYZ Corp. noticed an increase in late payments and bad debts from several key customers. The company's existing credit limits were no longer reflective of the customers' current financial health, leading to increased financial risk.

Solution:

XYZ Corp. implemented a comprehensive credit monitoring and adjustment strategy within Oracle ERP, focusing on the following steps:

- Conducted regular reviews of customer credit reports and payment behavior.

- Set up automated alerts for approaching credit limits and delinquent accounts.

- Established a standardized process for evaluating and approving credit limit adjustment requests.

- Involved multiple stakeholders in the decision-making process to ensure a balanced approach.

- Communicated changes to credit limits to all relevant internal teams.

Outcome:

By implementing these measures, XYZ Corp. achieved the following results:

- Reduced the incidence of late payments and bad debts by 20%.

- Improved cash flow and financial stability.

- Enhanced customer satisfaction by maintaining appropriate credit limits and avoiding unnecessary credit denials.

- Increased efficiency in credit management processes through automation and standardized procedures.

In conclusion, managing and adjusting credit limits within the Oracle ERP Accounts Receivable module is a critical aspect of maintaining a healthy financial environment. By leveraging technology, establishing clear policies, maintaining strong customer relationships, and staying informed about market conditions, businesses can effectively monitor and adjust credit limits to minimize risk and optimize cash flow.

6.3 Handling Delinquent Accounts

Managing delinquent accounts is a critical aspect of the Accounts Receivable (AR) function within Oracle ERP. Delinquent accounts can significantly impact an organization's cash flow and financial health. Therefore, it is crucial to have a systematic approach to identify, manage, and mitigate the risks associated with delinquent accounts.

6.3.1 Identifying Delinquent Accounts

Understanding Delinquency

Delinquency occurs when customers fail to meet their payment obligations within the agreed terms. Identifying delinquent accounts early helps in taking timely actions to recover dues and minimize potential losses. Delinquency can be classified based on the duration of the overdue payment:

- Current (0-30 days)

- Late (31-60 days)

- Delinquent (61-90 days)

- Seriously Delinquent (90+ days)

Setting Up Criteria for Delinquency

Oracle ERP provides flexible criteria to identify delinquent accounts. These criteria can be based on various factors such as:

- Payment Due Date: Comparing the payment due date with the current date.

- Invoice Age: Ageing of invoices to track overdue days.

- Customer Payment History: Analyzing past payment behaviors.

- Credit Terms: Considering the terms agreed upon with the customer.

Using Aging Reports

Aging reports are essential tools in Oracle ERP for identifying delinquent accounts. These reports categorize outstanding invoices based on the number of days they are overdue. The typical format of an aging report includes:

- Current: Invoices not yet due.

- 1-30 Days Past Due: Invoices overdue by up to 30 days.

- 31-60 Days Past Due: Invoices overdue by 31 to 60 days.

- 61-90 Days Past Due: Invoices overdue by 61 to 90 days.

- 90+ Days Past Due: Invoices overdue by more than 90 days.

Aging reports help AR managers quickly identify accounts that require immediate attention and prioritize collection efforts.

Configuring Delinquency Notifications

Oracle ERP allows the configuration of automated delinquency notifications. These notifications can be sent to customers and internal AR teams to alert them about overdue payments. Notifications can be configured to trigger based on:

- Invoice Due Date: Sending reminders a few days before or after the due date.

- Thresholds: Setting specific thresholds for sending reminders (e.g., 30 days overdue).

Implementing Delinquency Scoring

Delinquency scoring is a method used to assess the risk level associated with each customer based on their payment behavior. Oracle ERP can be configured to calculate a delinquency score for each customer by considering factors such as:

- Payment History: Frequency and extent of late payments.

- Invoice Amount: Larger overdue amounts may indicate higher risk.

- Customer Segment: Certain segments may have different risk profiles.

- Credit Limit Utilization: High utilization of credit limits could indicate potential payment issues.

Case Study: Identifying Delinquent Accounts in XYZ Corporation

XYZ Corporation implemented a robust system within Oracle ERP to identify delinquent accounts. They configured aging reports to run weekly, categorizing overdue invoices into specific buckets. Additionally, they set up automated email notifications to alert customers of upcoming and overdue payments. By implementing a delinquency scoring model, XYZ Corporation could prioritize high-risk accounts for immediate follow-up.

Challenges in Identifying Delinquent Accounts

Despite having automated tools and reports, organizations may face challenges in identifying delinquent accounts:

- Data Accuracy: Ensuring that customer and invoice data is up-to-date and accurate.

- Integration Issues: Seamless integration between AR and other modules like Sales and Billing.

- Customer Communication: Ensuring effective communication channels for reminders and notifications.

- System Limitations: Configuring Oracle ERP to handle complex scenarios and customized reporting needs.

Best Practices for Identifying Delinquent Accounts

1. Regular Monitoring: Schedule regular reviews of aging reports and delinquency scores.

2. Automation: Utilize Oracle ERP's automation features for notifications and reporting.

3. Data Quality: Maintain accurate and up-to-date customer and invoice records.

4. Customer Engagement: Establish clear communication channels with customers regarding payment terms and reminders.

5. Continuous Improvement: Periodically review and update delinquency criteria and scoring models.

By implementing these practices, organizations can effectively identify delinquent accounts, allowing them to take proactive measures to manage and mitigate financial risks.

Conclusion

Identifying delinquent accounts is a foundational step in managing the Accounts Receivable process. With Oracle ERP's robust tools and features, organizations can efficiently track overdue payments, prioritize collection efforts, and maintain healthy cash flow. Accurate identification and timely actions are crucial to minimizing the impact of delinquent accounts on the organization's financial stability.

6.3.2 Collection Actions for Delinquent Accounts

Managing delinquent accounts is a critical aspect of maintaining a healthy cash flow and ensuring the financial stability of an organization. Delinquent accounts, if not handled effectively, can lead to significant financial losses. Therefore, it is essential to have a robust strategy for taking collection actions on delinquent accounts. This section outlines the best practices, strategies, and steps for managing and collecting from delinquent accounts.

Understanding Delinquent Accounts

Before diving into the collection actions, it is important to understand what constitutes a delinquent account. A delinquent account is one where the customer has not made the payment within the agreed-upon terms. The aging of the receivables, which refers to how long the invoices have been outstanding, plays a crucial role in categorizing the accounts into various delinquency stages, such as 30, 60, 90, or more days past due.

Importance of Early Intervention

Early intervention is key to managing delinquent accounts. The earlier you begin the collection process, the higher the chances of recovering the overdue amounts. Proactive communication with the customer as soon as an invoice becomes overdue can prevent the situation from escalating. Here are some steps to take for early intervention:

1. Automated Reminders: Set up automated email or SMS reminders that notify customers of their overdue invoices. These reminders should be polite and include all necessary details, such as the invoice number, due date, and outstanding amount.

2. Personalized Follow-Up: If the automated reminders do not elicit a response, follow up with a personalized email or phone call. This personal touch can often prompt a quicker response from the customer.

3. Payment Plan Offers: For customers facing financial difficulties, offer to set up a payment plan that allows them to pay the overdue amount in installments. This shows flexibility and willingness to work with the customer, which can improve the chances of recovery.

Collection Strategies for Delinquent Accounts

Effective collection strategies are essential for handling delinquent accounts. Here are several strategies that can be employed:

1. Segmentation of Delinquent Accounts: Segmenting delinquent accounts based on the age of the receivable, the customer's payment history, and the amount owed can help in prioritizing collection efforts. High-value accounts or those with a history of timely payments should be handled with more care.

2. Dunning Process: Implement a structured dunning process, which is a series of communications (emails, letters, phone calls) that escalate in tone and urgency as the account remains unpaid. This process should be clearly defined and consistently followed.

3. Customer Relationship Management (CRM): Use a CRM system to track all interactions with delinquent customers. This helps in maintaining a record of communications, promises made by customers, and actions taken, which can be valuable in case of disputes.

4. Payment Reminders and Follow-Ups: Regular payment reminders and follow-ups should be part of the collection strategy. These should be sent at predetermined intervals and should become more frequent as the account becomes more overdue.

5. Incentives for Early Payment: Offering incentives for early payment, such as discounts or additional services, can encourage customers to settle their overdue accounts sooner.

Escalation of Collection Actions

When initial collection efforts fail, it is necessary to escalate the actions to recover the overdue amounts. The escalation process should be clearly defined and include the following steps:

1. Final Demand Letter: Send a final demand letter to the customer, which clearly states the overdue amount, the consequences of non-payment, and a final deadline for payment. This letter should be formal and convey the seriousness of the situation.

2. Involving a Collections Agency: If the customer does not respond to the final demand letter, consider involving a professional collections agency. Collections agencies have the expertise and resources to recover overdue amounts. However, it is important to choose a reputable agency and understand the fees involved.

3. Legal Action: As a last resort, legal action can be taken against the customer. This may involve filing a lawsuit or seeking a court judgment for the unpaid amount. Legal action should be considered carefully, as it can be time-consuming and costly.

Monitoring and Adjusting Credit Limits

Monitoring and adjusting credit limits based on the customer's payment behavior is an important part of managing delinquent accounts. Here are the steps to follow:

1. Regular Review of Credit Limits: Conduct regular reviews of credit limits for all customers. Customers who frequently become delinquent may require a reduction in their credit limit.

2. Temporary Credit Holds: Place temporary credit holds on accounts that are significantly overdue. This prevents the customer from making additional purchases until the overdue amount is settled.

3. Permanent Adjustments: For customers who consistently fail to pay on time, consider making permanent adjustments to their credit limits or requiring them to pay upfront for future purchases.

Customer Communication and Relationship Management

Maintaining a good relationship with customers, even when they are delinquent, is important for future business. Here are some tips for effective communication and relationship management:

1. Polite and Professional Communication: Always maintain a polite and professional tone in all communications. Aggressive or threatening language can damage the customer relationship and reduce the chances of recovery.

2. Understanding Customer Circumstances: Take the time to understand the reasons behind the customer's delinquency. In some cases, customers may be facing temporary financial difficulties and may appreciate a more empathetic approach.

3. Negotiating Payment Terms: Be open to negotiating payment terms that are feasible for the customer. This can include extending the payment deadline or setting up a payment plan.

4. Regular Check-Ins: Schedule regular check-ins with customers who have overdue accounts. This helps in keeping the lines of communication open and demonstrates your commitment to resolving the issue.

Using Technology for Collection Management

Leveraging technology can greatly enhance the efficiency and effectiveness of the collection process. Here are some ways technology can be utilized:

1. Accounts Receivable Software: Use specialized accounts receivable software that offers features such as automated reminders, aging reports, and payment tracking. This can

streamline the collection process and provide valuable insights into the status of overdue accounts.

2. Customer Portals: Implement customer portals that allow customers to view their account status, make payments, and communicate with your team. This can make it easier for customers to settle their overdue accounts.

3. Data Analytics: Use data analytics to identify patterns and trends in delinquent accounts. This can help in developing targeted collection strategies and improving overall collection performance.

Conclusion

Handling delinquent accounts requires a well-structured approach that combines early intervention, effective collection strategies, and escalation processes. By understanding the reasons behind delinquency, maintaining good customer relationships, and leveraging technology, organizations can improve their chances of recovering overdue amounts and maintaining a healthy cash flow. Implementing these best practices can help in managing delinquent accounts more efficiently and ensuring the financial stability of the organization.

6.3.3 Writing Off Bad Debts

In the realm of accounts receivable, writing off bad debts is an inevitable process that every business must contend with at some point. Despite robust credit policies and diligent collection efforts, there will always be some customers who are unable or unwilling to pay their outstanding balances. Writing off these uncollectible accounts is essential for maintaining accurate financial records and ensuring that the company's financial statements reflect its true financial position. This section delves into the intricacies of identifying, processing, and accounting for bad debts in the Oracle ERP system.

Understanding Bad Debts

Bad debts are amounts owed by customers that are deemed uncollectible after all reasonable efforts to collect them have been exhausted. These debts can arise from various situations, such as customer bankruptcy, disputes over goods or services, or simply a customer's inability to pay due to financial difficulties. Recognizing and writing off these bad debts promptly helps in maintaining the integrity of financial statements and ensures that the company's revenue and receivables are not overstated.

Identifying Bad Debts

The first step in the process is identifying which accounts are truly uncollectible. This involves a detailed review of the accounts receivable aging report, which categorizes outstanding invoices by the length of time they have been overdue. In Oracle ERP, the aging report can be generated to provide insights into the status of receivables. Accounts that have remained unpaid for a significant period, despite multiple collection efforts, are potential candidates for write-off.

Indicators of Bad Debts:

- Prolonged Overdue Status: Invoices that are significantly overdue, typically beyond 90 or 120 days, depending on the company's credit policy.

- Failed Collection Efforts: Multiple attempts to collect the debt, including phone calls, emails, and formal collection letters, have been unsuccessful.

- Customer Insolvency: The customer has declared bankruptcy or is in financial distress, making it unlikely that the debt will be paid.

- Legal Action: Even after legal proceedings, the likelihood of recovery is minimal or the cost of further legal action outweighs the potential recovery.

Approval Process for Write-Offs

Once potential bad debts have been identified, the next step is to obtain the necessary approvals to write them off. This process typically involves several layers of authorization to ensure that write-offs are justified and properly documented.

Steps in the Approval Process:

1. Initial Review: The accounts receivable team conducts an initial review of the accounts identified as uncollectible.

2. Documentation: Detailed documentation of all collection efforts and reasons for considering the debt as bad are compiled.

3. Managerial Approval: The documentation is reviewed by the accounts receivable manager or department head for preliminary approval.

4. Executive Approval: For larger amounts, approval from senior management or the finance director may be required.

5. Audit Committee Approval: In some organizations, the audit committee or board of directors must approve significant write-offs to ensure governance and oversight.

Oracle ERP can streamline this process by automating workflow approvals, ensuring that all necessary stakeholders review and approve the write-off before it is finalized.

Processing the Write-Off in Oracle ERP

After obtaining the required approvals, the actual process of writing off the bad debt in Oracle ERP involves several steps to ensure that the transaction is accurately recorded in the financial system.

Steps to Write-Off Bad Debts in Oracle ERP:

1. Adjusting the Customer Account: The first step is to create an adjustment to reduce the customer's outstanding balance. This is done by creating a debit memo or a write-off adjustment in the accounts receivable module.

2. Recording the Write-Off: The write-off is then recorded in the general ledger. This typically involves debiting the bad debt expense account and crediting the accounts receivable account.

3. Updating Reports: The accounts receivable aging report and other relevant financial reports are updated to reflect the reduction in outstanding receivables.

4. Notifying the Customer: Although the debt is written off, it is good practice to notify the customer that their account has been adjusted, both as a record and to maintain transparency.

Example Journal Entry for Writing Off Bad Debt:

- Debit: Bad Debt Expense

- Credit: Accounts Receivable

Oracle ERP provides robust functionality to handle these transactions, ensuring that all entries are accurately recorded and reflected in the company's financial statements.

Financial Reporting and Impact

Writing off bad debts has a direct impact on a company's financial statements, particularly on the income statement and the balance sheet. Understanding these impacts is crucial for financial analysis and reporting.

Impact on Financial Statements:

- Income Statement: The bad debt expense reduces the net income for the period. It is important to monitor the bad debt expense as a percentage of sales to gauge the effectiveness of credit policies and collection efforts.

- Balance Sheet: The accounts receivable balance is reduced, which also affects the total current assets. This reduction must be carefully monitored to ensure that the company maintains sufficient liquidity.

Regularly reviewing and analyzing the bad debt expense helps in refining credit policies and improving future collection efforts. Oracle ERP's reporting tools can be utilized to generate detailed reports on bad debts, providing insights for management to make informed decisions.

Best Practices for Managing Bad Debts

To minimize the occurrence of bad debts, it is essential to implement effective credit management and collection strategies. Here are some best practices that can help:

1. Rigorous Credit Evaluation: Conduct thorough credit checks before extending credit to new customers.

2. Clear Credit Policies: Establish and communicate clear credit policies to all customers.

3. Proactive Collections: Implement proactive collection strategies, such as early payment discounts and regular follow-ups on overdue accounts.

4. Regular Review: Regularly review the accounts receivable aging report and take timely action on overdue accounts.

5. Customer Relationship Management: Maintain good relationships with customers to encourage timely payments and resolve disputes quickly.

By adopting these best practices and leveraging the capabilities of Oracle ERP, businesses can effectively manage their accounts receivable, reduce the incidence of bad debts, and ensure healthier cash flows.

In conclusion, writing off bad debts is a critical aspect of accounts receivable management that requires careful identification, thorough documentation, and proper authorization. By following the outlined steps and best practices, companies can maintain accurate financial records and improve their overall financial health. Oracle ERP provides the necessary tools and functionalities to streamline this process, ensuring that bad debts are handled efficiently and effectively.

CHAPTER VII
Reporting and Analysis

7.1 Standard Reports in Accounts Receivable

7.1.1 Overview of Available Reports

In the Oracle ERP Accounts Receivable module, reporting is a critical component that enables businesses to track and analyze their financial data effectively. The module offers a comprehensive suite of standard reports designed to provide detailed insights into various aspects of accounts receivable operations. These reports help organizations monitor cash flow, manage customer accounts, assess credit risk, and ensure compliance with financial regulations.

The Importance of Standard Reports

Standard reports in the Accounts Receivable module are pre-built templates that offer consistent and reliable data output. These reports are essential for several reasons:

1. Accuracy and Consistency: Standard reports ensure that data is presented in a consistent format, reducing the risk of errors and discrepancies. This consistency is vital for accurate financial analysis and decision-making.

2. Time Efficiency: Using predefined templates saves time compared to creating reports from scratch. Users can quickly generate reports with the required information without spending hours on data compilation and formatting.

3. Compliance and Audit: Standard reports are designed to meet regulatory requirements and audit standards. They provide the necessary documentation for financial audits and help ensure compliance with accounting principles and industry regulations.

4. Actionable Insights: By providing detailed and accurate data, standard reports enable businesses to identify trends, assess performance, and make informed decisions. These insights are crucial for effective accounts receivable management and overall financial health.

Key Standard Reports in Accounts Receivable

The Oracle ERP Accounts Receivable module offers a variety of standard reports, each tailored to specific aspects of accounts receivable management. Some of the key reports include:

1. Aging Reports: Aging reports categorize outstanding receivables based on the length of time they have been unpaid. These reports are crucial for identifying overdue invoices and managing collections effectively.

2. Customer Account Statements: These statements provide a detailed summary of transactions for each customer, including invoices, payments, and outstanding balances. They are essential for maintaining accurate customer records and communication.

3. Invoice Register: The invoice register lists all invoices generated within a specified period. It includes details such as invoice numbers, dates, customer names, and amounts. This report helps track billing activities and ensure all invoices are accounted for.

4. Receipt Register: Similar to the invoice register, the receipt register records all receipts received within a specified period. It provides details on payment dates, amounts, and the corresponding invoices. This report is crucial for cash flow management.

5. Sales Reports: Sales reports provide an overview of sales activities, including the number of sales orders processed, total sales amounts, and sales trends over time. These reports help assess sales performance and identify opportunities for growth.

6. Credit Reports: Credit reports analyze customer credit limits, outstanding balances, and credit risk. They help businesses manage credit exposure and make informed credit decisions.

7. Collection Reports: Collection reports track the status of collection efforts, including overdue invoices, collection actions taken, and outstanding amounts. These reports are essential for monitoring collection performance and improving cash flow.

8. Tax Reports: Tax reports provide detailed information on tax liabilities and payments, ensuring compliance with tax regulations. They include data on tax codes, tax amounts, and jurisdictions.

Generating Standard Reports

Generating standard reports in the Accounts Receivable module is a straightforward process. Users can access the reporting functionality through the Oracle ERP interface, where they can select the desired report template and specify the parameters for the report. The steps typically involve:

1. Navigating to the Reporting Section: Users access the reporting section of the Accounts Receivable module through the main menu or a dedicated reporting dashboard.

2. Selecting the Report Template: The module offers a list of available standard report templates. Users select the template that matches their reporting needs.

3. Setting Report Parameters: Users specify the parameters for the report, such as date ranges, customer names, invoice numbers, and other relevant criteria. These parameters help filter the data and customize the report output.

4. Generating the Report: Once the parameters are set, users can generate the report by clicking a button or selecting an option from the menu. The system processes the data and generates the report in the chosen format (e.g., PDF, Excel, HTML).

5. Reviewing and Analyzing the Report: After the report is generated, users can review the data, analyze the results, and use the insights to make informed decisions. They can also save, print, or share the report as needed.

Customizing Report Templates

While standard reports provide a robust foundation for accounts receivable reporting, businesses may have unique requirements that necessitate customization. The Oracle ERP Accounts Receivable module allows users to customize report templates to meet their specific needs. Customization options include:

1. Adding or Removing Fields: Users can modify the report layout by adding or removing fields to include the necessary information. For example, they may add additional customer details or remove non-essential fields to streamline the report.

2. Changing Report Layouts: Users can adjust the layout and formatting of the report to improve readability and presentation. This may include changing column widths, font styles, and header formatting.

3. Applying Filters and Sorting: Custom filters and sorting options allow users to organize the data in a way that best suits their analysis needs. For instance, they can filter reports by specific customer segments or sort invoices by due dates.

4. Incorporating Visual Elements: Users can enhance reports with visual elements such as charts, graphs, and tables. These visual aids help convey complex data more effectively and make the reports more engaging.

5. Saving Customized Templates: Once a report template is customized, users can save it for future use. This feature allows for quick access to frequently used custom reports, saving time and effort in report generation.

Best Practices for Using Standard Reports

To maximize the benefits of standard reports in the Accounts Receivable module, businesses should follow these best practices:

1. Regular Review and Monitoring: Regularly review and monitor standard reports to stay updated on accounts receivable performance. This helps identify issues early and take corrective actions promptly.

2. Consistency in Reporting: Ensure consistency in report generation by using the same parameters and templates for similar reports. This consistency improves data accuracy and comparability over time.

3. Training and Support: Provide training and support to users on how to generate and interpret standard reports. A well-trained team can effectively utilize reporting tools to make informed decisions.

4. Integrate Reports with Other Modules: Leverage the integration capabilities of Oracle ERP to combine accounts receivable reports with data from other modules. This holistic view enhances overall financial analysis and decision-making.

5. Regularly Update Report Templates: Periodically review and update report templates to reflect changes in business processes, reporting requirements, and regulatory standards. Keeping templates up-to-date ensures relevance and accuracy.

By understanding and utilizing the standard reports available in the Oracle ERP Accounts Receivable module, businesses can gain valuable insights into their financial operations, improve cash flow management, and ensure compliance with regulatory requirements. These reports are indispensable tools for effective accounts receivable management and overall business success.

7.1.2 Generating Standard Reports

Generating standard reports in the Accounts Receivable (AR) module of Oracle ERP is a critical function for effective financial management, offering insights into the status of customer accounts, receivables aging, collection performance, and overall financial health. This section will delve into the step-by-step process of generating these reports, detailing the available report types, the importance of each, and how to customize them to meet specific business needs.

Overview of Report Types

Before we dive into the mechanics of generating reports, it's essential to understand the different types of standard reports available in the AR module. Commonly used reports include:

- Aging Reports: These reports provide a breakdown of receivables by age, helping businesses identify overdue invoices and manage collections more effectively.

- Customer Balance Reports: These reports show the current balance for each customer, offering insights into outstanding receivables.

- Transaction History Reports: These reports track all transactions related to AR, including invoices, payments, and adjustments.

- Receivables Reconciliation Reports: These reports help reconcile AR balances with the general ledger, ensuring data accuracy and consistency.

- Cash Receipts and Application Reports: These reports provide details on cash receipts and how they have been applied to customer accounts.

- Dunning Reports: These reports assist in the collections process by highlighting overdue accounts and generating dunning letters.

Steps to Generate Standard Reports

1. Accessing the Reporting Interface:

   - Navigate to the Accounts Receivable module in Oracle ERP.

   - Select the "Reports" option from the main menu.

   - Choose the specific report type you wish to generate from the list of available reports.

2. Selecting Report Parameters:

   - Each report will have a set of parameters that need to be defined. Common parameters include:

   - Date Range: Specify the start and end dates for the report.

   - Customer Information: Choose whether to include all customers or filter by specific customers.

   - Transaction Types: Select the types of transactions to be included (e.g., invoices, payments, adjustments).

   - Currency: If your business deals in multiple currencies, select the currency for the report.

3. Customizing Report Layout:

   - Oracle ERP allows for customization of the report layout to better meet the needs of your business. This can include:

   - Adding or Removing Fields: Modify which data fields are included in the report.

   - Changing Data Grouping: Adjust how data is grouped (e.g., by customer, by date).

   - Applying Filters: Set filters to narrow down the report results (e.g., only showing overdue invoices).

4. Running the Report:

- Once all parameters and customizations are set, click the "Run" button to generate the report.

- Oracle ERP will process the request and generate the report, which can then be viewed on-screen or exported to various formats (e.g., PDF, Excel).

5. Reviewing and Analyzing the Report:

  - After the report is generated, review the data to ensure it meets your requirements.

- Look for any discrepancies or unexpected results that might indicate data entry errors or issues with the AR processes.

6. Scheduling Reports:

- For reports that need to be generated regularly, Oracle ERP offers the option to schedule reports.

- Define the frequency (e.g., daily, weekly, monthly) and the system will automatically generate and distribute the report as per the schedule.

Practical Use Cases and Benefits

Generating standard reports in the AR module provides numerous benefits, including:

1. Improved Financial Visibility:

- Regularly generated reports offer a clear view of the financial status of receivables, helping management make informed decisions.

2. Enhanced Collections Management:

- Aging reports and dunning reports support effective collections by identifying overdue accounts and prompting timely follow-up actions.

3. Accurate Financial Reporting:

- Receivables reconciliation reports ensure that AR balances are accurately reflected in the general ledger, supporting overall financial integrity.

4. Strategic Customer Insights:

- Customer balance reports and transaction history reports provide valuable insights into customer behavior and payment patterns, aiding in strategic planning and customer relationship management.

5. Efficient Cash Flow Management:

- Reports on cash receipts and applications help track incoming cash flows and ensure that payments are properly applied, supporting efficient cash flow management.

Customizing Standard Reports

While Oracle ERP provides a robust set of standard reports, businesses often have unique requirements that necessitate customization. Customizing reports ensures that the information presented is relevant and actionable.

1. Using Report Builder:

- Oracle's Report Builder tool allows users to create custom report templates.

- Users can drag and drop fields, apply filters, and design the layout to match specific reporting needs.

2. Incorporating Business-Specific Metrics:

- Custom reports can include business-specific metrics and KPIs not covered in standard reports.

- This might include custom aging buckets, industry-specific compliance metrics, or detailed cash flow projections.

3. Data Visualization:

- Enhancing reports with visual elements like charts, graphs, and dashboards can make the data more accessible and easier to interpret.

- Oracle ERP's BI (Business Intelligence) tools facilitate the creation of visually rich reports.

Best Practices for Generating Standard Reports

1. Regular Review and Maintenance:

- Regularly review and update report parameters to ensure they reflect the current business environment.

- Periodically review the list of generated reports to eliminate any that are no longer relevant.

2. Training and Support:

  - Ensure that all relevant staff are trained on how to generate and interpret AR reports.

  - Provide ongoing support to help users troubleshoot issues and make the most of the reporting capabilities.

3. Data Quality and Accuracy:

  - Emphasize the importance of data quality in the AR process, as inaccurate data can lead to misleading reports.

  - Implement regular data audits to identify and correct discrepancies.

4. Integration with Other Systems:

  - Ensure that the AR module is properly integrated with other financial systems to provide a comprehensive view of financial performance.

  - Leverage integration to pull in data from sales, inventory, and procurement for more holistic reporting.

Conclusion

Generating standard reports in the Accounts Receivable module of Oracle ERP is a fundamental process that supports effective financial management and decision-making. By understanding the different types of reports available, the steps to generate them, and the customization options, businesses can leverage these tools to gain valuable insights, improve collections, ensure compliance, and enhance overall financial health. Implementing best practices and leveraging the full capabilities of Oracle ERP's reporting tools will ensure that the AR team can provide accurate, timely, and actionable information to support the organization's strategic goals.

7.1.3 Customizing Report Templates

Customizing report templates in the Accounts Receivable (AR) module of Oracle ERP allows organizations to tailor their reports to meet specific business needs and preferences. This customization can improve the clarity, relevance, and usefulness of reports, making it easier for stakeholders to understand and act upon the information presented. This section will guide you through the process of customizing report templates in the AR module, covering essential steps, tips, and best practices.

Understanding the Need for Customization

Every organization has unique reporting requirements driven by various factors such as industry standards, regulatory requirements, internal policies, and specific stakeholder needs. Standard reports provided by Oracle ERP offer a solid foundation, but they might not cover all aspects or present information in the most useful format for every situation. Customization allows you to:

- Highlight critical data points specific to your organization.

- Organize information in a more logical or actionable format.

- Add or remove fields to better align with your business processes.

- Improve the visual presentation of reports to enhance readability and comprehension.

Steps to Customize Report Templates

1. Identify Reporting Requirements

  - Engage Stakeholders: Collaborate with key stakeholders, including finance teams, auditors, and management, to understand their specific reporting needs.

  - Define Objectives: Clearly outline the objectives of the report, such as compliance, performance tracking, or operational insights.

2. Access the Report Template

  - Navigate to the Reports Section: In the Oracle ERP AR module, navigate to the reports section where the standard templates are stored.

- Select the Report to Customize: Choose the standard report template that closely matches your requirements as a starting point.

3. Use the Oracle BI Publisher Tool

- Open BI Publisher: Oracle BI Publisher (BIP) is a robust tool integrated within Oracle ERP for designing and customizing report templates.

- Load the Template: Load the selected report template into BI Publisher to begin customization.

4. Modify the Data Model

- Review Data Sources: Ensure that all necessary data sources are included in the data model. Add any additional data sources required for your customized report.

- Adjust Data Fields: Modify existing data fields or add new ones to capture all relevant information. This might include adding fields for specific financial metrics, customer details, or transaction types.

5. Design the Layout

- Customize Layout Components: Use BI Publisher's layout editor to arrange data fields, tables, charts, and other components. Adjust the layout to improve readability and highlight key information.

- Add Custom Elements: Incorporate logos, headers, footers, and other branding elements to align the report with your organization's standards.

- Use Conditional Formatting: Apply conditional formatting to highlight important data points, such as overdue invoices or high-value transactions, using colors or icons.

6. Incorporate Calculations and Formulas

- Add Calculated Fields: Define calculated fields to include custom calculations, such as aging buckets, percentage changes, or custom KPIs.

- Use Formulas: Incorporate complex formulas to derive meaningful insights from raw data. For example, you can calculate the average collection period or the invoice to payment ratio.

7. Test the Custom Report

- Run Sample Reports: Generate sample reports using historical data to verify the accuracy and completeness of the customized template.

- Validate Data Integrity: Ensure that all data is correctly pulled and displayed as intended. Check for any discrepancies or missing information.

- Gather Feedback: Present the sample reports to stakeholders for feedback and make necessary adjustments based on their input.

8. Deploy and Maintain the Custom Template

- Save and Deploy: Once finalized, save the customized template and deploy it within the Oracle ERP system.

- Schedule Reports: Set up automated scheduling for regular generation and distribution of the custom reports to relevant stakeholders.

- Regular Updates: Periodically review and update the custom template to reflect changes in reporting requirements, business processes, or regulatory standards.

Best Practices for Customizing Report Templates

- Consistency: Maintain a consistent format and design across all custom reports to ensure uniformity and ease of interpretation.

- Simplicity: Avoid over-complicating the report layout. Use clear, concise, and straightforward formats to present information effectively.

- Relevance: Focus on including only relevant data that meets the specific needs of the report's audience. Avoid cluttering the report with unnecessary information.

- Visualization: Utilize charts, graphs, and other visual aids to present data in an easily digestible format. Visualizations can help highlight trends, patterns, and anomalies.

- Security: Ensure that sensitive data is appropriately protected. Implement access controls to restrict who can view or modify the custom reports.

- Documentation: Document the customization process, including any changes made to the data model, layout, and formulas. This documentation can be invaluable for future reference and troubleshooting.

Examples of Customized Reports

1. Customer Aging Report

   - Purpose: To track overdue invoices and analyze the aging of receivables.

   - Customization: Include aging buckets (e.g., 0-30 days, 31-60 days), highlight overdue invoices, and add columns for contact information and payment terms.

2. Daily Sales Outstanding (DSO) Report

   - Purpose: To measure the average number of days it takes to collect payment after a sale.

   - Customization: Calculate DSO using custom formulas, present data in a trend line chart, and provide comparisons with industry benchmarks.

3. Invoice Dispute Report

   - Purpose: To monitor and manage disputed invoices.

   - Customization: Include fields for dispute reasons, status, and resolution timelines. Use conditional formatting to highlight unresolved disputes beyond a certain threshold.

4. Revenue Recognition Report

   - Purpose: To comply with revenue recognition standards and track recognized revenue.

   - Customization: Include fields for revenue recognition criteria, recognized and deferred revenue amounts, and period comparisons.

Conclusion

Customizing report templates in the Oracle ERP Accounts Receivable module empowers organizations to create tailored reports that meet specific business needs and enhance decision-making. By following a structured customization process and adhering to best practices, you can develop reports that provide valuable insights, ensure compliance, and support effective financial management. Regularly reviewing and updating these custom reports ensures they remain relevant and aligned with evolving business requirements.

7.2 Financial Analysis and Metrics

7.2.1 Key Performance Indicators (KPIs)

Key Performance Indicators (KPIs) are critical metrics used to evaluate the effectiveness and efficiency of various business processes, including Accounts Receivable (AR). In the context of AR, KPIs provide insights into the financial health of the organization, the efficiency of the collections process, and the overall management of receivables. Understanding and monitoring these indicators help in making informed decisions, optimizing processes, and improving cash flow.

1. Days Sales Outstanding (DSO)

Days Sales Outstanding (DSO) is one of the most important KPIs in AR. It measures the average number of days it takes for a company to collect payment after a sale has been made. A lower DSO indicates that the company is able to collect its receivables quickly, which is beneficial for cash flow.

- Formula: DSO = (Accounts Receivable / Total Credit Sales) Number of Days

- Interpretation: A low DSO is a sign of efficient collection processes and good credit management. Conversely, a high DSO may indicate issues with collections, customer payment habits, or credit policies.

2. Accounts Receivable Turnover Ratio

The Accounts Receivable Turnover Ratio measures how many times a company can turn its receivables into cash during a given period. It provides insight into the effectiveness of the company's credit policies and collection efforts.

- Formula: AR Turnover Ratio = Net Credit Sales / Average Accounts Receivable

- Interpretation: A higher turnover ratio indicates that the company is efficient at collecting its receivables and has a high-quality customer base that pays on time.

3. Average Collection Period

The Average Collection Period KPI indicates the average number of days it takes for a company to receive payments from its customers. It is similar to DSO but focuses more on the time aspect of collections.

- Formula: Average Collection Period = 365 / Accounts Receivable Turnover Ratio

- Interpretation: A shorter average collection period means quicker collection of receivables, which is beneficial for liquidity. A longer period suggests potential issues in the collection process.

4. Percentage of Overdue Invoices

This KPI measures the proportion of invoices that are past their due date. It helps in identifying trends and issues in the payment behavior of customers.

- Formula: Percentage of Overdue Invoices = (Total Overdue Invoices / Total Invoices) 100

- Interpretation: A high percentage of overdue invoices may indicate poor credit management or economic issues affecting customers. Reducing this percentage is crucial for maintaining healthy cash flow.

5. Bad Debt to Sales Ratio

The Bad Debt to Sales Ratio measures the proportion of bad debts (uncollectible receivables) to the total sales. It helps in assessing the effectiveness of the company's credit policies and risk management practices.

- Formula: Bad Debt to Sales Ratio = (Bad Debts / Total Sales) 100

- Interpretation: A low ratio indicates effective credit management and low risk of bad debts, while a high ratio suggests potential issues in credit policies or economic conditions affecting customers.

6. Collection Effectiveness Index (CEI)

The Collection Effectiveness Index (CEI) is a KPI that measures the effectiveness of the collections process over a specific period. It provides a more detailed analysis than DSO by considering the timing of collections.

- Formula: CEI = (1 - [(Total Beginning Receivables + Credit Sales - Total Ending Receivables) / Total Beginning Receivables]) 100

- Interpretation: A higher CEI indicates a more effective collections process, while a lower CEI may suggest inefficiencies or issues in collections.

7. Cash Conversion Cycle (CCC)

The Cash Conversion Cycle (CCC) is a comprehensive KPI that measures the time it takes for a company to convert its investments in inventory and other resources into cash flows from sales. It includes the time taken to collect receivables.

- Formula: CCC = DSO + Inventory Conversion Period - Payables Conversion Period

- Interpretation: A shorter CCC means that the company can quickly turn its resources into cash, which is advantageous for liquidity and operational efficiency.

8. Customer Payment Trend Analysis

Customer Payment Trend Analysis involves tracking the payment patterns of customers over time. This KPI helps in identifying trends and potential issues with specific customers or groups of customers.

- Methods: Analyze historical payment data, categorize customers based on payment behavior, and monitor changes over time.

- Interpretation: Identifying negative trends early can help in addressing issues proactively, such as adjusting credit terms or focusing collection efforts on specific customers.

9. Dispute Resolution Time

This KPI measures the average time taken to resolve disputes related to invoices and payments. Efficient dispute resolution is crucial for maintaining good customer relationships and ensuring timely payments.

- Formula: Dispute Resolution Time = Total Dispute Resolution Time / Number of Disputes

- Interpretation: A shorter resolution time indicates effective dispute management, while a longer time suggests potential inefficiencies or communication issues.

10. Percentage of Write-offs

The Percentage of Write-offs KPI measures the proportion of receivables that are written off as uncollectible. It is an important indicator of the quality of the receivables and the effectiveness of the credit policies.

- Formula: Percentage of Write-offs = (Total Write-offs / Total Receivables) 100

- Interpretation: A low percentage indicates good credit quality and effective collection practices, while a high percentage may suggest issues with credit policies or economic conditions affecting customers.

11. Customer Satisfaction Score

While not a direct financial KPI, the Customer Satisfaction Score (CSAT) is crucial for understanding the overall health of the AR process. Satisfied customers are more likely to pay on time and continue doing business with the company.

- Methods: Conduct surveys, gather feedback, and analyze customer satisfaction data.

- Interpretation: High customer satisfaction is associated with timely payments and lower dispute rates, while low satisfaction may indicate issues that need to be addressed.

12. Percentage of Early Payments

This KPI measures the proportion of invoices that are paid before their due date. Encouraging early payments can improve cash flow and reduce the risk of bad debts.

- Formula: Percentage of Early Payments = (Total Early Payments / Total Invoices) 100

- Interpretation: A high percentage of early payments indicates effective incentives for early payment and good customer relationships.

13. Aging Analysis

Aging Analysis involves categorizing receivables based on their age (e.g., 30 days, 60 days, 90 days, etc.). This KPI helps in understanding the distribution of receivables and identifying potential risk areas.

- Methods: Generate aging reports, categorize receivables, and analyze trends.

- Interpretation: A higher proportion of older receivables may indicate collection issues or potential bad debts, while a healthy aging distribution suggests effective collection practices.

14. Invoice Processing Time

The Invoice Processing Time KPI measures the average time taken to process and issue invoices after a sale is made. Efficient invoice processing is crucial for timely collections.

- Formula: Invoice Processing Time = Total Invoice Processing Time / Number of Invoices

- Interpretation: A shorter processing time indicates efficient invoicing processes, while a longer time suggests potential inefficiencies.

15. Percentage of Electronic Payments

This KPI measures the proportion of payments received electronically. Electronic payments are typically faster and more secure than traditional payment methods.

- Formula: Percentage of Electronic Payments = (Total Electronic Payments / Total Payments) 100

- Interpretation: A high percentage of electronic payments indicates efficient payment processing and modern payment methods, while a low percentage may suggest room for improvement in payment options.

Monitoring and analyzing these KPIs provide a comprehensive understanding of the performance of the Accounts Receivable process. By focusing on these indicators, organizations can identify areas for improvement, optimize their collections process, and enhance overall financial management. Effective use of KPIs also helps in setting realistic targets, benchmarking performance, and driving continuous improvement in the Accounts Receivable function.

7.2.2 Analyzing Accounts Receivable Data

Analyzing accounts receivable (AR) data is a crucial activity for any business that extends credit to its customers. This analysis provides valuable insights into the company's cash flow, customer payment behaviors, and overall financial health. By understanding AR data, organizations can make informed decisions, optimize their receivables management processes, and ultimately improve their financial performance. In this section, we will explore various techniques and tools for analyzing AR data, the key metrics to monitor, and how to interpret the results to drive business improvements.

Understanding the Importance of AR Data Analysis

Accounts receivable data analysis is important for several reasons:

1. Cash Flow Management: AR data helps businesses monitor the flow of cash coming in from customers. By analyzing this data, companies can predict cash inflows, manage working capital more effectively, and ensure they have enough liquidity to meet their obligations.

2. Customer Insights: Analyzing AR data provides insights into customer payment behaviors, such as payment timeliness and patterns. This information is valuable for assessing customer creditworthiness and managing credit risk.

3. Performance Measurement: Tracking AR metrics allows businesses to measure the efficiency and effectiveness of their credit and collections processes. By identifying areas for improvement, companies can enhance their receivables management strategies.

4. Financial Health Assessment: AR data is a key component of a company's financial health. High levels of overdue receivables can indicate potential liquidity issues or problems with credit policies, whereas low levels of overdue receivables suggest efficient receivables management.

Key Metrics for AR Data Analysis

To effectively analyze AR data, it is important to focus on several key metrics. These metrics provide a comprehensive view of the company's receivables performance and help identify areas that require attention:

1. Days Sales Outstanding (DSO): DSO measures the average number of days it takes for a company to collect payment after a sale has been made. It is calculated using the formula:

Days Sales Outstanding (DSO) = (Total Accounts Receivable / Total Credit Sales) × Number of Days

Components:

Total Accounts Receivable (AR): This represents the outstanding balance of all credit sales that have not yet been collected by the company. It's typically found on the balance sheet under the current assets section.

Total Credit Sales: This refers to the total value of all sales made during a specific period (month, quarter, year) where payment was not received at the time of sale. It can be obtained from the company's sales records or income statement.

Number of Days: This is the number of days in the period you're analyzing. For monthly DSO, use 30 days; for quarterly DSO, use 90 days; and for annual DSO, use 365 days.

A lower DSO indicates that the company is collecting receivables quickly, which is a positive sign. Conversely, a higher DSO suggests potential issues with collections.

2. Aging Schedule: An aging schedule categorizes receivables based on how long they have been outstanding. It typically includes categories such as 0-30 days, 31-60 days, 61-90 days, and over 90 days. The aging schedule helps identify overdue accounts and assess the effectiveness of the company's credit policies.

3. Collection Effectiveness Index (CEI): CEI measures the effectiveness of the collections process over a specific period. It is calculated using the formula:

CEI = (Beginning Accounts Receivable + Credit Sales - Ending Accounts Receivable) / (Beginning Accounts Receivable + Credit Sales - Current Accounts Receivable) x 100

In simpler terms, CEI indicates the percentage of cash a company collects from credit sales within a specific period.

Here's a breakdown of the variables in the formula:

Beginning Accounts Receivable: The total amount of accounts receivable outstanding at the beginning of the period being evaluated.

Credit Sales: The total amount of sales made on credit during the period being evaluated.

Ending Accounts Receivable: The total amount of accounts receivable outstanding at the end of the period being evaluated.

Current Accounts Receivable: The portion of accounts receivable that are considered to be "current" or not yet past due. This is typically defined as receivables that are outstanding for 60 days or less.

A higher CEI indicates better collections performance.

4. Bad Debt Ratio: This ratio measures the proportion of receivables that are written off as uncollectible. It is calculated using the formula:

Bad Debt Ratio = (Bad Debts / Total Credit Sales) x 100

Bad Debt Ratio: This ratio represents the percentage of credit sales that a company expects to be uncollectible.

Bad Debts: This refers to the total amount of money owed by customers that the company has given up on collecting. These are typically written off as an expense on the company's financial statements.

Total Credit Sales: This represents the total amount of sales made on credit during a specific period.

A lower bad debt ratio indicates better credit risk management.

5. Average Collection Period (ACP): ACP measures the average time it takes to collect receivables. It is similar to DSO but can provide a different perspective when analyzed over various periods. It is calculated using the formula:

Average Collection Period (ACP) = (Accounts Receivable / Total Credit Sales) × 365

Average Collection Period (ACP): This metric measures the average number of days it takes a company to collect payment for its credit sales. A lower ACP indicates a company collects its credit sales faster, which is generally considered positive as it improves cash flow. Conversely, a higher ACP suggests it takes longer for a company to collect payments, which could lead to cash flow issues.

Accounts Receivable: This refers to the total amount of money owed by customers for goods or services purchased on credit. It represents the amount of cash a company is waiting to collect from its customers.

Total Credit Sales: This represents the total amount of sales made on credit during a specific period. It reflects the total amount of credit sales that a company has generated over a given time frame.

A shorter ACP is desirable as it indicates quicker collections.

6. Receivables Turnover Ratio: This ratio measures how many times a company collects its average receivables during a period. It is calculated using the formula:

Receivables Turnover Ratio = Net Credit Sales / Average Accounts Receivable

Receivables Turnover Ratio: This metric measures how efficiently a company collects cash from its credit sales. A higher ratio indicates better collection practices and faster turnover of accounts receivable.

Net Credit Sales: This represents the total revenue earned from sales made on credit, after accounting for returns, allowances, and discounts.

Average Accounts Receivable: This is the average amount of money owed by customers on credit sales during a specific period. It's typically calculated as the average of the beginning and ending accounts receivable balances.

A higher ratio indicates efficient collections.

Techniques and Tools for Analyzing AR Data

To analyze AR data effectively, businesses can employ various techniques and tools. These methods help in organizing, visualizing, and interpreting the data for better decision-making.

1. Data Segmentation: Segmenting AR data by customer, region, industry, or product line can provide deeper insights into specific areas of receivables performance. This segmentation helps identify trends, spot outliers, and tailor collection strategies accordingly.

2. Trend Analysis: Analyzing AR data over time helps identify trends and patterns. For example, businesses can track changes in DSO, aging schedules, or bad debt ratios to understand seasonal variations, market conditions, or the impact of credit policies.

3. Comparative Analysis: Comparing AR metrics with industry benchmarks or peer companies provides a context for evaluating performance. This analysis helps identify areas where the company is performing well or lagging behind.

4. Variance Analysis: Variance analysis involves comparing actual AR data against budgets or forecasts. This technique helps identify discrepancies and understand the reasons behind them, enabling businesses to take corrective actions.

5. Root Cause Analysis: When issues are identified in AR data, conducting a root cause analysis helps determine the underlying reasons. This analysis involves investigating

factors such as customer behavior, credit policies, or internal processes to address the root causes of problems.

6. Visualization Tools: Using visualization tools such as dashboards, charts, and graphs makes it easier to understand and interpret AR data. Visual representations highlight key metrics, trends, and anomalies, facilitating better decision-making.

7. Software Solutions: Many ERP systems, including Oracle ERP, offer built-in tools and modules for AR data analysis. These solutions provide comprehensive reporting capabilities, customizable dashboards, and real-time data access, making it easier to monitor and analyze receivables performance.

Interpreting AR Data for Business Improvements

Once AR data has been analyzed, it is important to interpret the results and use them to drive business improvements. Here are some key considerations for interpreting AR data:

1. Identify Key Issues: Focus on identifying the key issues that impact receivables performance. This could include high DSO, a significant amount of overdue receivables, or a rising bad debt ratio. Prioritize these issues for immediate attention.

2. Assess Credit Policies: Evaluate the effectiveness of current credit policies. Are they too lenient, leading to high levels of overdue receivables, or too strict, potentially impacting sales? Adjust credit policies based on the analysis to strike the right balance between sales and collections.

3. Enhance Collections Strategies: Use the insights from AR data analysis to enhance collections strategies. This could involve segmenting customers for targeted follow-ups, implementing automated reminders, or offering flexible payment options to improve collections.

4. Optimize Cash Flow Management: Utilize the analysis to improve cash flow management. For example, by understanding payment patterns, businesses can better predict cash inflows and plan their expenditures accordingly. This helps ensure sufficient liquidity and avoid cash flow crunches.

5. Improve Customer Relationships: Analyze customer payment behaviors to identify high-risk customers or those with frequent payment delays. Implement proactive measures

such as credit limits, advance payments, or more stringent credit checks for these customers. Strengthening relationships with reliable customers through incentives or discounts can also improve collections.

6. Monitor Performance Continuously: Regularly monitor AR metrics and trends to ensure ongoing performance improvements. Set up periodic reviews and utilize dashboards for real-time tracking. Continuous monitoring helps identify emerging issues early and allows for timely interventions.

7. Leverage Technology: Invest in technology solutions that facilitate AR data analysis and management. Utilize the capabilities of Oracle ERP or other advanced analytics tools to streamline processes, enhance data accuracy, and gain deeper insights.

8. Train and Educate Staff: Ensure that the staff responsible for managing receivables are well-trained and knowledgeable about best practices in AR management. Provide continuous education and training to keep them updated with the latest tools, techniques, and industry trends.

Conclusion

Analyzing accounts receivable data is a vital process for maintaining the financial health of a business. By focusing on key metrics, employing effective analysis techniques, and leveraging technology, companies can gain valuable insights into their receivables performance. These insights enable businesses to optimize their credit and collections processes, improve cash flow management, and enhance overall financial stability. Regularly monitoring and interpreting AR data ensures that businesses can proactively address issues, make informed decisions, and drive continuous improvements in their receivables management strategies.

7.2.3 Using Dashboards for Financial Analysis

Dashboards are powerful tools that provide a visual representation of key financial data, enabling organizations to monitor and analyze their Accounts Receivable performance in real-time. The use of dashboards in financial analysis offers several benefits, including enhanced decision-making, improved efficiency, and better communication of financial information. This section explores the importance of dashboards, the types of dashboards commonly used in AR, and best practices for designing and utilizing dashboards effectively.

Importance of Dashboards

Dashboards are integral to modern financial management for several reasons:

1. Real-Time Data Access: Dashboards provide instant access to real-time data, allowing managers to monitor the current state of AR processes and respond quickly to any issues or trends.

2. Enhanced Visualization: By presenting data in graphical formats such as charts, graphs, and gauges, dashboards make it easier to understand complex data sets and identify patterns and anomalies.

3. Improved Decision-Making: Dashboards enable data-driven decision-making by providing a comprehensive view of key metrics and performance indicators.

4. Efficiency and Productivity: Automating data collection and visualization reduces the time and effort required to generate reports manually, freeing up resources for more strategic tasks.

5. Communication and Collaboration: Dashboards facilitate better communication of financial performance across departments and stakeholders, ensuring everyone has access to the same up-to-date information.

Types of Dashboards

There are several types of dashboards that can be used in Accounts Receivable to provide valuable insights:

1. Operational Dashboards: These dashboards focus on the day-to-day operations of the AR department. They provide real-time data on transactions, cash flow, and receivables management, helping managers ensure that processes are running smoothly and efficiently.

2. Analytical Dashboards: Analytical dashboards are designed for in-depth analysis of AR performance. They include historical data and trends, allowing users to identify patterns, forecast future performance, and make strategic decisions.

3. Strategic Dashboards: These dashboards provide a high-level view of AR performance, aligning with the organization's strategic goals. They typically include key financial metrics and KPIs that are critical to senior management and stakeholders.

4. Compliance Dashboards: Focused on regulatory compliance and audit requirements, these dashboards track compliance-related metrics, such as tax codes, payment terms, and adherence to internal policies.

Key Metrics and KPIs for Dashboards

When designing dashboards for Accounts Receivable, it is essential to include key metrics and KPIs that provide actionable insights. Some of the most important metrics to consider are:

1. Days Sales Outstanding (DSO): DSO measures the average number of days it takes for a company to collect payment after a sale has been made. Lower DSO indicates efficient receivables management.

2. Aging of Receivables: This metric breaks down outstanding receivables by the length of time they have been overdue. It helps identify potential collection issues and prioritize follow-up actions.

3. Collections Effectiveness Index (CEI): CEI measures the effectiveness of the collections process by comparing the amount collected within a specified period to the total amount due.

4. Average Days Delinquent (ADD): ADD calculates the average number of days receivables are past due, providing insight into the timeliness of collections.

5. Bad Debt Ratio: This ratio measures the percentage of receivables that are written off as bad debt, indicating the quality of the receivables portfolio.

6. Cash Conversion Cycle (CCC): CCC measures the time it takes for a company to convert its investments in inventory and other resources into cash flows from sales.

7. Customer Payment Performance: Tracking customer payment patterns and identifying those consistently paying late or early can help in renegotiating payment terms and managing cash flow more effectively.

Designing Effective Dashboards

To maximize the effectiveness of dashboards, it is crucial to follow best practices in design and implementation:

1. Define Clear Objectives: Start by defining the objectives of the dashboard. Understand the specific needs of the users and the key questions the dashboard should answer.

2. Select Relevant Metrics: Choose metrics and KPIs that align with the defined objectives. Avoid cluttering the dashboard with too much information; focus on what is most important.

3. Ensure Data Accuracy: The effectiveness of a dashboard depends on the accuracy of the underlying data. Implement robust data validation processes to ensure the data is reliable.

4. User-Friendly Design: Design the dashboard with the end-user in mind. Use intuitive layouts, clear labels, and appropriate visualizations to make the dashboard easy to understand and use.

5. Interactive Features: Incorporate interactive features such as drill-downs, filters, and dynamic data updates to allow users to explore the data in more detail and customize their views.

6. Regular Updates: Ensure that the dashboard is updated regularly to reflect the most current data. Real-time updates are ideal for operational dashboards, while analytical and strategic dashboards may require periodic updates.

7. Training and Support: Provide training and support to users to help them understand how to use the dashboard effectively and interpret the data correctly.

Implementing Dashboards in Oracle ERP

Oracle ERP offers robust tools for creating and managing dashboards within the Accounts Receivable module. Here are the steps to implement dashboards in Oracle ERP:

1. Identify Data Sources: Determine the data sources required for the dashboard. This may include AR transactions, customer records, payment histories, and other relevant data from Oracle ERP.

2. Data Integration: Integrate the data from various sources into a unified data repository. Use Oracle ERP's data integration tools to ensure seamless data flow and consistency.

3. Dashboard Development: Use Oracle ERP's built-in dashboard development tools to create the dashboard. Customize the layout, visualizations, and metrics to meet the defined objectives.

4. Testing and Validation: Test the dashboard thoroughly to ensure it meets the requirements and provides accurate insights. Validate the data and functionality before deploying it to end-users.

5. Deployment and Training: Deploy the dashboard to the relevant users and provide training to ensure they understand how to use it effectively. Offer ongoing support to address any issues or questions.

6. Monitoring and Maintenance: Continuously monitor the performance of the dashboard and make necessary updates and improvements. Ensure the data remains accurate and relevant to the users.

Case Study: Implementing Dashboards for Improved AR Management

A case study can provide practical insights into the implementation and benefits of dashboards in Accounts Receivable. Here is a hypothetical example:

Company X: Improving AR Efficiency with Dashboards

Background: Company X, a mid-sized manufacturing firm, faced challenges in managing its Accounts Receivable processes. The AR department struggled with high DSO, delayed collections, and limited visibility into receivables performance.

Objective: To improve AR efficiency and decision-making by implementing real-time dashboards.

Implementation:

1. Data Integration: Integrated AR data from various sources, including sales orders, customer records, and payment histories, into Oracle ERP's data repository.

2. Dashboard Development: Developed operational and analytical dashboards focusing on key metrics such as DSO, aging of receivables, and collection effectiveness. Customized visualizations to provide clear insights.

3. User Training: Conducted training sessions for AR staff to ensure they understood how to use the dashboards and interpret the data.

4. Deployment: Deployed the dashboards to the AR department and senior management, providing real-time access to critical AR data.

Results:

1. Reduced DSO: The operational dashboard helped identify bottlenecks in the collections process, leading to targeted actions that reduced DSO by 15%.

2. Improved Collections: The aging of receivables dashboard enabled the AR team to prioritize collections efforts, resulting in a 10% increase in collection rates.

3. Enhanced Decision-Making: The analytical dashboard provided valuable insights into customer payment patterns and credit risks, supporting better decision-making and credit management.

Conclusion: By implementing real-time dashboards, Company X significantly improved its AR efficiency, reduced DSO, and enhanced overall financial management.

Conclusion

Dashboards are invaluable tools for financial analysis and management in the Accounts Receivable module. They provide real-time insights, enhance decision-making, and improve the efficiency of AR processes. By selecting the right metrics, designing user-friendly dashboards, and leveraging Oracle ERP's capabilities, organizations can gain a comprehensive view of their AR performance and drive better financial outcomes.

7.3 Compliance and Audit Reports

7.3.1 Generating Compliance Reports

Compliance reports are essential in ensuring that an organization adheres to internal policies, industry standards, and legal requirements. In the context of Oracle ERP's Accounts Receivable (AR) module, generating compliance reports involves producing documentation that verifies adherence to financial regulations, tax laws, and internal controls. This section will guide you through the process of generating compliance reports within Oracle ERP, focusing on the tools and features available, best practices, and common challenges.

Understanding Compliance Reports

Compliance reports serve multiple purposes, including:

- Verification of Adherence: Ensuring that financial transactions comply with laws and regulations.

- Internal Controls: Demonstrating that internal processes and controls are functioning correctly.

- Audit Preparedness: Providing necessary documentation for external and internal audits.

- Risk Management: Identifying and mitigating compliance risks.

- Transparency: Offering stakeholders clear and accurate financial information.

In the AR module, compliance reports typically cover areas such as tax compliance, regulatory filings, and adherence to accounting standards.

Tools and Features in Oracle ERP for Compliance Reporting

Oracle ERP offers several tools and features that facilitate the generation of compliance reports. These include:

- Standard Reports: Pre-configured reports that meet common compliance needs.

- Custom Reports: Tailored reports created using Oracle's reporting tools to meet specific compliance requirements.

- Audit Trails: Logs of user activities and transaction histories to support compliance verification.

- Alerts and Notifications: Automated alerts that notify users of potential compliance issues.

- Integration with Third-Party Compliance Tools: Seamless integration with external tools for enhanced compliance reporting.

Steps to Generate Compliance Reports

Generating compliance reports in the Oracle ERP AR module involves several key steps:

1. Identify Compliance Requirements

   - Understand the specific regulations and standards that apply to your organization.

   - Consult with legal and compliance teams to ensure all requirements are identified.

2. Configure Reporting Tools

   - Set up Oracle ERP reporting tools to capture the necessary data.

   - Customize standard reports or create new reports using tools like Oracle BI Publisher or Oracle Reports.

3. Data Collection and Preparation

   - Ensure all relevant financial data is accurately recorded in the AR module.

   - Verify the completeness and accuracy of customer invoices, receipts, and adjustments.

4. Generate Reports

   - Run standard compliance reports available in Oracle ERP.

   - Customize or create new reports to meet specific compliance needs.

5. Review and Validate Reports

   - Review the generated reports for accuracy and completeness.

   - Validate the reports with internal stakeholders, such as finance and compliance teams.

6. Distribute and Archive Reports

   - Distribute the compliance reports to relevant stakeholders.

   - Archive the reports for future reference and audit purposes.

Common Compliance Reports in Accounts Receivable

Several types of compliance reports are commonly generated within the AR module:

- Tax Compliance Reports

  - Reports detailing sales tax, VAT, GST, and other tax liabilities.

  - Ensures accurate tax reporting and filing.

- Regulatory Compliance Reports

  - Reports required by regulatory bodies, such as the SEC or local financial authorities.

  - Includes financial statements and disclosures.

- Internal Control Reports

  - Reports that demonstrate adherence to internal controls and policies.

  - Includes segregation of duties and authorization controls.

- Audit Reports

  - Detailed transaction logs and audit trails.

  - Supports internal and external audit processes.

Best Practices for Generating Compliance Reports

To ensure the accuracy and effectiveness of compliance reports, follow these best practices:

1. Maintain Data Accuracy

   - Regularly review and update customer records, invoices, and receipts.

   - Implement validation checks to prevent data entry errors.

2. Automate Reporting Processes

   - Use Oracle ERP's automation features to schedule and generate reports.

   - Reduce manual intervention to minimize errors.

3. Regularly Update Reports

   - Periodically review and update compliance reports to reflect changes in regulations and standards.

   - Engage with legal and compliance teams to stay informed about regulatory changes.

4. Ensure User Training

   - Train users on the importance of compliance reporting and how to generate accurate reports.

   - Provide ongoing training to keep users informed about updates and new features.

5. Conduct Regular Audits

   - Perform internal audits to verify the accuracy and completeness of compliance reports.

   - Use audit findings to improve reporting processes and controls.

Challenges in Compliance Reporting

Generating compliance reports can present several challenges, including:

- Data Accuracy: Ensuring the accuracy of financial data is critical for compliance. Inaccurate data can lead to incorrect reports and potential legal issues.

- Regulatory Changes: Keeping up with changes in regulations and standards requires continuous monitoring and updates to reporting processes.

- Complex Reporting Requirements: Different regulatory bodies may have varying reporting requirements, making it challenging to produce comprehensive reports.

- Resource Constraints: Generating compliance reports can be resource-intensive, requiring significant time and effort from finance and compliance teams.

Addressing Compliance Reporting Challenges

To address these challenges, consider the following strategies:

1. Implement Robust Data Management Practices

   - Use Oracle ERP's data validation and error-checking features to maintain data accuracy.

   - Regularly review and reconcile financial data.

2. Stay Informed About Regulatory Changes

   - Subscribe to industry newsletters and updates to stay informed about regulatory changes.

   - Engage with legal and compliance experts to understand the implications of new regulations.

3. Leverage Reporting Tools and Automation

   - Utilize Oracle ERP's reporting tools to streamline the generation of compliance reports.

   - Automate routine reporting tasks to free up resources for more complex analyses.

4. Collaborate Across Departments

   - Foster collaboration between finance, compliance, and IT teams to ensure comprehensive and accurate reporting.

   - Share knowledge and best practices to improve reporting processes.

Conclusion

Generating compliance reports in Oracle ERP's Accounts Receivable module is a critical task that ensures adherence to regulatory requirements and internal controls. By leveraging Oracle ERP's robust reporting tools and following best practices, organizations can produce accurate and timely compliance reports, mitigate compliance risks, and maintain transparency with stakeholders. Regular updates, user training, and continuous improvement of reporting processes are essential to successfully navigating the complexities of compliance reporting.

7.3.2 Preparing for Financial Audits

Preparing for financial audits is a critical component of maintaining the integrity and accuracy of your Accounts Receivable (AR) data. Financial audits are designed to provide an independent assessment of the financial statements and ensure that the organization complies with all applicable accounting standards and regulatory requirements. This section will guide you through the process of preparing for financial audits, focusing on the steps you need to take to ensure that your AR records are accurate, complete, and compliant.

1. Understanding the Audit Process

Before diving into the specifics of preparing for an audit, it's essential to understand the audit process itself. Financial audits typically follow a standardized procedure, which includes the following steps:

- Planning: The auditor will outline the scope and objectives of the audit, including the specific areas to be examined.

- Fieldwork: This involves the collection of evidence through various methods such as reviewing documents, conducting interviews, and testing internal controls.

- Reporting: After analyzing the evidence, the auditor will prepare a report detailing their findings and providing an opinion on the financial statements.

- Follow-Up: The organization may need to address any issues or discrepancies identified during the audit.

Understanding these steps helps you anticipate what the auditors will be looking for and prepare accordingly.

2. Reviewing and Organizing AR Documentation

One of the first steps in preparing for a financial audit is to review and organize all relevant AR documentation. This includes:

- Invoices: Ensure all invoices are correctly issued, recorded, and stored. Verify that each invoice matches the sales order and delivery records.

- Receipts: Confirm that all customer payments are accurately recorded and applied to the corresponding invoices.

- Adjustments: Document any adjustments made to invoices or receipts, such as credits, write-offs, or refunds, and ensure they are justified and approved.

- Customer Statements: Review customer statements to ensure they accurately reflect the transactions and balances.

Organizing these documents in a systematic manner, either digitally or in physical files, makes it easier for auditors to access and review the necessary information.

3. Ensuring Data Accuracy and Completeness

Accurate and complete data is crucial for a successful audit. Here are some steps to ensure the integrity of your AR data:

- Reconcile Accounts: Regularly reconcile AR sub-ledgers with the general ledger to ensure consistency. Any discrepancies should be investigated and resolved promptly.

- Verify Balances: Check that all customer account balances are accurate and up-to-date. This involves verifying that all transactions have been posted correctly and that no unauthorized adjustments have been made.

- Validate Transactions: Perform periodic validation of transactions to ensure that they are recorded in the correct period and are in compliance with accounting standards.

- Internal Controls: Strengthen internal controls to prevent errors and fraud. This includes segregation of duties, regular reviews, and approval processes.

4. Preparing for Compliance Requirements

Compliance with accounting standards and regulatory requirements is a critical aspect of the audit process. Here are some key areas to focus on:

- Revenue Recognition: Ensure that revenue is recognized in accordance with applicable accounting standards, such as the IFRS 15 or ASC 606. This involves correctly identifying performance obligations and recognizing revenue when they are satisfied.

- Tax Compliance: Verify that all applicable taxes are correctly calculated, recorded, and reported. This includes sales tax, VAT, and other relevant taxes.

- Credit and Collection Policies: Review and document your credit and collection policies to ensure they are compliant with relevant regulations and industry standards.

5. Conducting Internal Audits

Internal audits are a proactive way to identify and address potential issues before an external audit. Here are some steps to conduct effective internal audits:

- Audit Plan: Develop a comprehensive audit plan that outlines the scope, objectives, and methodology of the internal audit.

- Risk Assessment: Identify and assess risks related to AR processes, such as credit risk, fraud risk, and compliance risk.

- Testing: Perform detailed testing of AR transactions and controls to ensure they are functioning as intended. This includes sample testing of invoices, receipts, and adjustments.

- Reporting: Document the findings of the internal audit and provide recommendations for improvement. Ensure that any identified issues are addressed promptly.

6. Collaborating with External Auditors

Effective collaboration with external auditors is essential for a smooth audit process. Here are some tips for working with auditors:

- Provide Documentation: Ensure that all requested documentation is readily available and organized. This includes invoices, receipts, customer statements, and internal policies.

- Answer Queries: Be prepared to answer any queries or provide additional information that the auditors may require. This includes explanations for any unusual transactions or adjustments.

- Timely Communication: Maintain open and timely communication with auditors to address any concerns or issues that may arise during the audit process.

7. Implementing Corrective Actions

Post-audit, it's important to implement any corrective actions recommended by the auditors. Here are some steps to ensure continuous improvement:

- Address Findings: Review the audit report and address any findings or recommendations. This may involve updating processes, improving controls, or providing additional training to staff.

- Monitor Progress: Regularly monitor the progress of corrective actions to ensure they are implemented effectively. This includes setting deadlines and assigning responsibilities.

- Continuous Improvement: Foster a culture of continuous improvement by regularly reviewing and updating AR processes to enhance efficiency and compliance.

8. Leveraging Technology for Audit Preparation

Modern technology can significantly streamline the audit preparation process. Here are some ways to leverage technology:

- Automated Reporting: Use ERP systems to generate automated reports that provide accurate and up-to-date information on AR transactions and balances.

- Data Analytics: Employ data analytics tools to identify trends, anomalies, and potential issues in AR data.

- Document Management: Utilize document management systems to organize and store AR documentation securely and efficiently.

Conclusion

Preparing for financial audits in the Accounts Receivable module involves a combination of meticulous documentation, data accuracy, compliance with accounting standards, and effective collaboration with auditors. By following the steps outlined in this section, you can ensure that your AR processes are audit-ready, thereby enhancing the integrity and reliability of your financial statements. Continuous improvement and leveraging technology further contribute to a streamlined and efficient audit preparation process, ultimately supporting the overall financial health of your organization.

7.3.3 Ensuring Data Accuracy and Integrity

Ensuring data accuracy and integrity within the Accounts Receivable (AR) module of Oracle ERP is crucial for maintaining reliable financial records, facilitating effective decision-making, and ensuring compliance with regulatory requirements. In this section, we will explore the various strategies, tools, and best practices that organizations can implement to guarantee the accuracy and integrity of their AR data.

Importance of Data Accuracy and Integrity

Accurate and reliable data is the cornerstone of effective financial management. Inaccurate AR data can lead to several issues, including:

- Misstated Financial Statements: Errors in AR data can cause significant discrepancies in financial statements, leading to inaccurate reporting of a company's financial health.

- Compliance Risks: Inaccurate data can result in non-compliance with regulatory standards, exposing the organization to legal and financial penalties.

- Decision-Making Implications: Management relies on accurate data to make informed business decisions. Data inaccuracies can lead to misguided strategies and actions.

- Customer Relationship Impact: Errors in customer invoices and payments can damage customer trust and satisfaction, affecting the organization's reputation.

Strategies for Ensuring Data Accuracy and Integrity

1. Data Validation and Verification:

  - Validation Rules: Implement strict validation rules at the point of data entry to ensure that all required fields are completed correctly. For example, ensure that customer names, addresses, invoice amounts, and dates are entered in the correct format and meet predefined criteria.

  - Automated Data Checks: Utilize Oracle ERP's built-in data validation tools to automate the verification of data accuracy. These tools can detect and flag anomalies, such as duplicate entries, inconsistent data, and missing information.

2. Regular Data Audits:

  - Internal Audits: Conduct regular internal audits of AR data to identify and rectify discrepancies. Internal audit teams should review invoices, receipts, and adjustments for accuracy and completeness.

  - External Audits: Engage external auditors to perform independent reviews of AR data. External audits provide an objective assessment of data accuracy and can identify areas for improvement.

3. Reconciliation Processes:

  - General Ledger Reconciliation: Regularly reconcile AR sub-ledger balances with the general ledger to ensure consistency. Discrepancies should be investigated and resolved promptly.

  - Bank Reconciliation: Perform monthly bank reconciliations to ensure that cash receipts and bank deposits match. This process helps identify unrecorded transactions and errors in the AR module.

4. Data Integrity Controls:

- Access Controls: Implement strict access controls to ensure that only authorized personnel can enter, modify, or delete AR data. Role-based access controls (RBAC) can help manage permissions and prevent unauthorized changes.

- Audit Trails: Maintain detailed audit trails that track all changes to AR data. Audit trails should capture information such as the user making the change, the nature of the change, and the date and time of the change.

5. Standard Operating Procedures (SOPs):

- Documentation: Develop and maintain comprehensive SOPs for all AR processes, including data entry, invoicing, payment processing, and adjustments. SOPs should outline the steps to be followed and the checks to be performed to ensure data accuracy.

- Training: Provide regular training to AR staff on SOPs and data accuracy best practices. Training should cover the importance of accurate data entry, common errors to avoid, and the use of Oracle ERP's validation tools.

6. Use of Technology:

- Data Integration Tools: Utilize data integration tools to ensure seamless data flow between the AR module and other ERP modules. Integration tools help eliminate data silos and reduce the risk of data discrepancies.

- Machine Learning and AI: Leverage machine learning and AI capabilities within Oracle ERP to identify patterns and anomalies in AR data. These technologies can automatically detect and flag potential errors for further investigation.

Best Practices for Ensuring Data Accuracy and Integrity

1. Consistent Data Entry Practices:

- Standardized Formats: Use standardized formats for data entry to ensure consistency. For example, standardize the format for dates, customer names, and invoice numbers.

- Drop-Down Lists: Utilize drop-down lists for data entry fields where applicable. This approach minimizes the risk of typographical errors and ensures consistency in data entry.

2. Regular Data Cleaning:

- Duplicate Records: Regularly review and eliminate duplicate customer records, invoices, and receipts. Duplicate records can cause confusion and inaccuracies in AR reporting.

- Inactive Accounts: Identify and archive inactive customer accounts to reduce clutter and maintain a clean AR database. Inactive accounts should be periodically reviewed and either reactivated or permanently removed.

3. Continuous Monitoring:

- Exception Reports: Generate and review exception reports that highlight unusual or inconsistent data. Exception reports can help identify potential errors and areas requiring further investigation.

- Key Performance Indicators (KPIs): Monitor KPIs related to AR data accuracy, such as the number of data entry errors, the time taken to resolve discrepancies, and the frequency of reconciliations.

4. Stakeholder Collaboration:

- Cross-Departmental Coordination: Foster collaboration between the AR team and other departments, such as sales, finance, and customer service. Effective communication and coordination help ensure that data is consistently accurate across the organization.

- Customer Feedback: Encourage customers to report any discrepancies or errors in their invoices and payments. Promptly address customer feedback to maintain data accuracy and improve customer satisfaction.

Tools and Technologies for Ensuring Data Accuracy and Integrity

1. Oracle Data Management Tools:

- Oracle Data Integrator (ODI): Use ODI to automate data integration processes and ensure consistent data flow between Oracle ERP modules. ODI provides robust data validation and transformation capabilities.

- Oracle Enterprise Data Quality (EDQ): Leverage EDQ to perform data profiling, cleansing, and matching. EDQ helps identify and rectify data quality issues, ensuring accurate and reliable AR data.

2. Third-Party Data Quality Tools:

 - Data Profiling Tools: Utilize data profiling tools to analyze AR data and identify potential quality issues. These tools provide insights into data patterns, anomalies, and completeness.

 - Data Cleansing Solutions: Implement data cleansing solutions to automatically correct errors, standardize data formats, and remove duplicates. Data cleansing tools help maintain a clean and accurate AR database.

3. Reporting and Analytics Platforms:

 - Oracle Business Intelligence (OBI): Use OBI to create comprehensive reports and dashboards that provide real-time insights into AR data accuracy and integrity. OBI's advanced analytics capabilities enable proactive monitoring and analysis.

 - Custom Reporting Tools: Develop custom reporting tools to address specific data accuracy and integrity needs. Custom reports can provide tailored insights and help identify data discrepancies.

Case Studies: Ensuring Data Accuracy and Integrity in AR

Case Study 1: Enhancing Data Accuracy Through Automation

Background: A mid-sized manufacturing company was facing issues with data accuracy in their AR module, leading to frequent discrepancies in financial statements and delayed payment processing.

Solution: The company implemented Oracle ERP's automation tools, including automated data validation and reconciliation processes. They also integrated machine learning algorithms to detect and flag anomalies in AR data.

Outcome: The automation initiative significantly reduced data entry errors and improved the accuracy of financial reporting. The company experienced faster payment processing times and enhanced customer satisfaction.

Case Study 2: Improving Data Integrity Through Standardized Practices

Background: A large retail organization was struggling with inconsistent data entry practices across multiple departments, resulting in inaccurate AR data and compliance risks.

Solution: The organization developed and implemented standardized operating procedures (SOPs) for all AR processes. They provided extensive training to AR staff and conducted regular internal audits to ensure adherence to SOPs.

Outcome: The standardized practices led to improved data accuracy and reduced compliance risks. Internal audits showed a significant decrease in data discrepancies, and the organization achieved better financial control.

Case Study 3: Leveraging Advanced Analytics for Data Integrity

Background: A global technology firm needed to ensure the accuracy and integrity of their AR data to support strategic decision-making and regulatory compliance.

Solution: The firm implemented Oracle Business Intelligence (OBI) to create real-time dashboards and reports. They used OBI's advanced analytics capabilities to monitor KPIs related to AR data accuracy and integrity.

Outcome: The use of advanced analytics provided the firm with actionable insights into data quality. They were able to proactively address data discrepancies, leading to more reliable financial reporting and improved compliance.

Conclusion

Ensuring data accuracy and integrity in the Accounts Receivable module of Oracle ERP is essential for maintaining reliable financial records, achieving regulatory compliance, and supporting effective decision-making. By implementing robust data validation, regular audits, reconciliation processes, and leveraging advanced technologies, organizations can guarantee the accuracy and integrity of their AR data. Adhering to best practices and fostering a culture of data quality can further enhance the reliability of financial management and contribute to the overall success of the organization.

CHAPTER VIII
Advanced Topics and Best Practices

8.1 Automating Accounts Receivable Processes

Automating accounts receivable (AR) processes within Oracle ERP can significantly enhance efficiency, accuracy, and compliance. This section delves into the tools and technologies that enable AR automation, discusses their benefits, and provides insights into common automation scenarios.

8.1.1 Implementing Automation Tools

Automation tools for accounts receivable in Oracle ERP streamline routine tasks, reduce manual errors, and improve overall productivity. Implementing these tools involves a series of steps, from selecting the right software to configuring and integrating it with existing systems.

1. Understanding the Need for Automation

Before implementing automation tools, it's essential to assess the current AR processes and identify areas that would benefit most from automation. Common pain points include:

- Manual data entry errors.

- Time-consuming invoice generation and distribution.

- Delayed payment processing and reconciliation.

- Inefficient customer communication regarding outstanding invoices.

- Difficulty in tracking and managing overdue accounts.

2. Selecting the Right Automation Tools

There are several automation tools available for AR processes, each offering different features and capabilities. Key considerations when selecting an automation tool include:

- Compatibility with Oracle ERP: Ensure the tool integrates seamlessly with Oracle ERP.

- Scalability: The tool should support the growing volume of transactions as the business expands.

- User-Friendliness: A user-friendly interface ensures quick adoption by AR staff.

- Customization: The ability to customize workflows to match specific business requirements.

- Support and Maintenance: Reliable vendor support and regular updates are crucial for long-term success.

Popular AR automation tools that integrate well with Oracle ERP include:

- Oracle Fusion Receivables: Part of the Oracle Fusion Cloud Applications suite, it provides comprehensive automation features for invoice processing, payment collections, and more.

- BlackLine: Offers robust AR automation capabilities, including automated cash application, collections management, and reconciliation.

- HighRadius: Provides AI-driven automation solutions for invoice presentment, collections, and deductions management.

3. Setting Up Automation Workflows

Once the appropriate tool is selected, the next step is to configure automation workflows. These workflows define how tasks are automated, ensuring consistency and efficiency. Key workflows in AR automation include:

a. Invoice Generation and Distribution:

- Automated Invoice Creation: Configure the system to automatically generate invoices based on predefined triggers, such as order fulfillment or service completion.

- Electronic Invoice Distribution: Enable electronic delivery of invoices via email or electronic data interchange (EDI) to expedite the billing process.

b. Payment Processing and Reconciliation:

- Automated Payment Reminders: Set up automated reminders for overdue invoices, sent to customers at regular intervals.

- Auto-Matching of Payments: Implement rules for automatic matching of incoming payments with open invoices, reducing the need for manual reconciliation.

- Bank Integration: Integrate with banks to automate payment receipt and reconciliation processes.

c. Collections and Dunning:

- Automated Collections Management: Define automated workflows for follow-up actions based on the aging of receivables, such as escalation to collections agencies.

- Dunning Letters: Configure the system to automatically generate and send dunning letters to customers with overdue accounts, following a predefined schedule.

d. Reporting and Analytics:

- Real-Time Dashboards: Implement dashboards that provide real-time visibility into AR metrics, such as outstanding receivables, days sales outstanding (DSO), and collection effectiveness index (CEI).

- Automated Reports: Schedule automated generation and distribution of AR reports to key stakeholders.

4. Integrating Automation Tools with Oracle ERP

Integration with Oracle ERP is crucial for seamless data flow and process synchronization. Key integration points include:

a. Master Data Synchronization:

- Customer Data: Ensure customer records are synchronized between the AR automation tool and Oracle ERP to maintain consistency.

- Product and Pricing Data: Synchronize product and pricing information to ensure accurate invoice generation.

b. Transactional Data Integration:

- Sales Orders and Invoices: Integrate sales orders from Oracle ERP with the AR automation tool for automatic invoice generation.

- Payment Data: Ensure payment information flows back into Oracle ERP for accurate financial reporting.

c. Real-Time Data Exchange:

- APIs and Web Services: Utilize APIs and web services to enable real-time data exchange between Oracle ERP and the AR automation tool.

- Batch Processing: Implement batch processing for high-volume data transfers, ensuring timely updates without impacting system performance.

5. Testing and Validation

Before full-scale implementation, it's essential to test the automation workflows in a controlled environment. This includes:

- Unit Testing: Test individual components of the automation tool to ensure they function correctly.

- Integration Testing: Verify that data flows seamlessly between the automation tool and Oracle ERP.

- User Acceptance Testing (UAT): Conduct UAT with AR staff to ensure the workflows meet business requirements and are user-friendly.

6. Training and Change Management

Successful implementation of AR automation tools requires proper training and change management. Steps include:

- Training Programs: Develop comprehensive training programs for AR staff, covering the functionalities and workflows of the automation tool.

- Documentation: Provide detailed documentation, including user manuals and quick reference guides.

- Change Management: Communicate the benefits of automation to all stakeholders and address any concerns or resistance to change.

7. Monitoring and Continuous Improvement

Post-implementation, it's crucial to monitor the performance of the automation tools and continuously seek improvements. This involves:

- Performance Metrics: Track key performance indicators (KPIs) such as invoice processing time, payment collection time, and error rates.

- Feedback Mechanism: Establish a feedback mechanism for AR staff to report issues and suggest improvements.

- Regular Audits: Conduct regular audits to ensure compliance with internal policies and external regulations.

- System Updates: Keep the automation tool updated with the latest features and security patches.

8. Case Studies and Success Stories

Learning from real-world examples can provide valuable insights into the implementation of AR automation tools. Consider including case studies or success stories from organizations that have successfully automated their AR processes. These examples can highlight:

- Challenges Faced: Common challenges encountered during implementation and how they were overcome.

- Benefits Realized: Quantifiable benefits such as reduced processing times, improved cash flow, and enhanced accuracy.

- Best Practices: Key takeaways and best practices that can be applied to other implementations.

9. Future Trends in AR Automation

The field of AR automation is constantly evolving, with new technologies and trends emerging. Staying informed about these trends can help organizations maintain a competitive edge. Some future trends to watch include:

- Artificial Intelligence (AI): AI-driven automation for predictive analytics, fraud detection, and intelligent decision-making.

- Robotic Process Automation (RPA): Using RPA to automate repetitive tasks such as data entry and reconciliation.

- Blockchain: Leveraging blockchain technology for secure and transparent transaction tracking.

- Advanced Analytics: Utilizing advanced analytics for deeper insights into AR performance and customer behavior.

Implementing automation tools in accounts receivable processes within Oracle ERP can significantly enhance efficiency, accuracy, and compliance. By carefully selecting the right tools, configuring workflows, integrating with existing systems, and continuously monitoring and improving the processes, organizations can achieve substantial improvements in their AR management.

8.1.2 Benefits of Automation in AR

Automating the Accounts Receivable (AR) processes within Oracle ERP offers numerous benefits that can significantly improve the efficiency and accuracy of financial operations. In this section, we will explore the key advantages of AR automation and how they contribute to the overall success of an organization.

1. Enhanced Efficiency and Productivity

One of the most significant benefits of automating AR processes is the substantial increase in efficiency and productivity. Manual processes are often time-consuming and prone to errors. Automation tools streamline repetitive tasks such as data entry, invoice generation, and payment processing. This allows AR staff to focus on higher-value activities such as customer relationship management and strategic financial planning. Automation reduces the need for manual intervention, leading to faster processing times and the ability to handle a larger volume of transactions with the same or fewer resources.

2. Improved Accuracy and Reduced Errors

Manual data entry and processing are susceptible to human errors, which can lead to discrepancies in financial records and delayed payments. Automation minimizes these errors by ensuring data is entered consistently and accurately. Automated systems can validate data against predefined rules and automatically flag inconsistencies or anomalies for review. This level of accuracy is critical for maintaining reliable financial records and avoiding costly mistakes that can impact cash flow and financial reporting.

3. Faster Invoicing and Payment Cycles

Automating the invoicing process speeds up the entire billing cycle. Automated systems can generate and send invoices immediately upon the completion of a sale or delivery of a service. This prompt invoicing reduces the time it takes for customers to receive and process bills, ultimately leading to quicker payments. Additionally, automated payment processing can expedite the receipt and application of payments, improving cash flow and reducing the days sales outstanding (DSO) metric.

4. Enhanced Cash Flow Management

Effective cash flow management is crucial for the financial health of any organization. Automation helps optimize cash flow by ensuring timely invoicing and payment collection. Automated systems can send payment reminders and follow-up communications to customers, reducing the likelihood of late payments. Moreover, automated cash application processes ensure that incoming payments are quickly and accurately matched to outstanding invoices, providing real-time visibility into cash flow status.

5. Better Customer Experience

Automation enhances the customer experience by providing faster and more accurate service. Automated invoicing and payment processing reduce the likelihood of billing errors, which can lead to customer dissatisfaction and disputes. Customers appreciate timely and accurate invoices, as well as the convenience of various payment options.

Automation also enables the AR team to respond more promptly to customer inquiries and issues, improving overall customer satisfaction and strengthening relationships.

6. Enhanced Data Security and Compliance

Data security and compliance with financial regulations are critical considerations for any organization. Automated AR systems offer robust security features such as encryption, access controls, and audit trails. These features help protect sensitive financial data from unauthorized access and ensure that the organization complies with regulatory requirements. Automation also facilitates the accurate and timely generation of compliance reports, reducing the risk of non-compliance and associated penalties.

7. Real-Time Reporting and Analytics

Automation provides real-time access to financial data, enabling organizations to generate up-to-date reports and perform in-depth analysis. Automated systems can produce a wide range of reports, from daily transaction summaries to detailed aging reports. This real-time visibility into AR metrics allows management to make informed decisions, identify trends, and take proactive measures to address potential issues. Advanced analytics tools can also help identify patterns and insights that can drive strategic improvements in AR processes.

8. Scalability and Flexibility

As organizations grow, their AR processes must scale to handle increased transaction volumes and complexity. Manual processes can quickly become bottlenecks, leading to delays and inefficiencies. Automated systems, on the other hand, are designed to scale seamlessly. They can handle a higher volume of transactions without compromising accuracy or speed. Additionally, automated systems offer flexibility, allowing organizations to easily adapt to changes in business processes, customer requirements, and regulatory standards.

9. Cost Savings

Automation can lead to significant cost savings by reducing the need for manual labor and minimizing errors that can result in financial losses. By streamlining AR processes, organizations can reduce operational costs and allocate resources more effectively. The initial investment in automation technology is often offset by the long-term savings achieved through increased efficiency, improved cash flow, and reduced error-related costs.

10. Improved Decision-Making

Acces to real-time, accurate financial data is essential for effective decision-making. Automated AR systems provide timely and reliable information that management can use to make informed decisions. Whether it's assessing the creditworthiness of customers, determining appropriate credit limits, or identifying opportunities for process improvements, automation equips decision-makers with the data they need to drive strategic initiatives and achieve business goals.

11. Enhanced Collaboration and Communication

Automation fosters better collaboration and communication within the AR team and across other departments. Automated workflows ensure that tasks are assigned and completed efficiently, reducing the need for constant follow-up and manual coordination. Additionally, automated systems can integrate with other modules and systems, facilitating seamless communication and data sharing. This integration enhances overall organizational efficiency and ensures that all stakeholders have access to the information they need.

12. Strategic Focus

By automating routine and repetitive tasks, AR staff can shift their focus to more strategic activities that add value to the organization. Instead of spending time on manual data entry and reconciliation, staff can engage in activities such as analyzing customer payment behavior, developing credit policies, and implementing strategies to improve cash flow. This strategic focus can drive continuous improvement in AR processes and contribute to the organization's long-term success.

Case Studies and Examples

To illustrate the benefits of automation in AR, consider the following case studies and examples:

Case Study 1: ABC Manufacturing

ABC Manufacturing implemented an automated AR system to streamline its invoicing and payment processes. Before automation, the company faced frequent billing errors, delayed payments, and high DSO. After implementing automation, ABC Manufacturing achieved a 50% reduction in billing errors, a 30% decrease in DSO, and improved cash flow. The AR team now spends less time on manual tasks and more time on strategic initiatives, such as credit management and customer relationship building.

Case Study 2: XYZ Services

XYZ Services, a professional services firm, struggled with manual invoice processing and collection efforts. By adopting an automated AR solution, the firm was able to automate invoice generation, send automated payment reminders, and implement a streamlined collection process. As a result, XYZ Services saw a significant improvement in on-time payments, reduced collection times, and enhanced customer satisfaction. The firm also benefited from real-time reporting and analytics, enabling better financial decision-making.

Conclusion

The benefits of automation in Accounts Receivable are clear and compelling. By leveraging automation tools and technologies, organizations can achieve greater efficiency, accuracy, and control over their AR processes. The improvements in cash flow, customer satisfaction, and compliance, coupled with cost savings and enhanced decision-making capabilities, make a strong case for the adoption of AR automation. As organizations continue to evolve and grow, the need for scalable and flexible AR solutions becomes even more critical, and automation will play a pivotal role in driving future success.

In the next section, we will explore the integration of Accounts Receivable with other modules within Oracle ERP, highlighting the benefits of seamless integration and the best practices for managing data flow between modules.

8.1.3 Common Automation Scenarios

Automation in the Accounts Receivable (AR) module can transform traditional, manual processes into streamlined, error-free, and efficient operations. Below are some of the most common scenarios where automation can be effectively applied in the AR module:

1. Invoice Generation and Distribution

Automation of invoice generation and distribution is one of the most significant time-savers in AR. This process involves automatically creating invoices based on predefined criteria and sending them to customers via email, electronic data interchange (EDI), or other electronic means.

- Implementation: Utilize Oracle ERP's invoicing functionalities to set up automatic invoice generation based on sales orders, contracts, or recurring billing schedules. Configure the system to extract necessary data, generate invoices, and distribute them according to customer preferences.

- Benefits: Reduces the time and labor involved in creating and sending invoices, minimizes errors, ensures timely delivery, and enhances customer satisfaction by providing accurate and prompt billing.

2. Payment Processing

Automated payment processing involves the electronic receipt and application of customer payments. This process can handle various payment methods, such as electronic funds transfer (EFT), credit cards, and checks.

- Implementation: Integrate payment gateways and banking systems with Oracle ERP to facilitate the automatic receipt of payments. Configure the system to match incoming payments with outstanding invoices, apply payments, and update customer balances.

- Benefits: Speeds up the payment application process, reduces manual data entry errors, improves cash flow visibility, and enhances reconciliation efficiency.

3. Dunning and Collection Management

Dunning refers to the process of communicating with customers about overdue payments. Automated dunning and collection management can streamline this process by sending reminders, escalating collection efforts, and managing follow-ups.

- Implementation: Set up dunning rules and schedules in Oracle ERP to automatically generate and send reminder notices to customers with overdue invoices. Configure escalation workflows to trigger additional actions, such as phone calls or third-party collections, based on predefined criteria.

- Benefits: Improves collection efficiency, reduces overdue balances, minimizes the risk of bad debts, and ensures consistent and professional communication with customers.

4. Credit Management and Credit Limit Monitoring

Automating credit management helps ensure that customers adhere to their credit limits and payment terms. This process involves monitoring customer credit limits, generating alerts for potential credit issues, and managing credit approvals.

- Implementation: Configure Oracle ERP to automatically monitor customer credit limits and payment behaviors. Set up alerts and approval workflows for exceeding credit limits or overdue balances, allowing for timely interventions and credit hold decisions.

- Benefits: Enhances risk management, reduces exposure to bad debts, and maintains healthy customer relationships by ensuring timely credit reviews and approvals.

5. Dispute Resolution and Chargeback Management

Automated dispute resolution and chargeback management streamline the handling of customer disputes and chargebacks. This process involves tracking disputes, assigning responsibility, and ensuring timely resolution.

- Implementation: Utilize Oracle ERP's dispute management functionalities to automatically log and track customer disputes. Set up workflows to assign disputes to the appropriate personnel, monitor resolution progress, and generate status reports.

- Benefits: Improves dispute resolution efficiency, enhances customer satisfaction by providing timely responses, and ensures accurate recording of chargebacks and adjustments.

6. Aging Analysis and Reporting

Automating aging analysis and reporting provides real-time visibility into the status of receivables, helping to identify overdue invoices and assess collection performance.

- Implementation: Configure Oracle ERP to automatically generate aging reports based on predefined criteria, such as invoice dates, due dates, and payment statuses. Set up dashboards and alerts to monitor key metrics and trends.

- Benefits: Enhances decision-making by providing up-to-date insights into receivables, improves collection prioritization, and supports proactive management of overdue balances.

7. Cash Forecasting and Analysis

Automated cash forecasting and analysis help predict future cash flows based on historical payment patterns, outstanding invoices, and customer behaviors.

- Implementation: Integrate Oracle ERP's AR data with cash forecasting tools to automatically generate cash flow projections. Configure the system to analyze trends, identify potential cash shortfalls, and recommend actions to optimize cash flow.

- Benefits: Improves financial planning and liquidity management, supports strategic decision-making, and enhances the accuracy of cash flow forecasts.

8. Reconciliation and Audit Trails

Automating reconciliation and audit trails ensures that all AR transactions are accurately recorded and easily traceable, facilitating compliance and audit readiness.

- Implementation: Utilize Oracle ERP's reconciliation tools to automatically match AR transactions with corresponding entries in the general ledger. Set up audit trails to log changes, approvals, and adjustments, ensuring transparency and accountability.

- Benefits: Reduces reconciliation errors, enhances audit preparedness, and supports regulatory compliance by maintaining accurate and traceable records.

9. Customer Communication and Self-Service Portals

Automated customer communication and self-service portals enable customers to access their account information, make payments, and interact with the AR department independently.

- Implementation: Set up self-service portals in Oracle ERP where customers can view invoices, payment histories, and account balances. Configure automated notifications for invoice generation, payment receipts, and overdue reminders.

- Benefits: Enhances customer experience, reduces administrative workload, and improves transparency by providing customers with real-time access to their financial information.

10. Integration with CRM and Sales Modules

Integrating AR automation with Customer Relationship Management (CRM) and sales modules ensures seamless data flow and improves overall customer management.

- Implementation: Configure Oracle ERP to synchronize AR data with CRM and sales modules, ensuring that customer information, sales orders, and payment histories are consistent across all systems.

- Benefits: Enhances data accuracy, supports cross-functional collaboration, and improves customer relationship management by providing a unified view of customer interactions and financial status.

Best Practices for Implementing AR Automation

When implementing AR automation, it is essential to follow best practices to maximize the benefits and ensure a smooth transition:

- Start with a Clear Plan: Define the objectives, scope, and timeline for AR automation. Identify the processes to be automated and the expected outcomes.

- Engage Stakeholders: Involve key stakeholders, including finance, IT, and customer service teams, in the planning and implementation process. Ensure that their requirements and concerns are addressed.

- Choose the Right Tools: Select automation tools and technologies that integrate seamlessly with Oracle ERP and meet your organization's needs. Consider factors such as scalability, ease of use, and vendor support.

- Focus on Data Quality: Ensure that data in the AR module is accurate, complete, and up-to-date before implementing automation. Cleanse and validate data to prevent errors and discrepancies.

- Train and Support Users: Provide comprehensive training and support to users involved in AR processes. Ensure that they understand how to use automation tools effectively and are aware of the benefits.

- Monitor and Optimize: Continuously monitor the performance of automated AR processes. Collect feedback from users, identify areas for improvement, and optimize workflows to enhance efficiency.

In conclusion, automating common scenarios in the Accounts Receivable module of Oracle ERP can lead to significant improvements in efficiency, accuracy, and overall financial management. By leveraging automation tools and following best practices, organizations can streamline AR processes, enhance customer satisfaction, and achieve better financial outcomes.

8.2 Integrating Accounts Receivable with Other Modules

Integration is a critical aspect of utilizing Oracle ERP effectively. In a well-integrated system, data flows seamlessly between modules, ensuring accuracy, efficiency, and real-time insights. In this section, we will delve into the key integration points of the Accounts Receivable (AR) module with other essential Oracle ERP modules.

8.2.1 Integration Points with Other Modules

The Accounts Receivable module does not operate in isolation; it interacts extensively with various other modules within the Oracle ERP suite. Effective integration facilitates better financial management, streamlined operations, and improved decision-making. Here are the primary integration points:

1. General Ledger (GL)

 - Transaction Posting: All financial transactions recorded in the AR module, such as invoices, receipts, adjustments, and write-offs, need to be posted to the General Ledger. This integration ensures that the financial statements reflect accurate and up-to-date information. The AR transactions are summarized and periodically transferred to the GL, where they are classified and reported in financial statements.

 - Reconciliation: The integration helps in reconciling the AR sub-ledger with the GL. Discrepancies between the two are identified and resolved, ensuring that the financial records are accurate and consistent. This process is vital for maintaining the integrity of financial data and supporting audit and compliance requirements.

2. Order Management (OM)

 - Sales Order Processing: The AR module is tightly integrated with the Order Management module, which handles sales orders. When a sales order is fulfilled and shipped, the corresponding invoice is generated in the AR module. This integration ensures that the invoicing process is automated and accurate, reducing manual errors and speeding up the billing cycle.

- Credit Management: Order Management relies on AR data to evaluate the creditworthiness of customers. Before confirming a new sales order, the system checks the customer's outstanding balances, credit limits, and payment history. This integration helps in mitigating credit risk and ensuring that sales are made to creditworthy customers.

3. Inventory Management

- Inventory Valuation: When inventory is sold and an invoice is generated, the corresponding cost of goods sold (COGS) is recorded in the AR module. This integration ensures that inventory levels and valuation are accurately reflected in financial records.

- Backorders and Partial Shipments: The AR module needs to handle scenarios where orders are partially shipped or backordered. The integration with Inventory Management allows the AR system to track these situations and generate invoices accordingly, ensuring that customers are billed correctly for the shipped quantities.

4. Cash Management

- Receipt Processing: Cash Management and AR modules collaborate closely to manage the receipt of customer payments. When a payment is received, it is recorded in Cash Management and applied to the corresponding invoices in the AR module. This integration ensures that cash flows are accurately tracked and that outstanding receivables are updated in real-time.

- Bank Reconciliation: The AR module provides data to Cash Management for reconciling bank statements with recorded receipts. This integration helps in identifying discrepancies between bank records and the ERP system, ensuring that cash records are accurate and up-to-date.

5. Procurement

- Supplier Payments and Customer Refunds: Although primarily dealing with suppliers, the Procurement module's integration with AR is crucial when issuing refunds to customers. The Procurement module processes these refunds, which are then reflected in the AR module as adjustments to the customer's account.

- Trade Receivables and Payables Offsetting: In some scenarios, businesses might offset receivables from a customer against payables to the same entity if they are also a supplier. This integration ensures that such transactions are accurately recorded and managed.

6. Project Accounting

- Billing for Project Deliverables: For companies involved in project-based work, the Project Accounting module integrates with AR to generate invoices for project deliverables. This integration ensures that billable milestones, time, and expenses are accurately captured and billed to clients.

- Revenue Recognition: The AR module helps in recognizing revenue based on project progress. This integration ensures compliance with accounting standards for revenue recognition, providing accurate financial reporting.

7. Customer Relationship Management (CRM)

- Customer Data Management: The CRM module maintains detailed customer profiles, including contact information, interaction history, and sales opportunities. This data is shared with the AR module to ensure that customer invoices and statements are sent to the correct addresses and that any special billing requirements are met.

- Dispute Resolution: When customers raise disputes regarding invoices, the CRM module tracks these issues. The integration with AR allows for efficient resolution by providing access to invoice details, payment history, and any previous interactions with the customer.

8. Human Capital Management (HCM)

- Employee Expense Reimbursements: While the primary focus of HCM is on employee management, it also handles expense reimbursements. These reimbursements are processed through AR, where they are recorded as receivables until paid. This integration ensures that employee-related financial transactions are accurately tracked.

- Sales Commissions: For sales-driven organizations, HCM may track sales commissions, which need to be integrated with AR for accurate payment processing. This ensures that commissions are calculated based on invoiced and collected amounts, maintaining alignment with sales performance.

9. Manufacturing

- Production Orders and Invoicing: For manufacturing firms, the integration between Manufacturing and AR modules is crucial for invoicing finished goods. As production orders are completed and goods are shipped, the corresponding invoices are generated in the AR module.

- Cost Tracking: The AR module integrates with Manufacturing to track the costs associated with producing goods. This ensures that the invoiced amounts reflect the actual costs incurred, providing accurate financial data for profitability analysis.

10. Tax Management

- Tax Calculation and Reporting: The AR module integrates with the Tax Management module to ensure accurate tax calculation on invoices. This integration ensures compliance with various tax regulations and simplifies tax reporting.

- Handling Tax Adjustments: When tax rates change or corrections are needed, the Tax Management module communicates these changes to AR. This integration ensures that invoices are updated with the correct tax amounts and that any adjustments are accurately recorded.

Benefits of Integration

Effective integration of the Accounts Receivable module with other Oracle ERP modules offers several key benefits:

- Improved Data Accuracy: By automating data exchange between modules, integration reduces the risk of manual errors and ensures that all financial data is accurate and up-to-date.

- Operational Efficiency: Integration streamlines processes across different functional areas, reducing duplication of efforts and improving overall operational efficiency.

- Enhanced Financial Reporting: With integrated data, financial reports provide a comprehensive view of the organization's financial health, supporting better decision-making.

- Real-Time Insights: Integration enables real-time data sharing, allowing stakeholders to access the latest information and make timely decisions.

- Compliance and Audit Readiness: Integrated systems ensure that financial records are consistent and accurate, supporting compliance with regulatory requirements and facilitating audit processes.

Conclusion

The integration of the Accounts Receivable module with other Oracle ERP modules is essential for achieving a cohesive and efficient financial management system. By understanding and leveraging these integration points, organizations can enhance their financial operations, improve data accuracy, and gain real-time insights into their business performance. In the next section, we will explore best practices for effective Accounts Receivable management, ensuring that your AR processes are optimized for success.

8.2.2 Benefits of Seamless Integration

In the context of enterprise resource planning (ERP) systems, seamless integration between the Accounts Receivable (AR) module and other modules is crucial for maximizing efficiency, accuracy, and overall business performance. The integration ensures that data flows smoothly across different functional areas, enabling better decision-making and streamlined processes. Below are the key benefits of seamless integration:

Improved Data Accuracy and Consistency

One of the primary benefits of seamless integration is the enhancement of data accuracy and consistency. When the AR module is integrated with other modules, such as Sales Order Management, General Ledger, and Inventory Management, data is automatically shared and updated in real-time across the entire ERP system. This reduces the likelihood of data entry errors, duplicate entries, and discrepancies. Accurate and consistent data ensures that all stakeholders have access to reliable information, which is critical for making informed decisions.

For example, when a sales order is processed, the details are automatically reflected in the AR module. This ensures that the invoicing process is based on accurate sales data, reducing the risk of billing errors. Additionally, payment receipts and customer account balances are updated in real-time, providing a clear and accurate picture of the company's financial status.

Enhanced Efficiency and Productivity

Seamless integration significantly enhances efficiency and productivity by automating routine tasks and reducing manual interventions. When the AR module is integrated with other modules, processes such as invoicing, payment processing, and financial reporting become more streamlined. This automation frees up valuable time for employees, allowing them to focus on more strategic activities that add value to the business.

For instance, once a sales order is fulfilled and the goods are shipped, the information is automatically transferred to the AR module to generate an invoice. This eliminates the need for manual data entry and reduces the processing time for invoices. Similarly, payment receipts can be automatically matched with outstanding invoices, accelerating the cash application process and improving cash flow management.

Better Financial Visibility and Control

Seamless integration provides better financial visibility and control by offering a unified view of the company's financial data. When the AR module is integrated with the General Ledger and other financial modules, it enables real-time tracking and monitoring of financial transactions. This comprehensive view helps finance teams to monitor cash flow, assess credit risks, and manage accounts receivable more effectively.

For example, finance managers can easily access consolidated financial reports that include data from the AR module, such as outstanding invoices, aging reports, and customer payment histories. This visibility allows for more accurate financial forecasting and planning, enabling the company to make proactive decisions to optimize cash flow and reduce credit risks.

Improved Customer Relationship Management

Integration of the AR module with Customer Relationship Management (CRM) systems enhances customer relationship management by providing a holistic view of customer interactions and transactions. Seamless integration ensures that customer data, such as contact information, purchase history, and payment behavior, is accessible across both the AR and CRM systems. This integration enables better customer service and support.

For instance, customer service representatives can access real-time information about a customer's outstanding invoices and payment history when addressing inquiries or disputes. This enables them to provide accurate and timely responses, enhancing customer satisfaction. Additionally, sales teams can leverage integrated data to identify cross-selling and up-selling opportunities based on customers' purchasing and payment patterns.

Streamlined Order-to-Cash Cycle

The order-to-cash (O2C) cycle encompasses the entire process from receiving a customer order to collecting payment. Seamless integration between the AR module and other modules involved in the O2C cycle, such as Sales Order Management, Inventory Management, and Shipping, streamlines the entire process. This integration ensures that each step of the O2C cycle is connected and automated, reducing delays and improving overall efficiency.

For example, when a customer places an order, the sales order details are automatically transferred to the Inventory Management module to check stock availability. Once the order is fulfilled and shipped, the information flows seamlessly to the AR module for invoicing. Payment receipts are then recorded and matched with the corresponding invoices, completing the O2C cycle. This streamlined process reduces the order-to-cash cycle time, improving cash flow and customer satisfaction.

Enhanced Compliance and Audit Readiness

Seamless integration between the AR module and other modules enhances compliance and audit readiness by providing a complete and accurate audit trail of financial transactions. Integrated systems ensure that all transactions are recorded and documented consistently across the ERP system, facilitating compliance with regulatory requirements and internal policies.

For instance, integrated data from the AR module and the General Ledger ensures that financial statements are accurate and reflect all receivables and revenue transactions. This integration simplifies the audit process by providing auditors with easy access to comprehensive and consistent financial records. Additionally, integrated systems can generate compliance reports and documentation required for regulatory filings, reducing the risk of non-compliance and associated penalties.

Improved Cash Flow Management

Effective cash flow management is critical for the financial health of any business. Seamless integration between the AR module and other financial modules enables better cash flow management by providing real-time visibility into receivables and payments. This visibility allows finance teams to monitor cash inflows and outflows accurately and take proactive measures to optimize cash flow.

For example, integrated systems can generate real-time aging reports that highlight overdue invoices and outstanding receivables. Finance teams can use this information to prioritize collection efforts and follow up with customers on late payments. Additionally, integrated data allows for accurate cash flow forecasting, helping businesses to plan for future cash needs and avoid liquidity issues.

Scalability and Flexibility

Seamless integration provides scalability and flexibility, enabling businesses to adapt to changing needs and growth. Integrated ERP systems can easily accommodate additional modules and functionalities as the business expands. This scalability ensures that the AR module can continue to support the company's operations and financial processes without disruption.

For instance, as a business grows and enters new markets, integrated systems can handle increased transaction volumes and complexities. New sales channels, payment methods, and customer segments can be seamlessly integrated into the existing ERP system, ensuring that the AR module remains aligned with the company's evolving requirements.

Enhanced Decision-Making

Seamless integration enhances decision-making by providing comprehensive and accurate data for analysis and reporting. Integrated ERP systems enable businesses to generate real-time reports and dashboards that offer insights into key financial and operational metrics. This data-driven approach empowers decision-makers to make informed choices and develop effective strategies.

For example, integrated systems can provide insights into customer payment behavior, sales trends, and receivables aging. Decision-makers can use this information to identify areas for improvement, optimize credit policies, and develop targeted collection strategies. Additionally, integrated data supports scenario analysis and predictive modeling, helping businesses to anticipate future trends and make proactive decisions.

Conclusion

In conclusion, the benefits of seamless integration between the Accounts Receivable module and other modules in an ERP system are manifold. Improved data accuracy and consistency, enhanced efficiency and productivity, better financial visibility and control, improved customer relationship management, streamlined order-to-cash cycle, enhanced compliance and audit readiness, improved cash flow management, scalability and flexibility, and enhanced decision-making are some of the key advantages. By leveraging these benefits, businesses can optimize their accounts receivable processes, enhance financial performance, and achieve greater operational excellence.

8.2.3 Managing Data Flow Between Modules

Effective management of data flow between the Accounts Receivable (AR) module and other Oracle ERP modules is crucial for maintaining accurate and up-to-date financial information. Seamless data flow ensures that all relevant modules have access to the most current data, enabling efficient operations and informed decision-making. In this section, we will explore best practices for managing data flow between the AR module and other modules, focusing on data synchronization, consistency, and error handling.

Understanding Data Flow

Data flow between modules refers to the movement of information from one module to another within the ERP system. In the context of AR, data flow typically involves the exchange of customer information, sales orders, invoices, receipts, and financial data with other modules such as Order Management, Inventory, General Ledger, and Cash Management. Proper management of this data flow is essential to ensure that all modules reflect the same information and that business processes operate smoothly.

Key Integration Points

To manage data flow effectively, it is important to understand the key integration points between the AR module and other modules:

1. Order Management and AR: Sales orders created in the Order Management module trigger the creation of invoices in the AR module. Ensuring that sales orders are accurately reflected in AR is critical for timely billing and revenue recognition.

2. Inventory and AR: Inventory module tracks the availability and movement of goods. When goods are shipped to customers, the AR module needs to generate corresponding invoices. This integration ensures that inventory reductions are matched with revenue recognition.

3. General Ledger and AR: Financial transactions in the AR module, such as invoice postings and receipt applications, impact the General Ledger (GL). Accurate data flow ensures that the financial statements are correct and up-to-date.

4. Cash Management and AR: Customer payments recorded in the AR module must be reflected in the Cash Management module to maintain accurate cash flow records and reconcile bank statements.

Best Practices for Managing Data Flow

1. Automate Data Synchronization

Automating data synchronization between modules reduces the risk of human error and ensures that data is consistently updated across the ERP system. Utilize Oracle ERP's built-in integration tools and APIs to automate the transfer of data. For example, when a sales order is created in Order Management, set up automated workflows to generate the corresponding invoice in AR.

2. Ensure Data Consistency

Data consistency is critical for accurate financial reporting and operational efficiency. Implement validation rules and data checks to ensure that data transferred between modules is accurate and complete. For example, ensure that all mandatory fields in sales orders and invoices are populated before data transfer.

3. Implement Real-Time Data Updates

Where possible, implement real-time data updates to ensure that information is always current. Real-time updates minimize the lag between transactions and data availability, enabling timely decision-making. For example, real-time updates between Inventory and AR ensure that invoices are generated as soon as goods are shipped.

4. Establish Clear Data Ownership

Define clear data ownership and responsibilities for each module to avoid conflicts and ensure accountability. For example, the Order Management team may be responsible for the accuracy of sales order data, while the AR team is responsible for invoice accuracy. Establishing clear ownership helps in resolving data discrepancies quickly.

5. Use Data Mapping and Transformation

Data mapping and transformation tools help in converting data formats and structures between modules. Use these tools to ensure that data transferred between modules is in the correct format and structure. For example, map customer fields from Order Management to AR to ensure that customer information is consistent.

6. Regularly Reconcile Data

Regular reconciliation of data between modules helps in identifying and resolving discrepancies early. Implement regular reconciliation processes to compare data in the AR module with other modules. For example, reconcile sales orders in Order Management with invoices in AR to ensure that all orders are billed.

7. Monitor Data Flow and Performance

Regularly monitor data flow between modules to identify any bottlenecks or issues. Use Oracle ERP's monitoring tools to track data transfer performance and ensure that data is flowing smoothly. Set up alerts and notifications for any data flow issues, such as failed data transfers or inconsistencies.

8. Provide Training and Support

Ensure that all relevant staff are trained in managing data flow between modules. Provide regular training sessions and resources to keep staff updated on best practices and any changes in processes. Establish a support system to assist staff with any issues they encounter in managing data flow.

Example Scenario: Sales Order to Invoice Process

To illustrate the importance of managing data flow, let's consider the process of converting a sales order to an invoice:

1. Sales Order Creation: A sales order is created in the Order Management module with all necessary details, including customer information, order items, quantities, and prices.

2. Data Transfer to AR: The sales order data is automatically transferred to the AR module, triggering the creation of an invoice. The data transfer includes all relevant information needed for the invoice.

3. Invoice Generation: The AR module generates the invoice based on the sales order data. The invoice includes details such as customer information, item descriptions, quantities, prices, and payment terms.

4. Data Validation: The AR module validates the invoice data to ensure accuracy and completeness. Any discrepancies are flagged for resolution.

5. Posting to GL: Once the invoice is validated, it is posted to the General Ledger. The financial impact of the invoice is recorded, updating revenue and accounts receivable balances.

6. Customer Notification: The customer is notified of the invoice, and the invoice is made available for payment.

7. Receipt Application: When the customer makes a payment, the receipt is recorded in the AR module and applied to the corresponding invoice. The payment information is also updated in the Cash Management module.

8. Reconciliation: Regular reconciliation processes are conducted to ensure that sales orders in Order Management match invoices in AR and that all payments are accurately recorded.

By following these steps and best practices, organizations can ensure that data flows seamlessly between the AR module and other Oracle ERP modules, leading to accurate financial records, efficient operations, and informed decision-making.

Handling Data Flow Errors

Despite best efforts, data flow errors can still occur. It is important to have a robust error handling and resolution process in place:

1. Identify and Log Errors: Implement mechanisms to identify and log data flow errors. Use Oracle ERP's error logging features to capture detailed information about the errors, including the source, affected data, and error messages.

2. Analyze and Resolve Errors: Analyze the logged errors to identify the root cause. Common issues may include data format mismatches, missing mandatory fields, or integration failures. Work with relevant teams to resolve the errors and prevent recurrence.

3. Implement Error Notifications: Set up notifications to alert relevant staff when data flow errors occur. Prompt notifications enable quick resolution and minimize the impact on business operations.

4. Document Error Resolution Procedures: Document standard procedures for resolving common data flow errors. Provide clear instructions and guidelines for staff to follow when addressing errors.

5. Review and Improve Processes: Regularly review data flow processes and error handling procedures. Identify areas for improvement and implement changes to enhance data flow management.

By effectively managing data flow between the AR module and other Oracle ERP modules, organizations can achieve accurate and timely financial information, streamline operations, and support strategic decision-making. Implementing best practices and having robust error handling procedures in place ensures that the ERP system operates efficiently and delivers maximum value to the organization.

8.3 Best Practices for Effective Accounts Receivable Management

Effective accounts receivable (AR) management is essential for maintaining a healthy cash flow, reducing bad debts, and ensuring timely collections. This section delves into best practices for AR management, beginning with the establishment of standard operating procedures (SOPs). These SOPs form the backbone of a structured and efficient AR process.

8.3.1 Establishing Standard Operating Procedures

Standard Operating Procedures (SOPs) are essential for ensuring consistency, efficiency, and compliance in accounts receivable management. SOPs provide clear instructions and guidelines for AR staff, helping to streamline processes and minimize errors. Here, we explore the key components and benefits of establishing robust SOPs for AR management.

The Importance of SOPs in Accounts Receivable

SOPs play a crucial role in AR management by:

- Ensuring Consistency: SOPs ensure that all AR tasks are performed consistently across the organization. This consistency helps in maintaining uniformity in customer interactions, invoicing, and collections.

- Enhancing Efficiency: By providing step-by-step instructions, SOPs streamline AR processes, reducing the time and effort required to complete tasks.

- Minimizing Errors: Clear guidelines help to minimize errors and discrepancies in AR processes, leading to more accurate financial records.

- Facilitating Training: SOPs serve as valuable training resources for new AR staff, helping them to quickly understand and perform their duties.

- Ensuring Compliance: SOPs help ensure compliance with internal policies, external regulations, and industry standards, reducing the risk of legal and financial penalties.

Developing Effective SOPs for Accounts Receivable

Developing effective SOPs for AR management involves several steps:

1. Identify Key AR Processes: Start by identifying the key processes involved in AR management, such as customer onboarding, invoicing, collections, and dispute resolution.

2. Document Each Process: For each key process, document the steps involved, the responsible parties, and the required inputs and outputs. Use clear and concise language to ensure that the SOPs are easy to understand.

3. Include Process Flowcharts: Use flowcharts to visually represent the steps involved in each process. Flowcharts help to clarify complex processes and highlight decision points.

4. Define Roles and Responsibilities: Clearly define the roles and responsibilities of each team member involved in the AR processes. This ensures accountability and helps prevent overlaps and gaps in task execution.

5. Establish Performance Metrics: Define performance metrics and key performance indicators (KPIs) for each process. These metrics help to measure the efficiency and effectiveness of AR processes and identify areas for improvement.

6. Review and Update Regularly: SOPs should be reviewed and updated regularly to reflect changes in policies, regulations, and business practices. Regular reviews help ensure that the SOPs remain relevant and effective.

Key Components of SOPs for AR Management

Effective SOPs for AR management should include the following components:

1. Customer Onboarding: SOPs for customer onboarding should cover the process of setting up new customer accounts, verifying customer information, and establishing credit terms. This process may include steps such as:

  - Collecting and verifying customer information

  - Conducting credit checks and risk assessments

  - Setting up customer accounts in the AR system

  - Communicating credit terms and payment expectations to customers

2. Invoicing: SOPs for invoicing should detail the process of creating, approving, and sending invoices to customers. This process may include steps such as:

  - Generating invoices based on sales orders or contracts

  - Reviewing and approving invoices for accuracy and completeness

  - Sending invoices to customers via email, mail, or electronic data interchange (EDI)

  - Recording invoices in the AR system and updating customer accounts

3. Collections: SOPs for collections should outline the process of managing overdue accounts and collecting payments from customers. This process may include steps such as:

  - Monitoring and identifying overdue accounts

  - Sending payment reminders and follow-up communications to customers

  - Implementing escalation procedures for delinquent accounts

  - Negotiating payment plans and settlements with customers

  - Recording payments and updating customer accounts in the AR system

4. Dispute Resolution: SOPs for dispute resolution should cover the process of handling and resolving customer disputes related to invoices, payments, and credits. This process may include steps such as:

  - Receiving and logging customer disputes

  - Investigating the validity of disputes and gathering supporting documentation

  - Communicating with customers to resolve disputes amicably

  - Making necessary adjustments to invoices or customer accounts

  - Recording dispute resolutions in the AR system

5. Reporting and Analysis: SOPs for reporting and analysis should detail the process of generating and analyzing AR reports to monitor performance and identify trends. This process may include steps such as:

  - Generating standard and custom AR reports, such as aging reports, collection reports, and dispute reports

- Analyzing report data to identify patterns and trends

- Using report insights to inform AR strategies and decision-making

- Presenting report findings to management and stakeholders

Implementing and Communicating SOPs

Once the SOPs have been developed, it is essential to implement and communicate them effectively:

1. Training and Onboarding: Provide comprehensive training to AR staff on the new SOPs. This training should cover the rationale behind the SOPs, the steps involved in each process, and the expected outcomes. Use training sessions, workshops, and hands-on exercises to ensure that staff understand and can apply the SOPs in their daily work.

2. Communication: Communicate the SOPs to all relevant stakeholders, including AR staff, management, and other departments that interact with AR processes. Use multiple communication channels, such as email, intranet, and meetings, to ensure that the SOPs are widely disseminated and understood.

3. Monitoring and Compliance: Establish mechanisms for monitoring compliance with the SOPs. This may include regular audits, performance reviews, and feedback sessions. Use these mechanisms to identify areas where compliance is lacking and take corrective actions as needed.

4. Continuous Improvement: Encourage a culture of continuous improvement by regularly reviewing and updating the SOPs. Solicit feedback from AR staff and other stakeholders to identify areas for enhancement. Use performance metrics and KPIs to measure the effectiveness of the SOPs and make data-driven improvements.

Benefits of Establishing SOPs for AR Management

Establishing SOPs for AR management offers several benefits:

1. Improved Efficiency: SOPs streamline AR processes, reducing the time and effort required to complete tasks. This leads to faster invoicing, collections, and dispute resolution.

2. Enhanced Accuracy: Clear guidelines help to minimize errors and discrepancies in AR processes, leading to more accurate financial records and fewer disputes.

3. Better Compliance: SOPs help ensure compliance with internal policies, external regulations, and industry standards, reducing the risk of legal and financial penalties.

4. Consistent Customer Experience: SOPs ensure that all customers are treated consistently and fairly, leading to improved customer satisfaction and stronger customer relationships.

5. Effective Training: SOPs serve as valuable training resources for new AR staff, helping them to quickly understand and perform their duties. This reduces the learning curve and enhances staff productivity.

6. Informed Decision-Making: SOPs provide a structured framework for AR processes, enabling better monitoring and analysis. This leads to more informed decision-making and improved financial performance.

By establishing and implementing robust SOPs for accounts receivable management, organizations can achieve greater efficiency, accuracy, and compliance. These benefits contribute to a healthier cash flow, reduced bad debts, and stronger financial performance.

8.3.2 Training and Development for AR Staff

Introduction

Effective management of the Accounts Receivable (AR) module in Oracle ERP requires a well-trained and knowledgeable team. The success of AR processes hinges on the competence of the staff handling these operations. Training and development are crucial for ensuring that AR staff are equipped with the skills and knowledge necessary to manage accounts receivable efficiently and accurately.

The Importance of Training and Development

Investing in training and development for AR staff has several benefits:

1. Enhanced Productivity: Well-trained employees can perform their tasks more efficiently, leading to faster processing of invoices, receipts, and other AR-related activities.

2. Reduced Errors: Proper training reduces the likelihood of errors in data entry and processing, which can prevent issues like incorrect billing, missed payments, and inaccurate financial reports.

3. Compliance and Security: Training ensures that staff are aware of compliance requirements and security protocols, helping to safeguard sensitive financial data and adhere to regulatory standards.

4. Employee Satisfaction and Retention: Providing opportunities for professional growth can improve job satisfaction and reduce turnover, ensuring continuity and stability in AR operations.

Developing a Training Program for AR Staff

Creating an effective training program involves several key steps:

1. Assess Training Needs

   - Conduct a skills assessment to identify the current capabilities and knowledge gaps of the AR staff.

   - Evaluate the specific requirements of the AR module in Oracle ERP, including any new features or updates.

   - Gather feedback from staff on areas where they feel they need more training or support.

2. Define Training Objectives

   - Set clear and measurable objectives for the training program. These should align with the overall goals of the AR department and the organization.

   - Objectives might include improving the accuracy of data entry, reducing the time required to process invoices, or increasing knowledge of compliance regulations.

3. Develop Training Materials

   - Create comprehensive training materials, including user manuals, process guides, video tutorials, and interactive e-learning modules.

- Ensure that the materials cover all essential aspects of the AR module, from basic operations to advanced features.

- Include real-life scenarios and practical exercises to help staff apply their learning in a practical context.

4. Implement Training Sessions

- Organize training sessions in various formats, such as in-person workshops, online webinars, and self-paced e-learning courses.

- Use a mix of instructional methods to cater to different learning styles, including lectures, demonstrations, hands-on practice, and group discussions.

- Provide access to a test environment where staff can practice using the AR module without affecting live data.

5. Monitor and Evaluate Training Effectiveness

- Use assessments, quizzes, and practical tests to evaluate the effectiveness of the training program.

- Collect feedback from participants to identify areas for improvement and make necessary adjustments to the training materials and delivery methods.

- Track performance metrics to measure the impact of training on key AR processes, such as invoice processing times and error rates.

Key Areas of Focus in AR Training

To ensure comprehensive coverage, the training program should focus on several key areas:

1. System Navigation and User Interface

- Familiarize staff with the layout and navigation of the Oracle ERP system.

- Teach staff how to access and use different features and functions of the AR module.

2. Data Entry and Management

- Train staff on accurate data entry techniques for creating and maintaining customer records.

- Emphasize the importance of data accuracy and consistency to avoid errors and discrepancies.

3. Invoice Processing

  - Provide detailed instructions on creating, posting, and adjusting customer invoices.

  - Cover different types of invoices, such as standard invoices, credit memos, and debit memos.

4. Receipt Management

  - Teach staff how to record, apply, and unapply customer receipts.

  - Explain different receipt methods, such as cash, checks, electronic transfers, and credit cards.

5. Collections and Credit Management

  - Train staff on setting up and implementing collection strategies.

  - Cover credit management practices, including establishing credit limits and handling delinquent accounts.

6. Reporting and Analysis

  - Instruct staff on generating and customizing standard reports in the AR module.

  - Teach staff how to use dashboards and other analytical tools to monitor AR performance and identify trends.

7. Compliance and Security

  - Educate staff on compliance requirements related to accounts receivable, such as tax regulations and data privacy laws.

  - Provide training on security protocols to protect sensitive financial information.

Continuous Development and Support

Training should not be a one-time event but an ongoing process to ensure that staff stay up-to-date with the latest features and best practices in AR management. Consider the following strategies for continuous development:

1. Regular Refresher Courses

 - Schedule regular refresher courses to reinforce key concepts and update staff on any changes or new features in the AR module.

2. Advanced Training Sessions

 - Offer advanced training sessions for experienced staff who want to deepen their knowledge and skills in specific areas.

3. Mentorship and Peer Support

 - Establish a mentorship program where experienced AR staff can provide guidance and support to new or less experienced team members.

 - Encourage peer support through regular team meetings and knowledge-sharing sessions.

4. Access to Resources

 - Provide access to a library of training materials, including user guides, video tutorials, and best practice documents.

 - Ensure that staff know how to access Oracle's online support resources and community forums for additional help.

5. Performance Monitoring and Feedback

 - Continuously monitor staff performance and provide constructive feedback to help them improve.

 - Use performance data to identify areas where additional training or support may be needed.

Conclusion

Investing in training and development for AR staff is essential for the effective management of the Accounts Receivable module in Oracle ERP. By providing comprehensive and ongoing training, organizations can enhance productivity, reduce errors, ensure compliance, and improve overall financial performance. A well-trained AR team is a valuable asset that contributes to the success and stability of the organization.

8.3.3 Continuous Improvement and Monitoring

Continuous improvement and monitoring are vital components of effective Accounts Receivable (AR) management. They ensure that the processes remain efficient, compliant, and aligned with the organization's financial goals. This section will explore the strategies, tools, and practices necessary for maintaining a dynamic and responsive AR system.

1. Understanding the Importance of Continuous Improvement

Continuous improvement is a systematic, ongoing effort to enhance products, services, or processes. In AR management, this means regularly reviewing and refining the processes to ensure they are as efficient and effective as possible. The key benefits include:

- Increased Efficiency: Streamlining processes to reduce time and effort.

- Enhanced Accuracy: Reducing errors and improving data integrity.

- Better Compliance: Ensuring adherence to regulatory and internal policies.

- Improved Customer Relationships: Faster, more accurate invoicing and collections enhance customer satisfaction.

- Optimized Cash Flow: Faster collections and fewer disputes contribute to a healthier cash flow.

2. Setting Goals for Improvement

To effectively improve AR processes, it is crucial to set clear, achievable goals. These goals should be Specific, Measurable, Achievable, Relevant, and Time-bound (SMART). Examples of AR improvement goals include:

- Reducing the average days sales outstanding (DSO) by a certain percentage.

- Increasing the percentage of on-time payments.

- Decreasing the number of disputed invoices.

- Enhancing the accuracy of invoice generation.

3. Monitoring Key Performance Indicators (KPIs)

KPIs are essential for measuring the effectiveness of AR processes. Regularly monitoring these indicators helps identify areas that need improvement. Key AR KPIs include:

- Days Sales Outstanding (DSO): Measures the average number of days it takes to collect payment after a sale.

- Collection Effectiveness Index (CEI): Evaluates the efficiency of collections over a specific period.

- Invoice Accuracy Rate: Tracks the percentage of invoices generated without errors.

- Dispute Resolution Time: Measures the average time taken to resolve invoice disputes.

- Percentage of Current Receivables: Indicates the proportion of receivables that are within the agreed payment terms.

4. Utilizing Technology and Automation

Technology plays a crucial role in continuous improvement. Implementing advanced AR software and automation tools can significantly enhance process efficiency and accuracy. Key technological solutions include:

- Automated Invoice Generation: Reduces manual errors and speeds up the invoicing process.

- Electronic Payment Processing: Facilitates faster, more secure payments.

- Advanced Reporting Tools: Provide real-time insights into AR performance.

- Artificial Intelligence (AI) and Machine Learning (ML): Predictive analytics can identify trends and potential issues before they become problems.

5. Conducting Regular Audits and Reviews

Regular audits and reviews are essential for identifying inefficiencies and areas for improvement. These reviews should include:

- Process Audits: Evaluating the efficiency and effectiveness of AR processes.

- Compliance Audits: Ensuring adherence to regulatory requirements and internal policies.

- Performance Reviews: Assessing the performance of the AR team and identifying training needs.

6. Implementing Feedback Mechanisms

Feedback from both internal and external stakeholders is invaluable for continuous improvement. Establishing feedback mechanisms helps gather insights from:

- Customers: Understanding their experiences with the invoicing and payment processes.

- AR Team Members: Identifying challenges and opportunities for process improvement.

- Other Departments: Collaborating with sales, customer service, and finance to ensure seamless AR processes.

7. Training and Development

Continuous training and development of the AR team are critical for maintaining high performance and adapting to new technologies and processes. Training programs should cover:

- Process and Policy Updates: Keeping the team informed about changes in AR processes and policies.

- Technology Training: Ensuring the team is proficient in using the latest AR software and tools.

- Soft Skills Development: Enhancing communication, negotiation, and customer service skills.

8. Leveraging Data Analytics

Data analytics provides powerful insights into AR performance and areas for improvement. Key data analytics practices include:

- Trend Analysis: Identifying patterns and trends in payment behavior and receivables.

- Predictive Analytics: Using historical data to predict future outcomes, such as potential payment delays.

- Root Cause Analysis: Investigating the underlying causes of issues, such as frequent disputes or late payments.

9. Establishing a Continuous Improvement Culture

Creating a culture of continuous improvement within the AR team and the broader organization is crucial for sustained success. This involves:

- Leadership Commitment: Ensuring senior management supports and advocates for continuous improvement initiatives.

- Employee Involvement: Encouraging team members to contribute ideas and participate in improvement projects.

- Recognition and Rewards: Acknowledging and rewarding contributions to process improvement.

10. Case Studies and Real-World Examples

Examining case studies and real-world examples of successful AR process improvements can provide valuable insights and inspiration. Examples might include:

- Company A: Implemented automated invoice generation, reducing invoice errors by 40% and speeding up the invoicing process by 30%.

- Company B: Utilized predictive analytics to identify at-risk accounts, resulting in a 20% reduction in late payments.

- Company C: Conducted regular AR team training sessions, leading to a 15% increase in collection effectiveness.

11. Developing an Improvement Plan

Developing a structured improvement plan ensures that continuous improvement efforts are organized and focused. An effective improvement plan should include:

- Objectives: Clear, measurable goals for improvement.

- Actions: Specific steps to achieve the objectives.

- Responsibilities: Assigning roles and responsibilities for each action.

- Timeline: Establishing a timeline for implementation and review.

- Evaluation: Setting criteria for evaluating the success of the improvement efforts.

12. Overcoming Challenges in Continuous Improvement

Continuous improvement in AR management can face several challenges, such as:

- Resistance to Change: Overcoming resistance from team members and stakeholders.

- Resource Constraints: Ensuring adequate resources, such as time, budget, and technology, are available.

- Maintaining Momentum: Keeping the improvement efforts ongoing and preventing complacency.

13. Celebrating Successes

Recognizing and celebrating the successes achieved through continuous improvement efforts is vital for maintaining motivation and engagement. This can include:

- Acknowledging Individual Contributions: Highlighting the efforts of team members who have contributed significantly to improvement initiatives.

- Sharing Success Stories: Communicating the achievements and benefits of improvement efforts to the broader organization.

- Rewarding Team Performance: Offering incentives and rewards for achieving improvement goals.

Conclusion

Continuous improvement and monitoring are essential practices for effective accounts receivable management. By setting clear goals, leveraging technology, conducting regular audits, and fostering a culture of improvement, organizations can optimize their AR processes, enhance efficiency, and achieve better financial outcomes. Embracing these best practices ensures that the AR function remains dynamic, responsive, and aligned with the organization's overall objectives.

CHAPTER IX
Troubleshooting and Support

9.1 Common Issues in Accounts Receivable

9.1.1 Identifying and Resolving Common Problems

In the realm of Accounts Receivable (AR) within Oracle ERP, users may encounter several common issues that can impede the efficiency of financial operations. This section aims to provide a comprehensive guide to identifying and resolving these problems, ensuring smooth and accurate AR management.

Identifying Common Problems

1. Data Entry Errors:

   Data entry errors are one of the most frequent issues in AR. These errors can occur when entering customer information, invoice details, or payment data. Incorrect data can lead to mismatched records, incorrect billing, and ultimately, customer dissatisfaction.

   Indicators:

   - Discrepancies between invoice amounts and received payments.

   - Incorrect customer information leading to misdirected invoices.

   - Frequent adjustments and corrections in AR records.

2. Invoice Discrepancies:

   Invoice discrepancies can arise from incorrect pricing, misapplied discounts, or errors in quantity billed. Such discrepancies can cause delays in payment processing and affect cash flow.

Indicators:

- Customer complaints about incorrect billing.

- High volume of invoice adjustments.

- Disputes over invoice amounts.

3. Delayed Payments:

Delayed payments can occur due to several reasons, including customer financial difficulties, disputes over invoice accuracy, or inefficient payment processing workflows.

Indicators:

- Aging receivables reports showing overdue invoices.

- Increased collection efforts and communications with customers.

- Cash flow issues due to pending payments.

4. Credit Management Issues:

Ineffective credit management can lead to extended credit to high-risk customers, increasing the risk of bad debts. Conversely, overly strict credit policies can hinder sales and customer relationships.

Indicators:

- High levels of bad debt write-offs.

- Frequent credit limit adjustments.

- Sales team feedback on lost sales due to credit policies.

5. Integration Issues:

Integration issues between AR and other modules (such as Sales, Inventory, and General Ledger) can lead to data inconsistencies and operational inefficiencies.

Indicators:

- Inconsistent data across modules.

- Delays in updating financial records.

- Difficulty in tracking transactions across the ERP system.

Resolving Common Problems

1. Data Entry Errors:

Implementing rigorous data validation processes and training staff on accurate data entry can significantly reduce errors.

Solutions:

- Utilize data validation rules in Oracle ERP to check for inconsistencies at the point of entry.

- Regularly audit data entries and correct any identified errors.

- Provide comprehensive training for staff on the importance of accurate data entry and the potential impact of errors.

2. Invoice Discrepancies:

Establishing clear guidelines for invoice creation and implementing a review process can help mitigate discrepancies.

Solutions:

- Implement standard operating procedures for invoice generation, including verifying pricing and discounts before issuing invoices.

- Use automated tools within Oracle ERP to cross-check invoice details against purchase orders and contracts.

- Establish a dedicated team to handle invoice disputes and ensure timely resolution.

3. Delayed Payments:

Streamlining payment processing and enhancing customer communication can improve payment timeliness.

Solutions:

- Set up automated payment reminders and follow-ups within Oracle ERP to prompt customers about upcoming and overdue payments.

- Offer multiple payment options to customers to facilitate easier payments.

- Review and optimize the payment processing workflow to reduce delays.

4. Credit Management Issues:

Implementing robust credit policies and regularly reviewing customer credit limits can help manage credit risks effectively.

Solutions:

- Use Oracle ERP's credit management features to set and enforce credit limits based on customer risk profiles.

- Regularly review and adjust credit limits based on customer payment history and financial health.

- Provide training for the credit management team on assessing credit risk and managing customer accounts.

5. Integration Issues:

Ensuring seamless integration between AR and other modules requires careful planning and regular monitoring.

Solutions:

- Conduct regular data synchronization checks to ensure consistency across modules.

- Use Oracle ERP's integration tools to automate data flow between modules and reduce manual intervention.

- Set up alerts and notifications for any integration failures to allow for immediate resolution.

Case Studies and Examples

Case Study 1: Resolving Data Entry Errors

Company A faced significant challenges due to frequent data entry errors in their AR module. Inaccurate customer information and incorrect invoice details were leading to delayed payments and customer dissatisfaction. By implementing a data validation tool within Oracle ERP, they were able to reduce errors by 75%. Additionally, conducting regular training sessions for their AR staff on the importance of accurate data entry resulted in improved data quality and faster payment processing.

Case Study 2: Addressing Invoice Discrepancies

Company B experienced a high volume of invoice disputes due to pricing errors and misapplied discounts. They established a cross-functional team to review and approve all invoices before they were sent to customers. This team utilized Oracle ERP's automated invoice matching feature to ensure that all invoice details were correct. As a result, invoice disputes dropped by 50%, and payment delays were significantly reduced.

Case Study 3: Enhancing Credit Management

Company C had a growing problem with bad debts due to ineffective credit management. They implemented Oracle ERP's credit management module to set strict credit limits based on customer risk profiles. By regularly reviewing customer credit limits and using automated alerts for overdue accounts, they were able to reduce bad debts by 40%. This proactive approach also helped in maintaining healthy customer relationships while managing credit risks effectively.

Case Study 4: Overcoming Integration Issues

Company D struggled with data inconsistencies between their AR and Sales modules. This was causing delays in financial reporting and difficulties in tracking transactions. They utilized Oracle ERP's integration tools to automate data flow between the modules and set up regular synchronization checks. By doing so, they achieved real-time data consistency and improved their overall financial reporting accuracy.

Best Practices for Ongoing Issue Management

1. Continuous Monitoring and Improvement:

   Regularly monitor AR processes and performance metrics to identify and address issues proactively.

   Actions:

   - Use Oracle ERP's reporting and analytics tools to track key performance indicators (KPIs) related to AR.

   - Conduct regular audits of AR processes to identify areas for improvement.

- Foster a culture of continuous improvement within the AR team, encouraging feedback and suggestions for enhancing processes.

2. Leveraging Automation:

Utilize automation tools within Oracle ERP to streamline AR processes and reduce manual intervention.

Actions:

- Implement automated invoice generation, payment reminders, and approval workflows.

- Use robotic process automation (RPA) to handle repetitive tasks and free up staff for higher-value activities.

- Regularly review and optimize automated processes to ensure they align with business needs.

3. Effective Communication and Training:

Ensure clear communication of AR policies and procedures and provide ongoing training for staff.

Actions:

- Develop and maintain comprehensive documentation of AR processes and guidelines.

- Conduct regular training sessions for AR staff on system updates, process changes, and best practices.

- Encourage open communication within the AR team to share knowledge and address challenges collaboratively.

By following these strategies, organizations can effectively identify and resolve common issues in the Accounts Receivable module, ensuring smooth and efficient financial operations within Oracle ERP.

9.1.2 Troubleshooting Invoice and Receipt Issues

In any Accounts Receivable (AR) system, issues with invoices and receipts can arise due to a variety of factors, ranging from data entry errors to system configuration problems. Effective troubleshooting is crucial to ensure smooth financial operations and maintain accurate records. This section will delve into common invoice and receipt issues, their potential causes, and step-by-step solutions to resolve them.

Understanding Common Invoice Issues

1. Invoice Discrepancies

- Symptoms: Differences between the amount billed and the amount received, missing line items, incorrect quantities, or prices.

- Causes: Data entry errors, incorrect customer or product details, issues during the invoice generation process, or discrepancies in the sales order.

2. Unposted Invoices

- Symptoms: Invoices that remain in an unposted state, causing delays in revenue recognition.

- Causes: Errors during invoice creation, missing mandatory information, or system configuration settings that prevent posting.

3. Duplicate Invoices

- Symptoms: Multiple invoices generated for the same transaction.

- Causes: System errors, accidental duplication during data entry, or batch processing issues.

4. Incorrect Invoice Dates

- Symptoms: Invoices showing incorrect billing or due dates.

- Causes: Errors in date selection during invoice creation, or incorrect system date settings.

5. Missing Invoices

- Symptoms: Invoices that are not generated or not found in the system.

- Causes: Failures in the batch processing system, data entry omissions, or system glitches.

6. Customer Disputes

- Symptoms: Customers contesting the amounts billed or the products/services listed.

- Causes: Errors in the sales order, miscommunications, or discrepancies between what was agreed and what was billed.

Understanding Common Receipt Issues

1. Unmatched Receipts

- Symptoms: Receipts that are not matched to the corresponding invoices.

- Causes: Data entry errors, incorrect application of payments, or system configuration issues.

2. Overpayments and Underpayments

- Symptoms: Receipts that do not match the invoice amounts, resulting in overpayments or underpayments.

- Causes: Customer payment errors, partial payments, or misapplication of receipts.

3. Duplicate Receipts

- Symptoms: Multiple entries for the same payment.

- Causes: Data entry duplication, errors during batch processing, or system bugs.

4. Unapplied Receipts

- Symptoms: Receipts recorded in the system but not applied to any invoice.

- Causes: Incomplete payment application process, errors in customer identification, or missing invoice references.

5. Misallocated Payments

- Symptoms: Payments applied to the wrong invoices or customer accounts.

- Causes: Data entry errors, incorrect customer or invoice selection, or system issues.

Step-by-Step Troubleshooting Guide

Step 1: Identify the Issue

- Review System Logs: Check the AR system logs for error messages or warnings.

- Analyze Reports: Run reports to identify anomalies in invoices and receipts.

- Communicate with Stakeholders: Gather information from customers, sales teams, and accounting staff.

Step 2: Investigate the Root Cause

- Check Data Entries: Verify the accuracy of data entered in the system.

- Review System Configuration: Ensure that the system settings are correct and aligned with business processes.

- Audit Transactions: Conduct a detailed audit of the transactions leading up to the issue.

Step 3: Implement Solutions

- Correct Data Entries: Update incorrect data entries and ensure all mandatory fields are filled.

- Reprocess Transactions: Re-run batch processes or re-generate invoices as needed.

- Adjust System Settings: Modify system configurations to prevent future occurrences.

Step 4: Validate the Fix

- Re-run Reports: Generate updated reports to confirm that the issues have been resolved.

- Monitor Transactions: Keep a close eye on subsequent transactions to ensure no new issues arise.

- Seek Feedback: Obtain feedback from users and customers to verify the resolution's effectiveness.

Detailed Troubleshooting Examples

1. Resolving Invoice Discrepancies

Step-by-Step Solution:

1. Identify the Discrepancy: Review the invoice and sales order details to identify specific discrepancies in amounts, quantities, or line items.

2. Verify Data Entries: Check the data entered during invoice creation against the original sales order or contract.

3. Correct Errors: Update the invoice to reflect accurate information. This may involve adjusting quantities, prices, or adding missing line items.

4. Reissue Invoice: If significant changes are made, reissue the invoice to the customer with a clear explanation of the adjustments.

5. Communicate with Customer: Inform the customer of the corrections and provide supporting documentation if necessary.

2. Addressing Unposted Invoices

Step-by-Step Solution:

1. Check Invoice Status: Review the status of unposted invoices to identify common patterns or errors.

2. Identify Missing Information: Ensure all mandatory fields (e.g., invoice date, customer details, amounts) are filled in correctly.

3. Review System Settings: Check system settings that might prevent posting, such as approval workflows or validation rules.

4. Update and Post Invoices: Make necessary updates and attempt to post the invoices again. If issues persist, consult system documentation or support.

3. Handling Duplicate Invoices

Step-by-Step Solution:

1. Identify Duplicates: Run a report to identify duplicate invoices by comparing key fields such as invoice number, date, and customer.

2. Determine Cause: Investigate the cause of duplication, whether it's data entry error, batch processing issue, or system bug.

3. Cancel or Merge Duplicates: Cancel or merge duplicate invoices, ensuring that only one invoice remains active.

4. Prevent Future Duplications: Implement checks and validations in the invoice creation process to prevent future duplications.

4. Correcting Incorrect Invoice Dates

Step-by-Step Solution:

1. Identify Incorrect Dates: Review invoices for incorrect billing or due dates.

2. Verify Date Settings: Check the system date settings and user input during invoice creation.

3. Update Invoice Dates: Correct the invoice dates in the system, ensuring consistency with the sales order or contract terms.

4. Reissue Invoices if Necessary: If date changes significantly impact the customer, reissue the invoice with the correct date.

5. Locating Missing Invoices

Step-by-Step Solution:

1. Run an Audit Trail: Check the audit trail to identify any system failures or omissions during invoice generation.

2. Verify Batch Processes: Ensure that batch processes for invoice generation ran successfully and captured all necessary transactions.

3. Reprocess Missing Invoices: Re-generate missing invoices from the original sales orders or transactions.

4. Communicate with Affected Customers: Inform customers of any delays or issues in invoicing and provide updated invoices promptly.

6. Resolving Customer Disputes

Step-by-Step Solution:

1. Gather Dispute Details: Obtain detailed information from the customer regarding the nature of the dispute.

2. Review Sales Order and Invoice: Compare the disputed invoice with the original sales order, contract, and any correspondence.

3. Investigate Discrepancies: Identify the root cause of the discrepancy, whether it's a data entry error, miscommunication, or other issue.

4. Resolve and Communicate: Correct the invoice as needed and communicate the resolution to the customer. Provide any necessary documentation to support the correction.

7. Unmatched Receipts

Step-by-Step Solution:

1. Identify Unmatched Receipts: Run reports to identify receipts that are not matched to invoices.

2. Review Payment Details: Check the details of the unmatched receipts and the corresponding customer accounts.

3. Match Receipts to Invoices: Apply receipts to the correct invoices, ensuring that payment amounts and references match.

4. Address Discrepancies: Resolve any discrepancies between the receipt amounts and invoice amounts.

8. Managing Overpayments and Underpayments

Step-by-Step Solution:

1. Identify Overpayments/Underpayments: Review customer accounts for overpayments or underpayments.

2. Verify Payment Details: Compare the payment details with the invoices to identify the source of the discrepancy.

3. Adjust Accounts: Apply adjustments to customer accounts to correct overpayments or underpayments.

4. Communicate with Customers: Inform customers of any adjustments made to their accounts and provide updated statements if necessary.

9. Handling Duplicate Receipts

Step-by-Step Solution:

1. Identify Duplicate Receipts: Run reports to identify duplicate entries for the same payment.

2. Determine Cause: Investigate the cause of duplication, such as data entry errors or system issues.

3. Cancel or Merge Duplicates: Cancel or merge duplicate receipts, ensuring accurate records.

4. Implement Preventive Measures: Implement checks in the receipt recording process to prevent future duplications.

10. Unapplied Receipts

Step-by-Step Solution:

1. Identify Unapplied Receipts: Run reports to identify receipts that have not been applied to invoices.

2. Verify Customer Accounts: Check customer accounts and payment details to identify the corresponding invoices.

3. Apply Receipts: Apply the receipts to the correct invoices, ensuring accurate matching.

4. Communicate with Customers: Inform customers of any changes made to their accounts and provide updated statements if necessary.

11. Resolving Misallocated Payments

Step-by-Step Solution:

1. Identify Misallocated Payments: Run reports to identify payments applied to the wrong invoices or customer accounts.

2. Review Payment Details: Check the details of the misallocated payments and the corresponding customer accounts.

3. Reallocate Payments: Correctly allocate payments to the appropriate invoices or accounts.

4. Prevent Future Misallocations: Implement process improvements and training to prevent future misallocations.

Best Practices for Preventing Invoice and Receipt Issues

1. Implement Robust Validation Checks

- Automated Checks: Use automated validation checks during data entry to ensure accuracy.

- Manual Reviews: Conduct regular manual reviews of invoices and receipts to catch errors early.

2. Train Staff Thoroughly

- Comprehensive Training: Provide comprehensive training for staff involved in the AR process.

- Regular Updates: Keep staff updated on any changes to processes or system configurations.

3. Utilize System Features

- Automated Matching: Use system features for automated matching of receipts to invoices.

- Error Reporting: Leverage error reporting tools to identify and address issues promptly.

4. Maintain Clear Documentation

- Process Documentation: Maintain clear and detailed documentation of AR processes.

- Issue Logs: Keep logs of common issues and their resolutions to aid in future troubleshooting.

5. Engage with Oracle Support

- Oracle Resources: Utilize Oracle support resources for guidance on resolving complex issues.

- Community Engagement: Engage with the Oracle community to share experiences and solutions.

By following these troubleshooting steps and best practices, organizations can effectively address and prevent common invoice and receipt issues in the Oracle ERP Accounts Receivable module. This ensures smoother financial operations, improved customer satisfaction, and enhanced accuracy in financial reporting.

9.1.3 Managing Data Discrepancies

Data discrepancies in Accounts Receivable (AR) can create significant challenges for financial management and reporting. Ensuring data accuracy is critical for maintaining the integrity of financial records, fostering trust with customers, and making informed business decisions. This section delves into the causes of data discrepancies, methods for identifying them, and strategies for effectively managing and resolving these issues.

Identifying Data Discrepancies

The first step in managing data discrepancies is to identify them accurately. Data discrepancies can arise from various sources, including data entry errors, system integration issues, and discrepancies in transaction records. Here are some common methods for identifying data discrepancies:

1. Reconciliation: Regularly reconciling AR records with bank statements, customer accounts, and other financial records can help identify discrepancies. Reconciliation involves comparing and matching transactions recorded in the AR module with external records to ensure consistency.

2. Exception Reports: Generating exception reports can highlight unusual or unexpected transactions. These reports can identify anomalies such as duplicate invoices, missing payments, or discrepancies between recorded and actual amounts.

3. Audit Trails: Maintaining audit trails for all transactions can help trace discrepancies back to their source. Audit trails provide a detailed record of all changes made to financial data, including who made the changes and when.

4. Automated Alerts: Setting up automated alerts in the ERP system can notify users of potential discrepancies. For example, alerts can be configured to flag transactions that deviate from predefined thresholds or patterns.

5. Manual Reviews: Periodic manual reviews of AR records by experienced staff can also help identify discrepancies. Manual reviews involve examining transaction details, supporting documents, and customer communications to detect errors or inconsistencies.

Common Causes of Data Discrepancies

Understanding the common causes of data discrepancies can help in developing effective strategies for managing them. Some typical causes include:

1. Data Entry Errors: Mistakes made during manual data entry, such as incorrect amounts, duplicate entries, or missing information, can lead to discrepancies. These errors are often the result of human error or lack of training.

2. System Integration Issues: Discrepancies can occur when data is transferred between different systems or modules within the ERP. Integration issues, such as data synchronization problems or incorrect mapping of data fields, can result in inconsistent records.

3. Timing Differences: Differences in the timing of transactions being recorded can create temporary discrepancies. For example, a payment might be recorded in the bank statement but not yet reflected in the AR module.

4. Discrepancies in Supporting Documents: Differences between the details in invoices, receipts, and other supporting documents can lead to discrepancies in AR records. These discrepancies may arise from incorrect or incomplete documentation.

5. Customer Disputes: Disputes raised by customers regarding invoices, payments, or terms can result in discrepancies. Resolving these disputes requires thorough investigation and communication with the customer.

Strategies for Managing Data Discrepancies

Effectively managing data discrepancies requires a combination of preventive measures, detection techniques, and resolution strategies. Here are some best practices for managing data discrepancies in Accounts Receivable:

1. Implementing Data Validation Rules: Setting up data validation rules within the ERP system can help prevent data entry errors. Validation rules can enforce mandatory fields, check for duplicate entries, and ensure data accuracy.

2. Regular Reconciliation: Conducting regular reconciliation of AR records with external statements, such as bank statements and customer account statements, can help identify and correct discrepancies promptly.

3. Using Automated Tools: Leveraging automated tools for data matching and reconciliation can enhance accuracy and efficiency. These tools can automatically compare records and highlight discrepancies for further investigation.

4. Training and Awareness: Providing training and awareness programs for AR staff on common causes of discrepancies and best practices for data entry and reconciliation can reduce the occurrence of errors.

5. Maintaining Detailed Documentation: Keeping detailed documentation for all transactions, including invoices, receipts, and communication with customers, can provide a reference point for resolving discrepancies.

6. Establishing Clear Policies and Procedures: Developing clear policies and procedures for handling discrepancies can ensure a consistent approach. These policies should outline the steps for identifying, investigating, and resolving discrepancies.

7. Enhancing System Integration: Ensuring seamless integration between different systems and modules within the ERP can reduce the risk of data discrepancies. Regularly testing and updating integration interfaces can help maintain data consistency.

8. Conducting Periodic Audits: Performing periodic audits of AR records by internal or external auditors can provide an independent assessment of data accuracy. Audits can help identify underlying issues and recommend improvements.

9. Resolving Customer Disputes: Addressing customer disputes promptly and professionally can help resolve discrepancies related to disputed invoices or payments. Clear communication and documentation of dispute resolution processes are essential.

10. Continuous Improvement: Continuously monitoring and improving AR processes can help prevent and manage data discrepancies. Implementing feedback loops and learning from past discrepancies can drive process enhancements.

Case Study: Managing Data Discrepancies in a Large Organization

To illustrate the importance of managing data discrepancies, let's consider a case study of a large organization that faced significant challenges with data discrepancies in its AR module.

Background: The organization, a multinational corporation with thousands of customers, experienced frequent discrepancies in its AR records. These discrepancies led to delays in payment processing, customer dissatisfaction, and inaccuracies in financial reporting.

Challenges:

- High volume of transactions made manual reconciliation time-consuming and error-prone.

- Integration issues between the AR module and other financial systems caused data inconsistencies.

- Lack of standardized procedures for handling discrepancies resulted in inconsistent resolution approaches.

Solutions Implemented:

1. Automated Reconciliation Tools: The organization implemented automated reconciliation tools that matched AR records with bank statements and customer account statements. This significantly reduced the time and effort required for reconciliation.

2. Enhanced System Integration: Integration interfaces between the AR module and other financial systems were updated and tested regularly to ensure data consistency. Real-time data synchronization was implemented to minimize timing differences.

3. Standardized Procedures: Clear policies and procedures for managing discrepancies were developed and communicated to all AR staff. These procedures outlined the steps for identifying, investigating, and resolving discrepancies.

4. Training Programs: Comprehensive training programs were provided to AR staff on data entry best practices, reconciliation techniques, and discrepancy resolution. This improved data accuracy and consistency.

5. Regular Audits: Periodic audits of AR records were conducted by internal auditors. The audits identified areas for improvement and recommended corrective actions to address underlying issues.

Results:

- The organization saw a significant reduction in data discrepancies and improved accuracy in AR records.

- Reconciliation processes became more efficient, leading to faster payment processing and improved cash flow management.

- Customer satisfaction improved as disputes were resolved promptly and accurately.

- Financial reporting accuracy was enhanced, providing reliable data for decision-making.

Conclusion: Managing data discrepancies in Accounts Receivable is crucial for maintaining financial accuracy and integrity. By implementing preventive measures, leveraging automated tools, and establishing clear procedures, organizations can effectively identify, manage, and resolve data discrepancies. Continuous improvement and regular audits can further enhance data accuracy and support efficient AR processes.

9.2 Getting Help and Support

9.2.1 Utilizing Oracle Support Resources

In managing the Accounts Receivable (AR) module within Oracle ERP, there will inevitably be times when users encounter challenges or require additional assistance. This is where Oracle Support Resources become invaluable. Oracle offers a comprehensive suite of support options to ensure users can efficiently resolve issues and optimize their use of the ERP system. This section will delve into the various support resources available, how to access them, and best practices for utilizing these resources effectively.

Understanding Oracle Support Resources

Oracle provides a robust support infrastructure designed to assist users at all levels of expertise. These resources include:

1. Oracle Support Portal (My Oracle Support - MOS)

2. Oracle Knowledge Base

3. Oracle Support Communities

4. Oracle University and Training

5. Technical Support via Service Requests (SRs)

6. Documentation and User Guides

1. Oracle Support Portal (My Oracle Support - MOS)

The Oracle Support Portal, also known as My Oracle Support (MOS), is the primary platform for accessing Oracle's technical support services. Here are the key features of MOS:

- Service Requests (SRs): Users can log, track, and manage service requests for technical assistance.

- Knowledge Base: A searchable repository of articles, troubleshooting guides, and technical notes.

- Patches and Updates: Access to software patches and updates to keep your ERP system up-to-date.

- Health Checks and Diagnostics: Tools for proactive system health checks and diagnostics.

- Community Forums: Interactive forums where users can engage with peers and Oracle experts.

To maximize the use of MOS:

- Create an Account: Ensure that all users who need access have registered accounts.

- Regular Logins: Encourage regular logins to stay informed about updates and available resources.

- Service Request Management: Train users on how to effectively log and manage service requests, including providing detailed descriptions and attaching relevant documentation.

2. Oracle Knowledge Base

The Oracle Knowledge Base within MOS is an extensive repository of information. It includes:

- Articles: Technical articles on a wide range of topics related to Oracle ERP and AR.

- How-to Guides: Step-by-step instructions for common tasks and troubleshooting.

- FAQs: Frequently Asked Questions to quickly address common issues.

- Technical Notes: Detailed notes on specific technical issues, including known bugs and their resolutions.

Best practices for utilizing the Knowledge Base:

- Keyword Searches: Use specific keywords related to your issue for more accurate search results.

- Bookmarking: Bookmark frequently referenced articles for easy access.

- Regular Reviews: Periodically review new articles and updates to stay informed.

3. Oracle Support Communities

Oracle Support Communities are interactive forums where users can discuss issues, share solutions, and network with peers. These communities include:

- Product-Specific Forums: Dedicated forums for different Oracle products and modules.

- Expert Participation: Oracle experts and experienced users often participate in these discussions.

- Searchable Archives: Past discussions and solutions are archived and searchable.

To get the most out of Oracle Support Communities:

- Active Participation: Encourage active participation by asking questions and sharing knowledge.

- Follow Topics: Follow topics relevant to your role and responsibilities.

- Utilize Community Expertise: Leverage the collective expertise of the community for complex issues.

4. Oracle University and Training

Oracle University provides a wide range of training resources to help users enhance their skills and knowledge. These include:

- Online Training: Self-paced courses covering various aspects of Oracle ERP and AR.

- Instructor-Led Training: Live, instructor-led courses for in-depth learning.

- Certifications: Professional certifications to validate expertise.

- Learning Paths: Structured learning paths for different roles and career goals.

For effective utilization of Oracle University:

- Identify Training Needs: Assess the training needs of your team and identify relevant courses.

- Set Learning Goals: Establish clear learning goals and timelines.

- Encourage Continuous Learning: Foster a culture of continuous learning and development.

5. Technical Support via Service Requests (SRs)

When issues cannot be resolved through self-service resources, users can log a Service Request (SR) for technical support. Key aspects of SR management include:

- Detailed Description: Provide a detailed description of the issue, including steps to reproduce it.

- Attachments: Attach relevant logs, screenshots, and documents to assist support engineers.

- Priority Levels: Set the appropriate priority level based on the impact of the issue.

- Regular Updates: Monitor the SR and provide regular updates to support engineers.

To ensure efficient SR resolution:

- Training: Train users on how to effectively log SRs.

- Escalation Processes: Establish clear escalation processes for critical issues.

- Follow-Up: Follow up on open SRs to ensure timely resolution.

6. Documentation and User Guides

Oracle provides comprehensive documentation and user guides for all its products. These include:

- User Manuals: Detailed manuals covering all aspects of the AR module.

- Implementation Guides: Guides for setting up and configuring the AR module.

- Technical References: Technical reference materials for advanced users.

Best practices for using documentation and user guides:

- Accessibility: Ensure that documentation is easily accessible to all users.

- Regular Updates: Regularly check for updates and new releases.

- Training Material: Use documentation as training material for new users.

Best Practices for Utilizing Oracle Support Resources

To maximize the effectiveness of Oracle Support Resources, consider the following best practices:

- Proactive Engagement: Engage with support resources proactively rather than reactively.

- Continuous Improvement: Continuously seek to improve your knowledge and skills through training and self-study.

- Documentation: Maintain comprehensive documentation of your system configurations and issues encountered.

- Community Engagement: Actively participate in community forums and share your knowledge with others.

- Feedback: Provide feedback to Oracle on support resources and suggest improvements.

By effectively utilizing Oracle Support Resources, users can ensure the smooth operation of the Accounts Receivable module and address any challenges promptly. This not only enhances the efficiency of AR processes but also contributes to the overall success of the organization's financial management efforts.

9.2.2 Engaging with the Oracle Community

Engaging with the Oracle community is an invaluable strategy for professionals working with Oracle ERP, particularly in the Accounts Receivable (AR) module. The community provides a wealth of knowledge, resources, and networking opportunities that can enhance your understanding, troubleshoot issues, and keep you updated on best practices. This section will delve into the various aspects of engaging with the Oracle community, including forums, user groups, events, and online resources.

The Importance of Community Engagement

Engaging with the Oracle community can yield numerous benefits:

1. Knowledge Sharing: Community members share their experiences and solutions to common problems, which can help you solve issues more efficiently.

2. Networking: Building relationships with other Oracle professionals can open up opportunities for collaboration, learning, and career advancement.

3. Staying Updated: The community often discusses the latest updates, features, and best practices, ensuring you stay informed about Oracle ERP advancements.

4. Support: When facing complex issues, community members can offer advice, solutions, and moral support.

5. Learning Opportunities: Many community events and forums provide training sessions, webinars, and workshops that can enhance your skills.

Oracle Community Forums

Oracle hosts several official forums where users can ask questions, share knowledge, and discuss various topics related to Oracle ERP and the AR module. Here's how to make the most out of these forums:

1. Oracle Technology Network (OTN): OTN is a hub for Oracle professionals, offering forums, articles, and documentation. You can join the AR-specific forums to discuss issues and share solutions.

2. My Oracle Support Community: This community is part of Oracle's official support portal. It provides a platform for users to collaborate on technical issues and best practices.

3. User Groups and Subforums: Many regions have Oracle user groups that host their own forums. These can be particularly useful for localized issues and networking.

Tips for Effective Forum Engagement:

- Search Before Posting: Use the search function to see if your question has already been answered.

- Be Specific: When posting a question, provide detailed information about your issue, including error messages, screenshots, and steps taken.

- Contribute Back: If you find a solution to your problem, post an update to help others who might face the same issue.

Oracle User Groups

Oracle user groups are regional or industry-specific groups that bring together Oracle users for networking, knowledge sharing, and support. Some prominent user groups include:

1. Oracle Applications User Group (OAUG): OAUG is one of the largest Oracle user groups, offering resources, events, and a platform for collaboration.

2. Independent Oracle Users Group (IOUG): IOUG focuses on Oracle database and technology users, providing training, events, and a community platform.

3. Regional User Groups: Many regions have their own Oracle user groups, such as the UK Oracle User Group (UKOUG) or the Asia Pacific Oracle User Group (APOUG).

Benefits of Joining User Groups:

- Events and Conferences: User groups often host events, conferences, and webinars that provide learning opportunities and updates on Oracle ERP.

- Networking: These groups offer a platform to meet and network with other Oracle professionals in your region or industry.

- Access to Exclusive Content: Many user groups provide members with access to exclusive content, such as white papers, case studies, and training materials.

Oracle Events and Conferences

Oracle hosts several events and conferences that provide opportunities for learning, networking, and staying updated on the latest developments in Oracle ERP and the AR module. Some notable events include:

1. Oracle OpenWorld: This is Oracle's flagship conference, featuring keynotes, sessions, and networking opportunities focused on Oracle's latest technologies and solutions.

2. Oracle CloudWorld: This event focuses on Oracle Cloud solutions, including ERP, providing insights into new features and best practices.

3. Regional and Industry-Specific Events: Oracle also hosts regional and industry-specific events that focus on local issues and sector-specific challenges.

Maximizing Your Event Experience:

- Plan Ahead: Review the agenda and plan which sessions to attend based on your interests and professional needs.

- Network Actively: Take advantage of networking opportunities to meet other professionals and share experiences.

- Follow Up: After the event, follow up with new contacts and review your notes to implement new knowledge and solutions.

Online Resources and Social Media

The internet offers a plethora of resources and platforms where Oracle professionals can engage and learn. Here are some key online resources:

1. Oracle Blogs: Oracle's official blogs provide insights, updates, and best practices on various Oracle ERP modules, including AR.

2. LinkedIn Groups: LinkedIn hosts several groups focused on Oracle ERP and AR where professionals share articles, discussions, and job opportunities.

3. YouTube Channels: Many experts and organizations post tutorial videos, webinars, and case studies on YouTube, providing visual learning opportunities.

4. Reddit and Stack Overflow: These platforms have active communities where you can ask questions, share solutions, and discuss Oracle ERP topics.

Best Practices for Using Online Resources:

- Stay Engaged: Regularly check and participate in discussions to stay informed and connected.

- Contribute: Share your own insights and experiences to help others in the community.

- Filter Information: Be discerning about the sources of information to ensure you're getting accurate and reliable content.

Professional Development and Certification

Continuous learning and certification can significantly enhance your proficiency in Oracle ERP and the AR module. Engaging with the Oracle community can provide opportunities for professional development, including:

1. Certification Programs: Oracle offers certification programs that validate your skills and knowledge in various Oracle ERP modules. Engaging with certified professionals in the community can provide insights and tips for exam preparation.

2. Webinars and Workshops: Many user groups and community forums host webinars and workshops that offer training on specific topics and new features.

3. Mentorship and Coaching: Networking with experienced Oracle professionals can lead to mentorship opportunities, where you can receive guidance and advice for your career development.

Steps to Enhance Professional Development:

- Set Goals: Identify your career goals and seek out learning opportunities that align with them.

- Stay Updated: Regularly participate in community events and forums to stay informed about the latest developments and best practices.

- Seek Feedback: Engage with mentors and peers to get feedback on your skills and areas for improvement.

Conclusion

Engaging with the Oracle community is a powerful strategy for enhancing your knowledge, solving issues, and advancing your career in Oracle ERP, particularly in the Accounts Receivable module. By actively participating in forums, user groups, events, and online platforms, you can leverage the collective knowledge and experience of the community to stay updated, solve problems, and implement best practices. Continuous learning and professional development, supported by the community, will ensure you remain proficient and competitive in the ever-evolving field of Oracle ERP.

9.2.3 Continuous Learning and Certification

Continuous learning and professional certification are pivotal to maintaining and enhancing your proficiency with the Oracle ERP Accounts Receivable (AR) module. The evolving nature of enterprise technology, coupled with the frequent updates and enhancements to Oracle ERP systems, necessitates a commitment to ongoing education. This section delves into the importance of continuous learning, explores various certification paths, and offers practical advice on leveraging these opportunities to advance your career and improve your organization's ERP implementation.

The Importance of Continuous Learning

The landscape of enterprise resource planning (ERP) systems is dynamic and ever-changing. Oracle frequently updates its software to incorporate new features, improve existing functionalities, and address security vulnerabilities. To stay ahead in such a rapidly evolving field, professionals must commit to continuous learning. Here are several reasons why ongoing education is critical:

1. Keeping Up with Technological Advances: New technologies and methodologies are continually being introduced. By engaging in continuous learning, you ensure that you are up-to-date with the latest advancements, which can be leveraged to enhance your organization's processes and efficiency.

2. Maximizing System Utilization: Understanding new features and updates allows you to fully utilize the capabilities of the Oracle ERP AR module. This can lead to more streamlined operations, better data management, and improved financial reporting.

3. Improving Problem-Solving Skills: Continuous learning equips you with advanced problem-solving skills. As you gain more knowledge, you become better at troubleshooting and resolving issues that may arise, ensuring the smooth operation of your AR processes.

4. Professional Growth and Career Advancement: Staying current with industry trends and best practices can significantly enhance your career prospects. Employers value professionals who demonstrate a commitment to their field and are proactive in their learning.

Certification Paths

Oracle offers a variety of certification programs designed to validate your expertise and proficiency in using their ERP systems. These certifications are recognized globally and can significantly boost your professional credibility. Here are some key certifications related to the Oracle ERP Accounts Receivable module:

1. Oracle Certified Associate (OCA): This is an entry-level certification that covers the fundamentals of Oracle ERP systems. It is ideal for individuals who are new to Oracle ERP and want to establish a solid foundation.

2. Oracle Certified Professional (OCP): The OCP certification builds on the knowledge gained at the OCA level and dives deeper into specific modules, including Accounts Receivable. This certification demonstrates a higher level of expertise and is suitable for professionals looking to advance their careers.

3. Oracle Certified Master (OCM): The OCM certification is the highest level of certification offered by Oracle. It is designed for experts who have extensive experience with Oracle ERP systems and can demonstrate advanced skills in managing and optimizing these systems.

4. Specialized Certifications: Oracle also offers specialized certifications that focus on particular aspects of their ERP systems. For instance, you might pursue a certification specifically in Oracle Financials Cloud: Accounts Receivable.

Preparing for Certification Exams

Successfully obtaining Oracle certifications requires thorough preparation. Here are some tips to help you get ready for your certification exams:

1. Understand the Exam Objectives: Familiarize yourself with the exam objectives and topics. Oracle provides detailed exam guides that outline what you need to know for each certification.

2. Take Advantage of Oracle's Training Resources: Oracle offers a wealth of training resources, including instructor-led courses, self-paced online training, and study guides. These resources are designed to help you prepare effectively for your certification exams.

3. Join Study Groups and Forums: Engaging with study groups and online forums can provide additional insights and support. You can learn from the experiences of others, share study materials, and gain valuable tips and advice.

4. Practice, Practice, Practice: Practical experience is crucial. Use Oracle's practice environments and labs to gain hands-on experience with the AR module. This will not only help you understand the concepts better but also prepare you for the practical aspects of the exams.

Leveraging Continuous Learning and Certification for Career Growth

Once you have obtained your certifications, it is important to continue learning and applying your knowledge to grow your career. Here are some strategies to leverage your continuous learning and certifications:

1. Stay Updated with Oracle's News and Updates: Regularly check Oracle's official website, blogs, and newsletters for news about updates, new features, and best practices. This will help you stay informed about the latest developments in the Oracle ERP ecosystem.

2. Attend Conferences and Workshops: Participate in industry conferences, workshops, and webinars. These events provide opportunities to learn from experts, network with peers, and discover new tools and techniques.

3. Engage in Professional Networks: Join professional organizations and networks related to ERP systems and financial management. These networks can provide support, resources, and opportunities for professional development.

4. Share Your Knowledge: Consider mentoring junior colleagues, conducting training sessions, or writing articles and blogs about your experiences with Oracle ERP AR. Sharing your knowledge not only reinforces your learning but also establishes you as a thought leader in your field.

5. Pursue Advanced Certifications: As you gain more experience, consider pursuing advanced certifications or specialized credentials. This can further enhance your expertise and open up new career opportunities.

Practical Tips for Implementing Continuous Learning in Your Organization

Encouraging continuous learning within your organization can lead to a more knowledgeable and capable workforce. Here are some practical tips for fostering a culture of continuous learning:

1. Create a Learning and Development Plan: Develop a comprehensive learning and development plan that outlines training goals, resources, and timelines. Ensure that this plan is aligned with the organization's objectives and individual career aspirations.

2. Provide Access to Training Resources: Invest in training resources, such as online courses, books, and software. Ensure that employees have access to these resources and are encouraged to utilize them.

3. Encourage Knowledge Sharing: Foster a culture of knowledge sharing by organizing regular training sessions, workshops, and discussion forums. Encourage employees to share their insights and learnings with their peers.

4. Recognize and Reward Learning Achievements: Recognize and reward employees who demonstrate a commitment to continuous learning. This could include certifications, participation in training programs, or contributions to knowledge-sharing initiatives.

5. Monitor and Evaluate Learning Outcomes: Regularly assess the impact of learning and development initiatives on employee performance and organizational goals. Use feedback and evaluation results to continuously improve the learning programs.

Conclusion

Continuous learning and certification are essential components of professional growth and success in managing the Oracle ERP Accounts Receivable module. By staying updated with the latest developments, pursuing relevant certifications, and actively engaging in learning opportunities, you can enhance your skills, improve your organization's ERP implementation, and advance your career. Implementing a culture of continuous learning within your organization can lead to a more knowledgeable, capable, and motivated workforce, ultimately driving business success.

Appendices

Appendix A: Glossary of Terms

In this appendix, we provide a comprehensive glossary of key terms and concepts related to Oracle ERP Accounts Receivable. This glossary serves as a quick reference guide for readers to better understand the terminology used throughout the book.

A

Accounts Receivable (AR): The amount of money owed to a company by its customers for goods or services delivered but not yet paid for. It is a key component of a company's balance sheet under current assets.

Aging Report: A report that categorizes a company's accounts receivable according to the length of time an invoice has been outstanding. It helps in identifying overdue invoices and assessing the financial health of the company's receivables.

AutoCash Rules: Rules used in Oracle ERP to automatically apply cash receipts to open invoices based on predefined criteria, reducing manual intervention and streamlining the cash application process.

B

Bad Debt: The portion of accounts receivable that is considered uncollectible and written off as an expense. Bad debts are typically accounted for when it becomes clear that the customer will not pay the amount owed.

Balance Forward Billing: A billing method where all charges are added to a single balance and a summary invoice is generated periodically. This method is often used for customers who receive regular, recurring services.

Billing Cycle: The regular interval at which a company issues invoices to its customers. Common billing cycles include monthly, quarterly, and annually.

C

Cash Application: The process of applying customer payments to their respective invoices, updating the accounts receivable balance and reducing the outstanding amount owed by the customer.

Credit Memo: A document issued to a customer to reduce the amount they owe, often due to returned goods, billing errors, or agreed-upon discounts. It is recorded as a reduction in accounts receivable.

Credit Limit: The maximum amount of credit that a company extends to a customer based on their creditworthiness and payment history. It helps manage credit risk and prevent overextension of credit.

Customer Master Record: A comprehensive record in Oracle ERP that contains all relevant information about a customer, including contact details, credit limits, payment terms, and transaction history.

D

Dunning: The process of communicating with customers to collect overdue payments. Dunning letters and calls are common methods used to remind customers of their outstanding balances and request payment.

Days Sales Outstanding (DSO): A financial metric that measures the average number of days it takes for a company to collect payment after a sale has been made. A lower DSO indicates more efficient accounts receivable management.

E

Early Payment Discount: A discount offered to customers who pay their invoices before the due date. It encourages prompt payment and improves cash flow for the company.

Electronic Data Interchange (EDI): The electronic exchange of business documents, such as invoices and purchase orders, between companies. EDI helps streamline transactions, reduce errors, and improve efficiency.

F

Factoring: A financial transaction where a company sells its accounts receivable to a third party (factor) at a discount, in exchange for immediate cash. It helps improve cash flow but involves a cost in the form of the discount.

Finance Charge: A fee charged to customers for late payments or for extending credit beyond the agreed-upon terms. It is calculated based on the outstanding balance and the duration of the overdue period.

G

General Ledger (GL): A central repository of a company's financial transactions, used to prepare financial statements and reports. The GL includes accounts for assets, liabilities, equity, revenue, and expenses.

H

Hold Codes: Codes used in Oracle ERP to place holds on customer accounts or specific transactions, preventing further processing until certain conditions are met or issues are resolved.

I

Invoice: A document issued by a seller to a buyer, detailing the goods or services provided and the amount owed. It serves as a formal request for payment and includes terms and conditions for payment.

Invoice Matching: The process of comparing an invoice with related documents, such as purchase orders and receiving reports, to ensure accuracy before approving the invoice for payment.

J

Journal Entry: A record of a financial transaction in the general ledger. Each journal entry includes the date, accounts affected, amounts, and a description of the transaction.

K

Key Performance Indicators (KPIs): Metrics used to evaluate the effectiveness and efficiency of accounts receivable management. Common KPIs include Days Sales Outstanding (DSO), collection effectiveness index, and average days delinquent.

L

Late Payment Fee: A penalty charged to customers who fail to pay their invoices by the due date. It is intended to encourage timely payment and compensate the company for the delay.

Lockbox: A service offered by banks to process payments received by a company. Customers send their payments to a designated post office box, and the bank collects, processes, and deposits the payments into the company's account.

M

Manual Invoice: An invoice created and processed manually, as opposed to being generated automatically by the ERP system. Manual invoices are typically used for special cases or corrections.

Matching Principle: An accounting principle that requires expenses to be recorded in the same period as the revenues they help generate. It ensures accurate representation of a company's financial performance.

N

Net Terms: Payment terms that specify the number of days within which the invoice amount must be paid in full. Common net terms include Net 30, Net 45, and Net 60, indicating payment is due 30, 45, or 60 days from the invoice date, respectively.

O

Open Invoice: An invoice that has been issued but not yet paid by the customer. It represents an outstanding receivable and remains in the accounts receivable balance until payment is received.

Oracle ERP: An enterprise resource planning system developed by Oracle Corporation, designed to streamline and integrate various business processes, including accounts receivable, across an organization.

P

Payment Terms: The conditions under which a seller will complete a sale, typically specifying the period allowed to the buyer to pay off the amount due. Payment terms can include early payment discounts and late payment penalties.

Proforma Invoice: A preliminary invoice sent to a customer before the delivery of goods or services. It outlines the expected costs and terms of the transaction, often used for customs and import purposes.

Q

Query: A request for information from the ERP system, typically used to retrieve specific data or generate reports. Queries can be predefined or custom-built to meet specific needs.

R

Receipt: A document acknowledging that a payment has been received. In accounts receivable, a receipt records the payment made by a customer against their outstanding invoices.

Reconciliation: The process of comparing and matching records from different sources to ensure accuracy and consistency. In accounts receivable, reconciliation involves matching payments received with outstanding invoices.

Remittance Advice: A document sent by a customer to a supplier to inform them that payment has been made. It provides details of the invoices being paid and the amount paid against each invoice.

Revenue Recognition: The accounting principle that dictates how and when revenue is recognized in the financial statements. Revenue is typically recognized when goods or services are delivered and payment is reasonably assured.

S

Sales Order: A document generated by the seller to confirm the sale of goods or services to the customer. It precedes the invoice and outlines the terms of the sale, including prices, quantities, and delivery details.

Statement of Account: A summary of all transactions between a company and its customer over a specified period. It includes details of invoices, payments, credits, and the outstanding balance.

T

Terms of Sale: The conditions agreed upon by the buyer and seller regarding the sale of goods or services. These terms include payment terms, delivery conditions, and any discounts or penalties.

Transaction Code: A code used in Oracle ERP to identify and classify different types of transactions, such as invoices, receipts, and adjustments. It helps in organizing and analyzing transaction data.

U

Unapplied Cash: Payments received from customers that have not yet been matched to specific invoices. Unapplied cash remains in a suspense account until it is properly allocated.

User Interface (UI): The part of the ERP system that users interact with to perform their tasks. A well-designed UI enhances usability and efficiency in managing accounts receivable.

V

Value-Added Tax (VAT): A type of indirect tax levied on the value added to goods and services at each stage of production or distribution. Companies must account for VAT in their invoices and remittances.

W

Write-Off: The process of removing an uncollectible account receivable from the books. It is recorded as an expense and reduces the accounts receivable balance.

X

XML (eXtensible Markup Language): A markup language used for encoding documents in a format that is both human-readable and machine-readable. XML is often used for data interchange between ERP systems.

Y

Yield: The income generated from an investment, typically expressed as a percentage. In accounts receivable, yield can refer to the effective return from early payment discounts or finance charges.

Z

Zero-Balance Account: An account that is used to manage payments and receipts but is designed to have a zero balance at the end of each day. It is often used for cash concentration and disbursement purposes.

This glossary of terms provides a foundational understanding of the key concepts and terminology used in the Oracle ERP Accounts Receivable module. By familiarizing yourself with these terms, you will be better equipped to navigate the system and effectively manage your accounts receivable processes.

Appendix B: Frequently Asked Questions (FAQs)

1. What is Oracle ERP and how does it support Accounts Receivable?

Oracle ERP is a comprehensive suite of integrated applications that help businesses manage their operations, finance, and human resources. The Accounts Receivable module within Oracle ERP allows businesses to manage their customer invoices, payments, and collections efficiently. It supports the entire accounts receivable process from invoicing to cash receipts and includes features for tracking and managing customer credit, handling disputes, and generating detailed financial reports.

2. How do I set up the Accounts Receivable module in Oracle ERP?

Setting up the Accounts Receivable module involves several key steps:

- Define Company Parameters: Set up basic company information, configure financial and reporting parameters.

- Establish Customer Relationships: Create and maintain customer records with all necessary information.

- Configure Payment Terms and Options: Define the payment terms for customers and configure various payment options.

- Set Up Tax Codes and Jurisdictions: Define tax codes and jurisdictions to ensure compliance and accurate tax calculations.

3. How can I create and manage customer invoices in Oracle ERP?

To create a customer invoice in Oracle ERP:

- Navigate to the Accounts Receivable module.

- Select the option to create a new invoice.

- Enter the required information, including customer details, invoice date, due date, item details, and amounts.

- Save and review the invoice for accuracy.

- Submit the invoice for approval if necessary.

- Once approved, the invoice can be posted to the general ledger.

Managing customer invoices involves:

- Tracking invoice status and due dates.

- Adjusting or correcting invoices as needed.

- Handling disputed invoices by reviewing and resolving discrepancies.

4. How do I record and apply customer receipts in Oracle ERP?

Recording customer receipts involves:

- Navigating to the Receipts section within the Accounts Receivable module.

- Entering receipt information such as receipt date, amount, and payment method.

- Matching the receipt to the corresponding customer invoice(s).

- Saving and applying the receipt to reduce the outstanding balance.

Applying receipts:

- Navigate to the receipt application screen.

- Select the receipt to be applied.

- Choose the invoices or transactions to apply the receipt against.

- Confirm and save the application.

5. What are the common issues encountered in Accounts Receivable and how can I resolve them?

Common issues include:

- Invoice Discrepancies: Review and correct invoice details to ensure accuracy.

- Unapplied Receipts: Verify and apply receipts to the correct invoices.

- Data Discrepancies: Regularly reconcile accounts and resolve any mismatches.

To resolve these issues:

- Use the troubleshooting tools and reports available in Oracle ERP.

- Perform regular audits and reconciliations.

- Engage with Oracle Support or the Oracle Community for guidance.

6. How can I handle delinquent accounts and manage collections in Oracle ERP?

Managing collections involves:

- Setting up collections strategies and defining collection policies.

- Monitoring accounts receivable aging reports to identify delinquent accounts.

- Implementing collection actions such as sending reminders, contacting customers, and negotiating payment terms.

- Utilizing automated collections tools within Oracle ERP to streamline the process.

For delinquent accounts:

- Identify and prioritize based on the level of delinquency.

- Engage in proactive communication with customers.

- Consider implementing payment plans or taking legal action if necessary.

7. What are the best practices for managing Accounts Receivable in Oracle ERP?

Best practices include:

- Establishing clear standard operating procedures for the accounts receivable process.

- Regularly training and updating staff on Oracle ERP features and procedures.

- Implementing automation where possible to reduce manual errors and increase efficiency.

- Continuously monitoring key performance indicators (KPIs) and using analytics to drive improvements.

- Ensuring data integrity through regular audits and reconciliations.

8. How can I generate reports and analyze financial data in the Accounts Receivable module?

Generating reports:

- Navigate to the reporting section within the Accounts Receivable module.

- Select the desired report template or create a custom report.

- Enter the relevant parameters (date range, customer, etc.).

- Run the report and review the generated data.

Analyzing financial data:

- Use standard and custom reports to track invoice aging, payment history, and collection performance.

- Utilize dashboards and analytics tools to gain insights into accounts receivable trends.

- Compare actual performance against targets and identify areas for improvement.

9. What is the process for handling customer refunds in Oracle ERP?

Handling customer refunds involves:

- Identifying the need for a refund, such as overpayment or returned goods.

- Creating a refund request within the Accounts Receivable module.

- Entering the necessary details, including the amount to be refunded and the reason.

- Submitting the refund request for approval.

- Once approved, processing the refund and issuing payment to the customer.

- Recording the refund transaction in the general ledger.

10. How do I integrate the Accounts Receivable module with other Oracle ERP modules?

Integration involves:

- Setting up integration points between the Accounts Receivable module and other modules such as Sales, Inventory, and General Ledger.

- Ensuring data flows seamlessly between modules to maintain accuracy and consistency.

- Configuring workflows to automate processes that span multiple modules.

- Regularly testing and validating integrations to prevent issues.

11. What are the key performance indicators (KPIs) for Accounts Receivable management?

Key KPIs include:

- Days Sales Outstanding (DSO): Measures the average number of days it takes to collect payment after a sale.

- Collection Effectiveness Index (CEI): Evaluates the effectiveness of the collections process.

- Accounts Receivable Turnover Ratio: Indicates how frequently receivables are collected during a period.

- Aging Reports: Show the age distribution of outstanding receivables.

- Bad Debt Ratio: Measures the proportion of receivables that are written off as bad debt.

12. How can I customize the Accounts Receivable module to meet specific business needs?

Customization options include:

- Configuring invoice and receipt templates to match business requirements.

- Setting up custom approval workflows for invoices and receipts.

- Defining custom fields and data points for customer records.

- Implementing custom reports and dashboards to provide specific insights.

- Working with Oracle Support or a certified consultant for advanced customizations.

13. What resources are available for learning more about Oracle ERP and Accounts Receivable?

Resources include:

- Oracle's official documentation and user guides.

- Online training courses and certifications offered by Oracle University.

- Oracle community forums and user groups for peer support.

- Webinars, workshops, and conferences hosted by Oracle and industry experts.

- Books and publications on Oracle ERP best practices.

14. How do I stay updated with the latest features and updates in Oracle ERP?

Staying updated involves:

- Subscribing to Oracle's newsletters and update notifications.

- Participating in Oracle's user community and forums.

- Attending Oracle's webinars, workshops, and conferences.

- Regularly checking Oracle's official website and support portal for new releases and patches.

- Enrolling in continuous learning and certification programs offered by Oracle University.

15. How can I troubleshoot common technical issues in the Accounts Receivable module?

Troubleshooting involves:

- Identifying the issue using error messages and logs.

- Reviewing Oracle's documentation and knowledge base for solutions.

- Utilizing Oracle Support to report and resolve technical issues.

- Engaging with the Oracle community for peer assistance.

- Performing regular system maintenance and updates to prevent technical problems.

16. What are the benefits of using Oracle ERP for Accounts Receivable management?

Benefits include:

- Streamlined and automated accounts receivable processes.

- Improved accuracy and efficiency in invoicing and receipt management.

- Enhanced visibility into financial data and performance.

- Better integration with other business processes and modules.

- Robust reporting and analytics capabilities for informed decision-making.

- Scalability to support growing business needs and complexities.

17. How do I ensure data security and compliance in the Accounts Receivable module?

Ensuring data security and compliance involves:

- Implementing role-based access controls to limit user access.

- Regularly updating security settings and applying patches.

- Encrypting sensitive data to protect against unauthorized access.

- Monitoring user activity and system logs for suspicious behavior.

- Conducting regular audits and reviews to ensure compliance with regulations.

- Staying informed about industry standards and regulatory requirements.

18. What are the key steps to implement Oracle ERP's Accounts Receivable module in a business?

Key steps include:

- Assessing business requirements and defining objectives.

- Configuring the Accounts Receivable module to meet specific needs.

- Setting up customer records, payment terms, and tax codes.

- Training staff on the use of the module and its features.

- Testing the system thoroughly before going live.

- Monitoring performance and making adjustments as needed post-implementation.

19. How can I manage multiple currencies in the Accounts Receivable module?

Managing multiple currencies involves:

- Setting up currency codes and exchange rates in Oracle ERP.

- Configuring customer records to handle transactions in different currencies.

- Creating invoices and receipts in the applicable currency.

- Converting and posting transactions to the general ledger using current exchange rates.

- Generating reports and financial statements that reflect multi-currency transactions.

20. What are the different types of invoices that can be created in the Accounts Receivable module?

Types of invoices include:

- Standard Invoices: Regular invoices for goods or services sold.

- Credit Memos: Invoices issued to correct or cancel a previous invoice.

- Debit Memos: Invoices issued to charge additional amounts to customers.

- Recurring Invoices: Invoices generated automatically on a regular basis for ongoing services or subscriptions.

- Proforma Invoices: Preliminary invoices issued before finalizing the sale.

21. How do I handle partial payments and installment payments in Oracle ERP?

Handling partial payments:

- Record the partial payment as a receipt.

- Apply the partial payment to the outstanding invoice, reducing the balance.

- Monitor and track the remaining balance for follow-up.

Handling installment payments:

- Set up installment payment terms for the customer.

- Create and schedule invoices according to the installment plan.

- Record and apply each installment payment as received.

- Ensure accurate tracking of the installment schedule and balances.

22. What is the role of credit management in the Accounts Receivable process?

Credit management involves:

- Assessing the creditworthiness of customers before extending credit.

- Setting credit limits and terms for each customer.

- Monitoring customer credit balances and usage.

- Managing credit holds and releases based on payment history and outstanding balances.

- Implementing policies and procedures to mitigate credit risk and minimize bad debt.

23. How can I optimize the cash flow management process using the Accounts Receivable module?

Optimizing cash flow involves:

- Implementing efficient invoicing and receipt processes to reduce payment delays.

- Offering flexible payment terms and options to encourage timely payments.

- Regularly monitoring accounts receivable aging reports to identify and address overdue accounts.

- Utilizing automated reminders and collections tools to streamline the collections process.

- Analyzing cash flow patterns and adjusting strategies to improve liquidity.

24. What are the common reasons for invoice disputes and how can I resolve them?

Common reasons for invoice disputes include:

- Incorrect or incomplete invoice information.

- Discrepancies between the invoice and purchase order or contract.

- Quality or delivery issues with the goods or services provided.

- Disagreement over pricing or terms.

To resolve invoice disputes:

- Review and verify the disputed invoice details.

- Communicate with the customer to understand the issue.

- Correct any errors or discrepancies in the invoice.

- Negotiate a resolution with the customer, such as issuing a credit memo or adjusting the invoice.

- Document the resolution process and update records accordingly.

25. How do I manage the end-of-period closing process for Accounts Receivable in Oracle ERP?

Managing the end-of-period closing involves:

- Reconciling accounts receivable balances with the general ledger.

- Reviewing and resolving any outstanding discrepancies.

- Ensuring all invoices and receipts for the period are recorded and posted.

- Generating and reviewing financial reports for accuracy.

- Closing the accounts receivable period in Oracle ERP to prevent further transactions.

- Preparing for the next accounting period by setting up necessary configurations.

Thank You

Thank you for embarking on this journey through the comprehensive landscape of the Oracle ERP Accounts Receivable module. Our goal was to provide you with a robust understanding of the functionalities, processes, and best practices associated with managing accounts receivable using Oracle ERP. From setting up your company parameters and establishing customer relationships to managing sales orders and invoices, we hope this guide has equipped you with the knowledge and tools necessary to optimize your accounts receivable processes.

The successful implementation of the Accounts Receivable module can significantly enhance your organization's financial management capabilities, improve cash flow, and streamline your operations. By leveraging the features and best practices outlined in this book, you can ensure accurate financial reporting, efficient customer transactions, and effective credit management.

Remember, the journey to mastering Oracle ERP is ongoing. As you continue to explore and utilize the module, stay updated with the latest developments and enhancements from Oracle. Engage with the broader Oracle ERP community, participate in training sessions, and seek support whenever needed. Continuous learning and adaptation will help you maximize the benefits of your Oracle ERP system.

We trust that the insights and guidance provided in this book will serve as a valuable resource for your organization, empowering you to achieve excellence in your accounts receivable management.

Acknowledgements

We extend our heartfelt gratitude to you, our readers, for choosing "Oracle ERP Essentials: Accounts Receivable: From Basics to Advanced." Your decision to invest in this book is greatly appreciated, and we hope it has met your expectations and provided you with valuable insights.

We also want to acknowledge the contributions of the Oracle ERP community, whose shared knowledge and experiences have greatly enriched this guide. Special thanks to the Oracle support team for their unwavering assistance and dedication to helping users navigate the complexities of the Oracle ERP system.

Lastly, to the countless professionals who continue to innovate and push the boundaries of what is possible with Oracle ERP, your efforts inspire us all. Thank you for your commitment to excellence and for driving forward the field of enterprise resource planning.

We encourage you to share your feedback and experiences with us. Your input is invaluable and helps us improve future editions of this book. We wish you the best in your journey with Oracle ERP and hope that it brings you continued success and growth.

Warm regards,

www.ingramcontent.com/pod-product-compliance
Lightning Source LLC
LaVergne TN
LVHW081328050326
832903LV00024B/1068